WORKS OF BERTOLT BRECHT

The Grove Press Edition

General Editor: Eric Bentley

Translators

Lee Baxandall

Eric Bentley

Martin Esslin

N. Goold-Verschoyle

H. R. Hays

Anselm Hollo

Christopher Isherwood

Frank Jones

Charles Laughton

Carl R. Mueller

Desmond I. Vesey

Previously Published

BERTOLT BRECHT

JUNGLE OF CITIES
and other plays

Jungle of Cities *Translated by Anselm Hollo* / Drums in the Night *Translated by Frank Jones* / Roundheads and Peakheads *Translated by N. Goold-Verschoyle*

GROVE PRESS   NEW YORK

The English translation of *Roundheads and Peakheads* first appeared in *International Literature*, No. 5, Moscow, May 1937.

ISBN: 0-8021-5149-3

Library of Congress Catalog Card Number: 65-23860

Manufactured in the United States of America

GROVE PRESS, 841 Broadway, New York, NY 10003

10   9   8   7

CONTENTS

JUNGLE OF CITIES

*Two men fighting
in Chicago, the
gigantic city*

TRANSLATOR'S NOTE

According to Bertolt Brecht himself,* *Jungle of Cities*
was to be the round-by-round account of a savage, gratui-
tous, "unmotivated" fight to the death between two men
in that colorful "gigantic city Chicago" the young playwright had created for himself, out of material found in
popular "gangster" novels of the period. He specifically
mentions one of these, *The Wheel* by J. V. Jensen,† but
also Rimbaud's cycle of prose poems, *A Season in Hell*,
as well as that melodramatic German classic *The Robbers*
by Friedrich Schiller. Brecht's Chicago of 1912, as he
saw it in the 1920's, is less of a specific place in time
than a state of mind—though some of its quieter surrealistic
touches may not have been that to their author, at the time.

In Schiller's *Robbers*, Brecht says, a similar battle is
waged: but it is waged for a clearly defined prize, a
"bourgeois inheritance," even if the protagonists resort to
fairly unbourgeois methods. Here, in the great city jungle
on the other side of the Atlantic, the combatants are
simply out to prove themselves, to decide who is "the
better man." Originally, Brecht did not want to engage
them in the class struggle—though he has (again, later)
claimed that this was, after all, the real issue: his intention
was to pit them against each other like two gunfighters
walking down the archetypal dusty Main Street, fingers

---

* "Bei Durchsicht meiner ersten Stücke" ("On looking at
my first plays") from *Bertolt Brecht, Stücke*, Band I, Suhrkamp
Verlag, 1954.

† For more details on J. V. Jensen (and Rimbaud), see
Seven Plays by Bertolt Brecht, edited by Eric Bentley, Grove
Press, 1961.

curled for the kill. (There are several references to this "Western" obsession in the play, as when Garga accuses Shlink of reverting to "prairie" codes.)

But: are they simply out to prove themselves? When Paul Verlaine fired two shots at Arthur Rimbaud in a Brussels hotel room, that wasn't just plain old-fashioned gunslinging: it was the end of a long and harrowing love affair, by all accounts as violent and one-sided as the one described in *Jungle of Cities*. . . . Quoting from *A Season in Hell* Garga, whose speeches abound in straight quotes from and allusions to Rimbaud, actually refers to Shlink as his lover: and in the final desolate encounter by the shore of Lake Michigan the men's true relationship emerges in savage and memorable clarity.

The real reason for their inability to "come to grips," as Brecht puts it, is not so much the degeneration of man's fighting spirit in a climate of rampant capitalism, as it is an inability to live with their own secret desires. It is a play of desire: Brecht tells us he wrote most of it on long lonely walks in his native Augsburg, by the old town moat, with its swans in the calm, black water among yellow chestnut leaves: wrote it on small folded sheets of thin typing paper, "mixing phrases like cocktails, creating entire scenes out of words appealing to the senses and evocative of certain textures and colors"—the genuine Rimbaudian method. It is, perhaps, for all its metaphysical gunplay and shadowboxing, a poetic re-creation of Brecht's own season in hell: "To be alone—that's a good thing to be. The chaos has been used up. And it was the best time."

The present translation follows the original edition, *Im Dickicht der Städte,* Propyläen-Verlag, Berlin, 1927. In later editions Brecht has made one significant change: Garga's letter of denunciation, central to Scenes 8 and 9, was given a different address—not "Police Headquarters," but a newspaper, *The Examiner*. Brecht was probably not so much concerned to remove the taint of corruption from the police force as to give an indication of the "power (*and* corruption) of the Press."

—Anselm Hollo

London, 12 April 1965

CHARACTERS

Shlink, *the lumber dealer, a Malay*
George Garga
John Garga, *his father*
Mae Garga, *his mother*
Marie Garga, *his sister*
Jane Larry, *his girl friend*
Skinny, *a Chinaman, Shlink's clerk*
Collie Couch, *known as The Baboon, a pimp*
J. Finnay, *known as The Worm, hotel proprietor*
Pat Manky, *Ship's First Mate*
A Salvation Army Officer
The Snubnose
The Saloonkeeper
C. Maynes, *owner of a lending library*
Waiter
R.R. Workers

It is the year 1912 in the city of Chicago: you are witnessing an inexplicable wrestling match, and the destruction of a family that has come from the prairie lands to the great city jungle. In observing this battle, do not rack your brains for motives: concern yourself with the human element, evaluate the antagonists' fighting spirit impartially and concentrate your interest on the showdown.

1

C. MAYNES'S LENDING LIBRARY IN CHICAGO
The morning of the 8th of August 1912

GARGA *behind the counter. The doorbell rings, enter* SHLINK *and* SKINNY.

SKINNY: If we read that sign right, this is a lending library, correct? Well . . . lend us a book.

GARGA: What kind of book, sir?

SKINNY: A big fat one.

GARGA: For yourself, sir?

SKINNY (*who turns to look at* SHLINK *every time before he answers*): No. it's not for me; for this gentleman here.

GARGA: Your name, sir?

SKINNY: Shlink, lumber dealer, Number Six, Mulberry Street.

GARGA (*writes the name down*): Five cents a book for a week. You take your choice, sir.

SKINNY: No, we want you to pick one for us.

GARGA: That's a crime story. It isn't a good book. That one there is better, it's a travel book.

SKINNY: So you're saying, it's a bad book—just like that?

SHLINK (*stepping forward*): Is that an opinion of yours? I'd like to buy it off you. Would ten dollars be enough?

GARGA: You can have it for free, sir.

SHLINK: Does that mean you are changing your opinion to say that it is a good book after all?

GARGA: No, sir.

SKINNY: You could buy yourself some clean linen for that money.

GARGA: I'm only here to wrap up the books people take out, that's all.

SKINNY: It isn't good for business, you know.

GARGA: Now what do you want of me? I don't know you, I never saw you before.

SHLINK: I'm offering you forty bucks for your opinion on this book. I don't know the book, it could be any damn book.

GARGA: I'll sell you the opinions of Mr. V. Jensen and Mr. Arthur Rimbaud, but I won't sell you my own opinion.

SHLINK: Your opinion is immaterial too—except that I want to buy it.

GARGA: I think I can afford having and keeping my own opinions.

SKINNY: You the son of a transatlantic millionaire?

GARGA: No. Rotten fish, that's what my family have to live on.

SHLINK (*pleased*): A fighter! So one would think you could bring yourself to say the words that would give me pleasure and provide your family with better fare. . . .

SKINNY: Forty dollars! That's a lot of new clean shirts and things, for yourself and your folks.

GARGA: I'm not a prostitute.

SHLINK (*in good humor*): I don't think I'm violating your soul, by giving you fifty bucks.

GARGA: So you're raising the offer? That is a fresh insult, and you know it.

SHLINK (*as if naive*): A man ought to know what to choose: a pound of fish, or an opinion—or, on the other hand, two pounds of fish, or that opinion. . . .

SKINNY: My dear sir, watch out!

GARGA: I'll have you thrown out on your ear.

SKINNY: So you have opinions. Well, that's because you don't know about life.

SHLINK: Miss Jane Larry tells me you're raring to go to Tahiti.

GARGA: I'd like to know how you got to know Jane Larry.

SHLINK: She's close to starving, as she doesn't get paid any more for the shirts she has been sewing. It is three weeks now since you've last been to see her.

GARGA *drops a stack of books on the floor.*

SKINNY: Watch it! You're the salesman here!

GARGA: Gentlemen, I can't defend myself against your importunities.

SHLINK: You're a poor man.

GARGA: Rice and fish is what I live on, I don't care who knows it.

SHLINK: So it's a deal!

SKINNY: Are you the oil king?

SHLINK: The people in your street feel sorry for you.

GARGA: I can't go and gun down the whole goddamn street.

SHLINK: Your family, having come here from the flat country . . .

GARGA: Sleep their nights, three in a room, next to a burst sewage pipe. I have a long smoke every night, to be able to go to sleep in that stench. We keep the windows closed: Chicago is a cold place, if any of that seems amusing to you.

SHLINK: Yes, your mistress . . .

GARGA: Is sewing shirts, at two dollars apiece: net profit, twelve cents. I'd like to recommend her services. Sundays we get together, the pint of whisky is eighty cents, no more no less, eighty cents, if that's of any interest. . . .

SHLINK: But you aren't giving us the whole story.

GARGA: No, I'm not.

SHLINK: Well, who could live off those twelve cents she makes.

GARGA: Every man to his taste. And I am in love with Tahiti. Any objections?

SHLINK: You're well advised: that certainly is the simple life. Now and then there are a few storms, at Cape Hay, but farther south there are the tobacco islands, with green fields all a-rustle. . . . A lizard's life.

GARGA (*looking out the window; tonelessly*): Ninety-four degrees in the shade. Traffic, noise from the Milwaukee Bridge. A morning, like any other.

SHLINK: And on this morning, which isn't just like any other, I declare war on you! I'll begin the fight by shaking the foundations of your life.

The bell rings. Enter MAYNES.

Your man here, he's on strike.

MAYNES: Why aren't you attending to these gentlemen, George?

SKINNY (*aggressively*): He seems to have some grudge against us.

MAYNES: What does that mean?

SKINNY: Well, we made some remarks about his greasy shirt. . . .

MAYNES: Is this the way you come to work in my store, Garga? What do you think this is—an eating establishment? Gentlemen, it won't happen again, I assure you.

SKINNY: What's he saying! Cursing down his shirt sleeve. Why don't you speak up, with your own god-given voice?

GARGA: May I ask you to provide me with better linen, Mr. Maynes. You can't start a whorehouse for five dollars a week.

SHLINK: Why not go to Tahiti? Nobody ever has a wash there.

GARGA: Thank you kindly. Your concern for me is most touching. I'll tell my sister to say a prayer for you.

SHLINK: By all means—she has nothing better to do: Manky, who'd make an excellent husband for her, is wearing his boots out chasing after her. And your sister doesn't even blink, while her parents are starving.

GARGA: Are you running a detective agency? I hope your interest in our family has some flattering motive.

SHLINK: You just close your eyes, that's all. Your family is heading straight for a crack-up: you're the only one who's earning any money, and yet you think you can afford to have opinions. That, while you have a chance to go to Tahiti. (*Shows him a sea chart which he has brought with him.*)

GARGA: I never even saw you before.

SHLINK: These are the two shipping lines that go there.

GARGA: You only just bought that map, eh? It's brand-new.

SKINNY: Just you think of it—the great Pacific!

GARGA (*to* MAYNES): Please, Mr. Maynes, show these gentlemen the door. They aren't buying anything, they are holding up business, and they've been spying on me. I don't even know them.

Enter J. FINNAY, *known as* THE WORM. SHLINK *and* SKINNY *retreat into the background without giving any sign of recognition.*

THE WORM: Is this C. Maynes's Lending Library?

MAYNES: Yes, that's me. In person.

THE WORM: A most sinister establishment, this is.

MAYNES: What can I serve you with, sir—books, magazines, postage stamps?

THE WORM: So that's what they are, books? A slimy business. Why have them at all? There're enough lies in the world as it is. "The sky grew dark, the clouds were heading east." And why not south? My God, how gullible these people are.

MAYNES: I'll wrap it up for you, sir.

SKINNY: Why don't you give the man time to catch his breath? And does he look like a bookworm—I ask you?

GARGA: This is a conspiracy.

THE WORM: Now fancy that! Here she says: "When you kiss me, I always see your beautiful teeth." How can you see anything, when you're kissing? But that's the way she is, and now posterity knows it. What a bitch! (*He tramples the books with his boot heel.*)

MAYNES: Now wait a minute, sir, you'll have to pay for those damaged copies!

THE WORM: Books! What's the use of them? Did libraries stop the San Francisco earthquake?

MAYNES: Call the sheriff, George.

THE WORM: I keep a liquor store—now that's an honest man's business.

GARGA: He isn't drunk, either.

THE WORM: Just looking at bums like you makes me tremble like an aspen leaf.

GARGA: It's a frame-up. And it's me they're out to get.

Enter COUCH, *known as* THE BABOON, *accompanied by* JANE LARRY. THE WORM *retreats without a sign of recognition.*

THE BABOON: Just walk in, my little white hen. This is C. Maynes's Lending Library.

GARGA: Better close the store, Mr. Maynes. Strange creatures are crawling over your papers. In a minute you'll have the moths in your magazines.

THE WORM: Stare life in the eye! That's what I always say.

THE BABOON: Wipe that face off your head! I can't stand paper. I can't bear newsprint either.

GARGA: Get the gun, sir!

SHLINK (*stepping forward*): Allow me to repeat my offer.

GARGA (*sees* JANE): No!

JANE: George, is this your store? Why are you staring

like that? I only had a little outing with this gentleman.

GARGA: Go on, Jane, have another.

THE BABOON: Hey, that's a bit thick. Or don't you think so? Bejazus, my hands get to shake so this book falls into pieces. Or, you still don't think so?

MAYNES: All I can say is you're fired, if you don't apologize! All my books are going to the devil!

GARGA: Go home, Jane, I ask you to go home. You're drunk.

JANE: I don't know what's wrong with you, George. These gentlemen are being nice to me. (*She has a drink from The Baboon's flask.*) They've been buying me cocktails and things. It's—ninety-four degrees today, you know, George. That tears through your body like lightning.

GARGA: Go home now. I'll come and see you tonight.

JANE: It's three weeks now you haven't been to see me. I'm not going home any more. I'm fed up with just sitting there, with stacks of shirts all around.

THE BABOON (*pulls her down on his lap*): You won't have to, any more.

JANE: Oh, you're tickling me. Don't do it now! George doesn't like it!

THE BABOON: In short: she's got a body that's worth a few dollars. Can you pay for it, sir? Love and cocktails, that's what it is all about.

THE WORM: Or are you trying to preserve the young lady's chastity? You like to see her scrubbing floors? You want her to become a laundrywoman?

SKINNY: Are you asking a good little white grouse to become an angel?

GARGA (*to* SHLINK): What are you trying to do, start a frontier town all over again? Knives? Guns? Cocktails?

THE WORM: Hold it! You won't move out of here that fast. Or else maybe someone gets it. You take that offer, and now!

GARGA: Strange . . . Everybody seems to know what it's
  all about, only I don't. . . . Jane!

THE BABOON: You answer him.

JANE: Don't look at me like that, George! Maybe this is
  my only chance. Can you buy me cocktails? Oh, it
  isn't for the drink, it is that I look at myself in the
  mirror, George, in the mornings. It's two years now.
  You always go away to work for a month, and when
  you are really fed up and need a drink, too, then it is
  my turn. But I can't take it any longer! The nights,
  George . . . I'm not the worse for that, not me. You
  have no right to look at me like that!

THE BABOON: Well said. Here, have another, you'll become
  even wiser.

GARGA: That whisky has ruined your mind. Can you still
  hear me? I say: let's go away, together. To San
  Francisco, wherever you want to go. I don't know if
  a man can stay in love forever, but listen, I promise
  you this: I'll stay *with* you.

JANE: But you can't do it, Georgie, you just can't.

GARGA: I can do anything. I can make money, if that's
  what you want. I have a feeling for you—damn it,
  there aren't any words! But we'll get through again,
  to one another, I'll come and see you tonight, this
  evening I'll come to you!

JANE: I can hear everything you say, you don't have to
  shout, and you don't have to tell these gentlemen that
  you never loved me. What you are saying now are
  the bitterest things you know, and I have to listen,
  I know it, and you know it too.

THE WORM: What a bunch of monkeys! Why don't you
  just tell him that you've been in bed with this gentleman here—from nine till half-past ten.

JANE: Maybe that isn't so good. But it is good that you
  should know: it isn't the whisky, and it isn't the heat.

SHLINK: Come on, let's make it a deal now! I double the
  offer, once more. Enough of this.

GARGA: No go. What is nine to half-past ten, against two years?

SHLINK: Let me assure you that two hundred dollars don't mean a thing to me. I hardly dare offer you that pitiful amount.

GARGA: Perhaps you would be kind enough to dismiss your friends.

SHLINK: As you please. I only ask you to consider the conditions on this planet, and to accept my offer.

MAYNES: You're a fool, a sluggard, an apathetic coolie. Just think . . .

SKINNY: Of your innocent, grief-stricken parents!

THE WORM: Your sister!

THE BABOON: Your mistress! This pretty young thing, right here!

GARGA: No! No! No!

SHLINK: Tahiti!

GARGA: I'm not having it.

MAYNES: You're fired!

SHLINK: Your living! Now watch the foundations—they're heaving!

GARGA: And that—is freedom. Here's my coat! (*He takes it off.*) You share it! (*Takes a book from the shelf.*) "Idolatory! Lies! Lewdness! I am an animal, a Negro. But I am capable of being saved. You, maniacs, wild beasts, misers, are Negroes in disguise. Merchant, you're a Negro, general, you're a Negro. Emperor, you old scabby itch, you're a Negro: you have drunk untaxed liquor, Satan's moonshine. . . . This people is inspired by fever and cancer!" (*Drinks.*) "I have no knowledge of metaphysics, I do not understand the laws, I have no moral sense, I am an animal: you are making a mistake!"

SHLINK, SKINNY, THE WORM *and* THE BABOON *are crowding round* GARGA *and applauding, as if this had been a performance.*

SHLINK (*smoking*): How excited you get! Nothing is going
to happen to you.

JANE (*her arms around his neck*): George, is it that bad?

GARGA: Here, my boots! So you're smoking a little black
cigar, sir? Here, my handkerchief—the spittle might
run down your jowls. Yes, I'll auction her off, this
woman! I'll fling these papers into your faces! I'm
only asking for the tobacco fields of Virginia, and
for a ticket to the South Sea Islands. I'm asking, I'm
asking for my freedom. (*Runs out, barefoot and in
his shirt sleeves.*)

SHLINK (*calls after him*): My name is Shlink. Shlink the
lumber dealer! Number Six, Mulberry Street!

SKINNY: He sure is making tracks. How much for the bits
of paper?

THE WORM: Are you really going to pay him?

MAYNES: Those were ten dollars' worth of books.

SKINNY: Here's twenty.

THE BABOON (*to* JANE *who is crying*): I—see! Now you're
waking up! Save your tears for the gutter.

THE WORM: You have to stare life in the eye, is what I say.

SHLINK: How much are the rags?

MAYNES: The clothes? The coat? The tie? The boots? They
aren't really for sale. . . . Ten dollars.

SKINNY: So we finally got him to shed his skin: let's take
it along.

SHLINK *has already begun a slow exit, backstage.*
SKINNY *follows, carrying the bundle of clothes.*

2

THE OFFICES OF C. SHLINK,
THE LUMBER DEALER, IN CHICAGO
The 27th of August, in the evening, around 7 o'clock

SHLINK, *standing at a small table.*

SKINNY'S VOICE (*backstage left*): Seven cars from Kentucky!

THE WORM: All here.

SKINNY: Two cars of timber, cut lengths.

THE WORM: There's a man here, he wants to see Mr. Shlink.

SHLINK: Show him in.

THE WORM: That's Mr. Shlink.

GARGA *enters.*

SHLINK (*pleased*): So there you are! Here—your clothes. You can put them on again.

GARGA: You've been waiting for me? You've brought those clothes over here? Those filthy rags? (*Kicks the bundle of clothes.*)

SHLINK *strikes a small gong.* MARIE *enters.*

MARIE: George!

GARGA: Marie, you're here?

MARIE: George, where have you been? They were all very worried about you. And don't you look terrible!

GARGA: What the hell are you doing here?

MARIE: I take care of their washing. . . . It's a living, for us. Why are you staring at me like that? You do look as if you've had a bad time. I'm all right here. They said they chased you away.

23

GARGA: Listen, Marie! You get your things together and go home, right away. (*Walks around.*) I don't know what they plan to do to me. I've been harpooned, I've been dragged here, with God knows what ropes. And so, I'll just stick around, dear sir. But leave my sister out of this!

SHLINK: Whatever you say. (*To* MARIE:) But before you leave, please get him a fresh change of linen and a suit. If you don't mind.

MARIE: My brother tells me I have to go. I don't understand him.

SHLINK: And I ask you to go home, as soon as you've brought us those things. I don't know anything about clothes.

MARIE *goes*.

SHLINK: You have been drinking?

GARGA: Any objections? Just tell me.

SHLINK: The only stuff I have here is rice-liquor. But I'll send for any other poison you'd rather have—I guess you like to mix your drinks?

GARGA: Yes, that's my method: take care of everything at once. What I like is drinking, making love and smoking, all at once, a couple of weeks at a time.

SHLINK: No doubt you spare a few moments to leaf through a dictionary, too . . .

GARGA: . . . you just know everything, don't you.

SHLINK: When I was informed of your habits, here's what I said to myself: that one, he's a good fighting man.

GARGA: She sure takes her time over those clothes.

SHLINK: I'm sorry. (*Gets up and strikes the gong.*)

MARIE (*enters*): Here's the fresh linen, George. And the suit.

GARGA: You can wait here, we'll leave together. (*Changes his clothes behind a screen.*)

MARIE: So I'll say good-by, Mr. Shlink. I didn't get the

last lot quite done, but . . . And thanks for your
hospitality!

GARGA (*behind the screen*): There're no pockets in this
suit.

SHLINK *starts whistling to himself.*

(*Comes out again.*) Who you whistling for? I wish
you'd stop whistling for people like they were dogs.
At least, for these last couple of weeks of your life . . .

SHLINK: Aye aye, sir.

GARGA: It's you who started all this frontier business. I
say, all right—let's have it that wild and woolly.
You've skinned me, just for the hell of it. And I'll
settle my accounts with you. (*A gun in his hand.*)
An eye for an eye, a tooth for a tooth.

SHLINK: So you're really joining battle?

GARGA: Yes, I am. Which is not to say I can't pull out of
it again, whenever I feel like it.

SHLINK: You don't even want to know what it is all about?

GARGA: I don't even want to know what it is all about. I
don't want to know why you need a fight that bad.
I'm sure your reasons for it are rotten, anyway. For
me it's enough to know that you think you're the
tougher guy. . . .

SHLINK: Well then, let us consider. I have a house, I have
a lumber business; and so I could have you hounded
to hell's gate. Money, that's what counts. All right.
But my house is yours now: this lumber business
belongs to you. As from today, Mr. Garga, I put my
fortune into your hands. I don't even know you. But
from this day I am your slave. I'll tremble at every
look you give me. Every wish you have, even those
wishes I can't yet know, they'll find me your willing
servant. Your troubles are my troubles, and my
power will be your power. All my feelings will go out
to you, and you will rage at me.

GARGA: I take you up on that offer. And I hope you won'
find much reason for laughing, either.

THE BABOON, SKINNY *and* THE WORM *enter, withou
a sound.* GARGA *sees that their suits are the same a
his, and grins.*

SHLINK: Today, this building and this lumber business
registered in Chicago, under the name of Shlink
will be transferred to Mr. George Garga, of Chicago

GARGA (*to* SHLINK): That's me, all right. Good. You hav
any peeled logs in stock? How many?

SHLINK: About four hundred, I should think. I don't kno
the exact figure.

SKINNY: Going to Messrs. Broost & Co., down in Virginia

GARGA: Who sold those logs to them?

THE WORM: It was me, The Worm. I run the Chines
Hotel, in the coal-miners' part of town.

GARGA: You sell those logs once more, all right?

THE WORM: Sell them twice! But that's a crooked deal—

GARGA: And so it is.

THE WORM: Who'll be responsible for that order?

GARGA: You go ahead and sell those logs in San Francisc
or somewhere, and make it official, on the behalf o
Mr. Shlink's firm. Then you hand the money to Mr
Shlink: he'll keep it for me until I ask him for it
Any objections, Mr. Shlink?

SHLINK *shakes his head.*

THE WORM: But, but that's stupid—that's so stupidl
crooked, we'll have the law down on us in no time

GARGA: When, do you think?

SHLINK: Six months, at the latest. (*He carries the busines
ledger over to* GARGA.)

THE BABOON: But that's a gutter business!

GARGA: The tough rats make out all right, in the gutter. . .

THE BABOON: Man, I'd rather work with a razor than wit

crooked papers. And don't forget, Chicago's a cold place!

GARGA: You were talking about your proper lumber business, Shlink, or weren't you? About the house, the lumber, the fixtures?

SHLINK: Yes. Here is the ledger.

GARGA: You—come on over, and pour some ink on that ledger.

SKINNY: Me?!

SHLINK *hands him an ink bottle.*

SKINNY (*standing by the book*): All those entries! All the deals!

GARGA: Come on, just let it pour!

SKINNY *pours the ink, carefully.*

THE BABOON: Well, good-by!

THE WORM: Twenty years—and that's the end! Some joke! I don't get it. This was a lumber business.

GARGA: And now, stop the sawmill. Then it's all over.

THE BABOON: Okay, boss. (*Leaves the room.*)

The sound of the saws ceases. The men take off their overalls and stand against the wall. GARGA *bursts out laughing.*

MARIE: George, what are you doing?

GARGA: Keep your mouth shut! Mr. Shlink, now you fire that one!

SHLINK: All right, you go.

SKINNY: Go? I've been sitting here in your office for twenty years, come April. . . .

SHLINK: You've been fired.

MARIE: George, I don't think you're doing right by these folks.

GARGA: Please, Marie, go home now.

MARIE: But you'll come with me. How are you ever going

    to get out of this mess again! Let him go, Mr. Shlink!

SHLINK: You're the one that gives the orders, Garga.

GARGA: Right. So, now, seeing there's no more work for you to do, I'd like to see you sit down to a friendly game of poker with your former business managers.

SHLINK *and the men sit down at the card table.*

MARIE: George, let's go home now. It's all a big joke, and you just don't understand it.

GARGA: We grew up in the flat country, Marie. We're the suckers here.

MARIE: We are? But what can they want from us?

GARGA: I tell you: it's not you they're after. They just want to drag you into it, too. I come here to take a look at the guy who spit a cherry pit into my eye, two weeks ago. I come here with a gun in my pocket. And what do I see? He's kowtowing to me, he's offering me his business. So, I don't get it, but I take him up on it. I'm loning it on these plains—and there's nothing I can do for you now, Marie.

THE WORM (*speaking over their shoulders*): He's playing like a paper dragon. I bet he's cheating.

GARGA (*to* SHLINK): I don't understand a thing, sir, I stand here like a dumb nigger, I've come with the white flag, and now I unfold it as a banner. You hand me your papers, covering the property, all the private monies, so I can put them in my pocket!

SHLINK: But of course, please don't disdain them, modest as they are.

Exit SHLINK *and* GARGA.

SKINNY: True, it ain't been all that wonderful here, what with the rain running down your neck and all; but to get the sack, like that—it just ain't right.

THE WORM: Oh, shut your trap. (*With sarcasm.*) He still believes it's all on account of the dry rot in the floorboards.

SKINNY: Lady, listen, I've fallen in love with you. You have such a way of giving your hand. . . .

THE WORM: Hey! Now that he doesn't even have a bed anymore he wants to share it with a woman!

SKINNY: You come with me, I'll work for you. Come with me.

THE BABOON (*also stepping forward*): Jeezus! There's such as are black, or golden-yellow and white, like apple peel! Negro women! drawn straight and true from hip to heel! And with good round thighs too, dammit, not bloody butcher's scissors like those there! Yahoo for Papua! Forty bucks to get there!

SHLINK (*in the door, calls back over his shoulder*): Yes, that is all.

THE WORM: Come on, you're a barbarian, an ingrate! The lady's innocent as a lamb, and does she smoke a pipe maybe? Maybe she hasn't been around so much, but who can say she hasn't got it in her? Forty bucks and all for the lady.

SKINNY: I'll pay whatever you ask for!

THE BABOON: Wipe that powder off, of course; don't cook her, let's have it good naked meat. What latitudes, hey! Seventy bucks for the lot!

MARIE: Mr. Shlink, please, protect me!

SHLINK: I am ready to protect you.

MARIE: Are you telling me I should go with him?

SHLINK: No one loves you here. He does.

GARGA (*having re-entered*): How do you like it, on the market? There's a lot of wood around, and now we're auctioning off a few pounds of flesh for a change! And look at that jujitsu—that's the easy, merry art of whatever, isn't it?

SHLINK (*moves toward him with a worried face*): But aren't you making it a little too easy for yourself?

MARIE (*to GARGA*): You should have been here to help me. Now you'll come with me, George, right away. Something terrible has happened here, and perhaps it won't be over even if I leave now. You must be blind not to see how you're losing, losing, in this fight.

Backstage, two guitars and a drum; girls' voices singing "Ye Sinners Come Unto Jesus."

GARGA: I see. You want to lose yourself already. That's the sewer that'll swallow you up. Hey, this is something for you, Marie: the Salvation Army, heading straight for you, Marie! (*He gets up from the small table, goes to back of stage.*) Hey there! Come on! Christian soldiers!

THE WORM (*to* MARIE): They've drained a river from below here, and at night the place is swarming with the ghosts of all the rats that drowned. Now, go home to your folks!

GARGA: Clean the place up! Hide the booze!

SHLINK *pretends to obey, but* MARIE *does the work.*

Come on in, boys!

SHLINK *has already opened the tall wooden door, with a deep bow. Enter, a young man in Salvation Army uniform; two girls with guitars, and an old sinner with a drum; they halt a few steps behind him.*

SALVATION ARMY OFFICER: You called me?

THE WORM: Hallelujah! The Salvation Army!

GARGA: I don't think much of what you're up to: but if you need a house, I'll let you have this one.

SALVATION ARMY OFFICER: The Lord will bestow His blessings upon you.

GARGA: Maybe. (*To* SHLINK:) Did you inherit this house, and the rights?

SHLINK: No.

GARGA: You worked for it? Forty years?

SHLINK: Scratched it out of the ground, with my fingernails. I never slept more than four hours.

GARGA: So you were a poor man, when you came over?

SHLINK: I was seven years old. And I've been working ever since.

GARGA: And this is all your property, all there is?

SHLINK: This is all of it.

GARGA (*to* OFFICER): And so I'll make you a donation of this man's property—on one condition: on behalf of the orphans and drunkards that will be housed here, I want to spit into your disgusting puss!

SALVATION ARMY OFFICER: I am a servant of the Lord.

GARGA: So line it up, then.

SALVATION ARMY OFFICER: I am not permitted to do such a thing.

GARGA: Listen, bud, the orphans are drowning in the snow. The drunkards are rotting away, big piles of them. And you go on protecting your face. . . .

SALVATION ARMY OFFICER: I am ready. I have kept my face clean. I am twenty-one years old. You must have your reasons. But please, understand: ask that woman to turn away.

MARIE: I'll despise you if you let him do that to you.

SALVATION ARMY OFFICER: I expect you to despise me. There are better faces than mine, but there isn't a single one in the world that would be too good for this.

GARGA: Shlink, you spit him one in the mug, if you like.

MARIE: That's no good, George. That won't change my mind.

GARGA: A tooth for a tooth, if you please.

SHLINK *walks coolly over to the* OFFICER *and spits straight into his face.* THE WORM *gives a cackling laugh, the converted sinner booms his drum.*

SALVATION ARMY OFFICER (*shakes his fists, in tears*): Forgive me.

GARGA (*flings the deed papers at his feet*): That's the deed of gift. For the Army. And this, for you. (*Gives him the gun.*) Now get out of here, you pig!

SALVATION ARMY OFFICER: I thank you, on behalf of my
Mission. (*Exits, with an awkward bow. The hymn-
singing fades away, surprisingly fast.*)

GARGA: You ruined my joke. There's no beating you, for
brutality. I'll keep some of the folding money. I'm
not staying around. Because that's the point, Mr.
Shlink from Yokohama: now I'm off for Tahiti!

MARIE: That is cowardly, George. When that clergyman
went, I saw you, and you looked cross-eyed, you're
desperate!

GARGA: I came here, peeled and pared to the bone. I've
still got the shakes from all that's been cooking in my
mind the last two weeks. I spit into his face, many
times. He takes it. I say, the hell with him. That's all.

MARIE: Shame on you!

GARGA: And you, you didn't stand by me. A tooth for a
tooth.

MARIE: Now you want to fight me, too? You never knew
when to stop. God will punish you; I don't want anything from you; just leave me alone.

GARGA: And go and get your parents some bread. Bake
it in a whore's bed, sell them that horsey smell and
then say: It isn't me, it isn't me! That you may
prosper in bed, and long live on this earth. (*Exits
with the others.*)

MARIE: I really cannot understand you, Mr. Shlink. But,
you have a choice, haven't you, the four points of the
compass, where others only have one way to go?
People get many chances, don't they? I can see it
now, people get lots of chances. . . .

SHLINK *shrugs, turns, goes toward back of stage.*
MARIE *follows him.*

3

THE GARGAS' LIVING ROOM
The 22nd of August, in the evening, after 7 P.M.

A shabby loft. At the back, a curtained window, leading to a rooftop balcony. JOHN GARGA, MAE. MANKY, *singing a song.*

JOHN: Something's happened here, it ain't easy to talk about.

MANKY: They say your boy George got involved in one of those businesses no one can tell how how they're going to end. . . . They say, it's something with a Chink. That a Chink's been putting the hex on him, somehow.

MAE: We must keep out of it.

JOHN: If he's been kicked out of his job, we'll just have to scrape the mold off the bread, and have that for dinner.

MAE: He never could stand anyone bossing him, he couldn't, not even as a little child.

MANKY: They say you shouldn't have let your girl Marie go and work for this Chinaman.

MAE: Well, yes. She's stayed away for more than a week, too.

MANKY: So I guess it's pretty obvious, it's all part of the same business.

MAE: When our daughter left, she said she'd been offered a job at a lumber dealer's place. Ten dollars a week, just for doing the laundry.

MANKY: A Chink, and laundry!

JOHN: These here cities, you can't tell what's going on in

the house next door. And you can't even tell what it really means, when you read one of their damn papers.

MANKY: Or when you have to buy a ticket to go somewhere.

JOHN: Those people, riding around in them electric cars, they'll god knows end up with . . .

MANKY: Cancer of the stomach.

JOHN: You just can't tell. But ain't it true, here in the States you can grow wheat all year round, summer and winter. . . .

MANKY: But all of a sudden, and nobody's going to tell you, there is no dinner to eat. Or you go and take a walk with your kids in the street, and everything's fine and dandy, all according to the Fourth Commandment, and all of a sudden you find you're just holding the hand of your son or daughter, just the hand, and your son and your daughter have already sunk down, into that sudden gravel, way above their heads . . .

JOHN: Hey! Who's that?

GARGA *stands in the door.*

GARGA: Setting the world to rights, as usual?

JOHN: At last, you've come with the money for these two weeks?

GARGA: Yes.

JOHN: Now you tell me, do you still have that job, or don't you? And a new jacket! I guess you must've been paid good money, for something or the other?— Yes? That is your mother, George. (*To* MAE:) What you standing for like that, like Lot's Wife or something? Look, your boy's back. Our boy's come back, to take us all out to dinner in the Metropolitan Bar or someplace. You think he looks a little pale, your beloved son? A little drunk, maybe? Come on, Manky, let's go. Let's smoke our pipes on the stairs. (*Exit both.*)

MAE: George, please tell me: have you gotten into trouble
    with somebody?

GARGA: Someone been here?

MAE: No . . .

GARGA: I have to go, anyway.

MAE: But where are you going?

GARGA: Somewhere. Come on, don't always get so scared,
    the least little thing I say.

MAE: But you mustn't leave us here!

GARGA: Yeah, I have to leave you. You know, there's a
    man: now he insults another, right? That isn't so
    pleasant for the other guy. But under certain condi-
    tions this same man is ready and willing to give away
    a whole lumber business, just for the privilege of in-
    sulting another man. And sure, that makes things even
    less pleasant. The way I see it, the insulted party ought
    to get out in such a case; but even that would be too
    pleasant for him, and maybe he's not able to get out,
    anymore. At least, he would have to be free.

MAE: And aren't you?

GARGA: No, I'm not. (*Pause.*) We aren't free. It starts with
    coffee in the morning, and blows for being such a bad
    monkey, and mother's tears are salt to season the
    children's meal; and she washes their little shirts in
    her sweat, and you are all taken care of and safe,
    safe, until the Ice Age comes, while the root grows
    right through your heart. And when he's grown up,
    and wants to do something, wants to go the whole
    hog, what does he find out? He'll find he's already
    been consecrated, paid for, stamped and sold at a
    good price, so he isn't even free to go and drown
    himself!

MAE: George, tell me, what is it that makes you suffer so
    much?

GARGA: You can't help me.

MAE: But I can. And don't run away from your father.
    How are we going to live here?

GARGA (*gives her money*): They fired me. But here, this should last for half a year or so.

MAE: And we're so worried about your sister, we haven't heard from her at all, but we hope she still has her job. . . .

GARGA: That I don't know. I told her to get away from that yellowface.

MAE: Oh, I know. I'm not allowed to tell you how other mothers arrange these things. . . .

GARGA: Yeah, all those other people: all the good people, all the other, good people—standing at their lathes, and earning their bread, and turning out all the good tables for all the good bread-eaters, all the other good table-makers and bread-eaters and all their good families, so many of them, so goddamn many of them, and there's no one would spit into their soup, and no one to give them a good, solid kick across into the good other world, no deluge to drown them with a "Stormy is the night and the seas go high". . . .

MAE: Oh, George! .

GARGA: Don't Oh George me! I can't stand it any more, I don't want to hear it.

MAE: You don't want it any more? But what about me? How am I supposed to live? How filthy the walls are in this place. . . . And that stove won't last another winter.

GARGA: Listen, my dear mother, isn't it plain to see? Nothing is going to last long anymore, nothing, not the stove and not the wall either.

MAE: And you can say that to me! Are you blind?

GARGA: Neither will the bread last long in the cupboard, nor the dress on your body, and it won't be long before your daughter is done for too!

MAE: Go on shouting and ranting! Just you tell it to everybody who wants to listen. How it's all in vain, and all of it too much, too much trouble, and how it

wears you out! But how am I going to live? And I
still have such a long time to live. . . .

GARGA: Well, if it's that bad, why don't you say it. Why
is it so bad?

MAE: You know it.

GARGA: Yes, I know. I know.

MAE: The way you say that . . . What did you think I
meant? I don't want you to look at me like that—
I gave you birth, and I fed you with my milk, and
later with bread, and I beat you, and you can't look
at me like that. A husband, that's different. He is
the way he wants to be, I'm not saying anything
about him. He has worked for us all.

GARGA: Come with me, please.

MAE: What are you saying?

GARGA: I'm asking you to come with me, to the South. I'll
work, I can cut down trees and build a log cabin,
and you do the cooking. So you see, I really need you.

MAE: Who are you telling that to? To the wind? But when
you come back, you can come here and see where
it was we had to live out our last days. (*Pause.*)
When are you leaving?

GARGA: Right now.

MAE: Don't tell them anything. I'll get everything ready
for you, I'll put the bundle under the staircase.

GARGA: Thank you, mother.

MAE: You are welcome. (*Exit both.*)

THE WORM *enters cautiously, sneaks around.*

MANKY: Hey, who's that?

Enters, with JOHN.

THE WORM: Just me, a gentleman, for sure . . . Mr. Garga,
Mr. John Garga, I presume?

MANKY: What do you want here?

THE WORM: Me? Nothing! But maybe I could have a

word with your son, I mean, if he's had his bath
already?

JOHN: What do you want to see him about?

THE WORM (*shaking his head in mock sadness*): How in-
hospitable! But where, sir, if I may ask without
causing you undue strain, where is your son having
his siesta?

JOHN: He's gone. And you get the hell out of here! This
ain't no information bureau.

Enter MAE.

THE WORM: Oh, what a pity! A pity! We miss him, your
son, we really miss him, sir. And it's also on account
of your daughter, if you're at all interested.

MAE: Where is she?

THE WORM: She's staying in a Chinese hotel, madam, in a
Chinese hotel.

JOHN: What did you say?

MAE: Marie!

MANKY: What's that mean? What is she doing there?

THE WORM: Nothing, or, just eating. Mr. Shlink asked me
to tell you and your son, he ought to come and
take her home, she's getting too expensive, he can't
afford it, the lady's got such a blessed appetite. She
doesn't walk at all, not a single step. But she perse-
cutes us all with immoral propositions, yes, she's de-
moralizing the whole place. We'll end up having the
cops in, sir.

MAE: John!

THE WORM (*yells*): In short, she's like a millstone round
our necks!

MAE: Christ!

MANKY: Where is she? I'll go there right away and bring
her back.

THE WORM: Well yes, bring her back. . . . Are you a
dachshund? How can you tell which hotel it is? It
isn't all that simple, my young friend. You ought

to have kept an eye on the lady! And it's all that boy's fault—let him come and get the bitch, let him take care of her. Or we'll get the cops in, tomorrow night.

MAE: Oh, my God! But please, tell us where she is. I don't know where the boy has gone, he's left us—please, don't be so cruel! Oh, Marie! John, please ask him! What has happened to Marie? What is going to happen to me? George! John, what a terrible city this is! What terrible people! (*Exit.*)

SHLINK *appears in the doorway.*

THE WORM (*frightened, under his breath*): Yes, I have . . . The house has two doors. . . . (*Slinks out.*)

SHLINK (*matter-of-factly*): My name is Shlink. I was a lumber dealer once, now I'm just something to catch flies with. . . . I don't have to worry about anybody. Would you people have a bed for me? I'll pay for my board. You see, I saw the name of a man I know, downstairs, on the doorplate.

MANKY: So you are Shlink? You're the man who is holding the daughter of these folks imprisoned somewhere!

SHLINK: Who's their daughter?

JOHN: Marie Garga, sir, my daughter, Marie Garga.

SHLINK: Don't know her. I don't know your daughter.

JOHN: There was a gentleman here just now. . . .

MANKY: And my guess is, it was you who sent him.

JOHN: He disappeared, just as you came in.

SHLINK: I do not know that gentleman.

JOHN: But, but my boy, and you, you've . . .

SHLINK: All right, all right, have your joke at a poor man's expense. It's safe enough to insult me. I've gambled away all I had, sometimes I don't even know how it happened.

MANKY: Well . . . All I say is: when I take my brig into port, I know how deep the water is.

JOHN: Can't trust anybody.

SHLINK: You're alone now—and by your own awkward-
ness you're old enough to wish the ground would
close, so the snow doesn't fall into the cracks. . . . I
see your breadwinner has deserted you. I'm capable
of compassion, you know; and besides, it would give
some meaning to my work.

JOHN: You can't fill your belly with reasoning, you know.
And we aren't beggars. And herrings' heads don't
make much of a meal, either. But, you know, your
loneliness doesn't meet with hearts of stone here.
What you want is to lean your elbows on a family
table. But we're poor people.

SHLINK: I'm not particular. I can eat flint stones.

JOHN: There ain't much space, either. Already we're lying
here in layers, like haddock. . . .

SHLINK: I'll sleep on the floor, I can make do with a
space only half my length. As long as the weather
can't get at me, I'm happy, like a child. I'll pay half
of your rent.

JOHN: All right, I understand. You don't want to stand
out there in the wind and cold, in front of the door.
Come on in, there's a roof for you.

MAE (*enters*): I'm in a hurry, I have to get to town before
it gets dark.

JOHN: You're never home when I need you. I have told
this man he can stay with us. He's lonely, and seeing
that your boy has run away, there's room for one
more. Give him your hand.

MAE: Our home was in the flat country.

SHLINK: I know how it is.

JOHN: What are you doing, over there in the corner?

MAE: I'll bed down here, under the stairs.

JOHN: Where's your stuff?

SHLINK: I don't carry anything. Let me sleep over there
under the staircase, madam. I don't want to intrude.
I won't touch you: I know my hand has a yellow skin.

MAE (*coldly*): Here, I give you mine.

SHLINK: I don't deserve it. I meant what I said. And I know you didn't mean my skin. I'm sorry.

MAE: I'll leave the staircase window open for the night. (*Exit.*)

JOHN: She's a good old soul.

SHLINK: God bless her. I'm a simple man: don't expect any words out of my mouth. All I have in my mouth is teeth.

4

THE CHINESE HOTEL
The 24th of August, in the morning

SKINNY. THE BABOON. JANE.

SKINNY (*in the door*): Aren't you guys even thinking about starting up a new business?

THE BABOON (*in a hammock, shakes his head*): The boss just walks about in the harbor, that's all he does—checking up on the passengers leaving for Tahiti. . . . Seems this kid got away with his soul and all his money, maybe heading for Tahiti. So now he's looking for him. He's carted all the remains of his stuff here, to store it here; just about every cigar butt he brought here. (*Referring to* JANE.) That creature over there he's been feeding for free, these last three weeks. And he brought that kid's sister here too. God knows what he's up to, with her. Often he sits up all night, talking to her.

SKINNY: And you, you let him give you the sack, and now you're paying for his food and for his harem too?

THE BABOON: Well, he makes a couple of bucks, carrying coal, but those he hands over to the kid's folks; like he's a roomer there, but he can't stay, they don't like him too much it seems. That kid, Jesus; he just cleans him out, gets himself a cheap trip to Tahiti. Besides he rigged it up so there's like a great big tree, ready to crash down and break Shlink's neck any minute: the law's going to get him, in five months' time at the latest, for selling the same lot of lumber twice.

SKINNY: And that kind of wreck you're paying out money to keep?

THE BABOON: Well, he had to have a good time. Guys like him deserve a bit of credit. If that kid don't turn up any more, Shlink's going to be the biggest shot in the lumber business all over again, give him three months or so.

JANE (*half-dressed, making up her face*): I always thought I'd end up like this—in a Chink flophouse.

THE BABOON: You don't know half of what's in store for you, sweetie.

Two voices are heard from behind a partition.

MARIE: Why don't you ever touch me? And why are you always wearing that smoke-stained sack? I have a suit for you, one like the other gentlemen wear. . . . I can't sleep nights any more. I love you.

JANE: Sshh! Listen! There she goes again.

SHLINK: I'm not good enough for you. I don't know anything about virgins. And besides, I've been so conscious of the smell of my race, for many years.

MARIE: Yes, it is evil. Evil, that's what it is.

SHLINK: You shouldn't tear yourself to pieces like that. Now look: my body's gone numb, it affects even my skin. You know, in its natural state human skin is too thin for this world. So men take care to see it grows thicker. There would be nothing wrong with the method, if only you could stop it from growing. Take a piece of tanned leather: it stays the way it is. But the living skin grows, it grows thicker and thicker.

MARIE: Is it because you can't find anyone to fight you?

SHLINK: Or take a table: in the first stage, it still has corners: but later—and that's the unpleasant thing about it—later the table turns into rubber. But when your skin's grown really hard, there is no table, no rubber, nothing any more.

MARIE: Oh . . . When did you get this sickness?

SHLINK: Got it when I was a young boy, rowing junks on the Yangtze River. The Yangtze was murdering the junks, and the junks were murdering us. There was a man, every time he walked across the rowing-deck he stepped on our faces, trod them down. And at night we were too weary to turn them away. Strangely enough that man never got too weary. . . . We, for our part, we had a cat we could murder, bit by bit: she drowned while we were teaching her to swim— although she'd been saving us from getting eaten by the rats. All those people had the sickness.

MARIE: When did that happen—on the Yangtze-kiang?

SHLINK: We lay there, among the reeds, and day was breaking, and we could feel the sickness growing inside us. . . .

THE WORM (*enters*): That kid, the wind must've blown him to dust—there isn't a trace of him in all of Chi.

SHLINK: It would be best for you to get some sleep. (*Comes out.*) Again, nothing?

SHLINK *goes out. Through the open door you can hear the sounds of Chicago waking up, cries of milk- men, meat trucks rumbling.*

MARIE: Now Chicago awakens, with the milkmen shout- ing and the meat trucks rumbling through the streets, with the newspapers, with the fresh morning air. To go away would be a good thing, and to wash your- self in water is good—and prairie or asphalt, both yield a harvest. Just now, for instance, there's a cool wind rising down there in the flat country where we used to live; I'm sure of that.

THE BABOON: You still know the Little Catechism, Jane?

JANE (*puts on a whining voice*): It's getting worse, it's getting worse, it's getting worse.

They start cleaning the place up, raising the blinds, rolling up the mats.

MARIE: Me, I'm a little out of breath now. I want to sleep
with a man, and I don't know how to do it. There
are women like there are dogs: yellow ones, black
ones: and I can't do it. I feel as if I had been sawed
to pieces. And these walls, they're like paper—you
can't breathe, you feel like setting fire to it all. Where
are the matches, a black box, let the waters rush in.
. . . Oh, when I float away it is in two parts, each
going its own way. . . .

JANE: Where's he gone?

THE BABOON: Gone to study the faces of those who are
getting out of this town—who find it too tough here,
you know.

JANE: An easterly wind. And the ships for Tahiti, weigh-
ing anchor. . . .

5

THE SAME HOTEL
One month later, the 19th or 20th
of September

A dirty bedroom. A hallway. A gin mill type saloon.
THE WORM. GEORGE GARGA. MANKY. THE BABOON.

THE WORM (*talking from the hallway into the saloon*): So he hasn't set sail, after all. The harpoon stuck deeper than we thought, believing the kid had been swallowed up by the earth. . . . But there he is now, lying in Shlink's room, licking his wounds.

GARGA (*in the bedroom*): "In my dreams, I call him my Infernal Bridegroom"—that dog Shlink. "We do not share bed and board any more, he does not have a room of his own. But his little bride smokes cigarillos and earns herself something to tuck in the tops of her stockings." That's me! (*Laughs.*)

MANKY (*in the saloon, behind a frosted glass pane*): Life's pretty strange. Like for instance a man I knew, he was a first-rate guy, but he was in love with a woman. His people were starving. Two thousand bucks he had on him, but he let them die of hunger, in front of his own eyes. Because he had to make that woman with the two thousand bucks on him: otherwise he wouldn't have got her. A goddamn shame. But he's insane.

GARGA: "Look here: I am a sinner. I loved the desert, orchards ravaged by fire, neglected little shops, hot drinks. You are mistaken. I am just a small human being." What's Mr. Shlink from Yokohama to me!

THE BABOON: Yeah, but take the lumber boss. He never had a heart. But then one day he lost his business—lock, stock, and barrel, on account of some mad passionate thing. And now, he's lugging sacks of coal down there. And at one time he was boss of the whole section!

THE WORM: And we've given him shelter, like he was a starving pedigree dog. But if he doesn't lay off it soon, that bone he's so happy to have found again—we won't stand for it much longer.

GARGA: "One day I will be his widow, yes: the day, I am sure, has been marked already in our calendar. And I'll walk behind his corpse in my clean underwear, my legs well apart, in the beloved sun."

MARIE (*enters with a basketful of groceries*): George!

GARGA: Who's that? (*Recognizes her.*) God, you look like a dirty rag!

MARIE: Yes.

THE WORM (*speaking to the saloon*): He's drunk out of his mind. Now he got a visitor, his sister. He's already told her she's dirty. Where's the old man?

THE BABOON: He'll be here today. I've brought Jane along, for bait, I guess. We're gambling for the highest stakes.

JANE (*shakes her head*): I don't understand you. Give me a drink. Gin.

MARIE: I'm glad to know you had a better opinion of me, you're so surprised to see me here now. But I'd like to remind you, too—of when you were the idol of all the girls, doing the shimmy, playing ragtime, with a sharp crease in your pants on Saturday nights, and your only vices tobacco, whisky and the love of women, all of them permitted to men. I would like you to think back on those times, George. (*Pause.*) How is it with you?

GARGA (*lightly*): Gets a little cold here, at night. Anything you want? Are you hungry?

MARIE (*in the same tone of voice, shaking her head and looking at him*): Oh George, those vultures; they've been circling above our heads for some time now. . . .

GARGA (*as before*): When did you go home last?

MARIE *is silent.*

I heard that you usually hang out here.

MARIE: You did? Who do you think is taking care of the old folks?

GARGA (*coolly*): I've got good news for you. I've heard that someone is indeed taking care of them. And I've also been told the tricks you're up to, these days. I also know a thing or two about a certain Chinese hotel.

MARIE: Is it pleasant to be so cold-blooded, George?

GARGA *stares at her.*

Don't look at my face. I know, you're a faithful Catholic.

GARGA: Go ahead!

MARIE: I love him. Why don't you say anything?

GARGA: Love him, yes, good! That'll soften him up!

MARIE: Please, don't stare at that ceiling all the time. . . . But I can't have him.

GARGA: That's a disgrace!

MARIE: I know it. Oh, George, I'm all broken inside. Because I can't make him come to me. When I see him, I start shaking inside my dress, and then I say the wrong things to him.

GARGA: And I can't tell you the right words, either. A woman, and she gets scorned that way! I had one, she wasn't worth a bottle of rum, but she knew how to get her men! She was worth the investment. She knew her stuff, too.

MARIE: You say such violent things, they float into my head like strong drink. But are they any good? That you have to know, if they're good or not. But I can understand you now.

SHLINK *appears in the hallway.*

THE WORM: I tell you, and I've been around: all these people in the world, they're all of them suckers for dreams out of nothing but paper; they fall for it like a ton of bricks. And there's nothing so papery as real life!

MARIE *turns and bumps into* SHLINK.

SHLINK: You are here, Miss Garga?

MARIE: If a woman tells her love to a man, people say she's indecent. But I want to tell you now that my love for you doesn't prove a thing. There's nothing I want from you. And it isn't easy for me, to tell you that, and maybe it's only too obvious.

GARGA (*comes out of the bedroom*): Stay here, Marie. We've been marooned in this city, with our country faces. You mustn't act easy like that. You must only do what you want to do.

MARIE: Yes, George.

GARGA: The fact is, he's working like a dray-horse, while I'm laying on my back in my own little pool of absinthe. . . .

SHLINK: The conquistadores of this world enjoy lying on their backs.

GARGA: And the owners have to work.

SHLINK: Do you have worries?

GARGA (*to* SHLINK): Every time I look at your face I see you're sizing me up. You backed the wrong horse? Your face has grown old.

SHLINK: I thank you for not forgetting me. I already thought you had gone south, somewhere. I have to apologize. You see, I took the liberty of supporting your unfortunate family, with the work of my hands.

GARGA: Is that true, Marie? That I did not know. So you're digging in, are you? Relishing that vicious idea—to support my family? You make me laugh! (*Exits, left, into the bedroom, throws himself on the bed, laughs.*)

SHLINK (*follows him*): Go on, laugh, I love your laughing. Your laughter is my sunshine. It has been so gray here. It has made me sad, not being able to see you. It is three weeks now, Garga.

GARGA: I've been doing all right, when all is said and done.

SHLINK: Yes, you're living in clover.

GARGA: Only my back gets thin like a fishbone, from all this lazing around.

SHLINK: What a miserable thing life is: you're living in clover, only the clover isn't good enough.

GARGA: I've got better things to do than to go on wearing out my boots on your ass.

SHLINK: But I ask you, do leave my humble person and my intentions out of your considerations. Only, I'm still here. If you have to give up, you can't leave the battlefield without guilt.

GARGA: But I do give up. I go on strike. I throw in the towel. Why should I go on worrying you, like a dog? You're a hard little betel nut, I ought to spit you out—everybody knows they're harder than teeth, and nothing but a shell.

SHLINK (*pleased*): I'm trying my best to provide you with all the light you may need for that. Mr. Garga, I'm willing to put myself into any kind of light. (*Steps into the light.*)

GARGA. What are you trying to do? Auction off that pockmarked soul of yours? So you can take on any amount of suffering? Or are you simply callous?

SHLINK: Crack it, crack the nut now!

GARGA: You're just falling back on my positions. You're staging a metaphysical battle, and leaving a shambles behind.

SHLINK: You mean this affair with your sister? I haven't slaughtered anything you've held your hand over.

GARGA: I only have two hands. What I see as a human being, you devour like a hunk of meat. You open my eyes to resources I didn't know I had; by appropriating them. You turn members of my family into resources, you live off my supply. And I'm getting leaner and leaner, I'm drifting away into metaphysics! Yet you dare spew all this into my face!

MARIE: George, please, can't I go now? (*She retreats.*)

GARGA (*pulls her back*): But not at all! We've only started discussing you. I only noticed you just now.

SHLINK: It's my bad luck: always to tread on the soft ground. I'll go now. You only realize the worth of your affections when their objects lie in the morgue. And I feel compelled to make you familiar with these affections. But, go on, please; I already know what is in your mind.

GARGA: But I do make sacrifices. Have I said I wouldn't?

MARIE: You should let me go. This frightens me.

GARGA: Come on! (*Runs out in the hallway.*) Let's start a family!

MARIE: George!

GARGA: Stay here! (*Back in.*) A little human involvement, sir!

SHLINK: I don't shrink from it. Not for a minute.

GARGA: You love this man? And he doesn't do anything about it?

MARIE *is crying.*

SHLINK: I hope you don't overestimate your power. (*Runs back into the bedroom.*)

GARGA: Don't worry, it'll be an improvement. It's Thursday night, right? And this is the Chinese hotel. Now, this one here, she's my sister, Marie Garga, right? (*Runs outside.*) Come on, Marie! Sister! This is Mr. Shlink from Yokohama. He has something to tell you.

MARIE: George!

GARGA (*goes and pours himself a drink*): "I have retreated to the city precincts where the women, all white, squat in the fiery bramble bush, with their lopsided mouths the color of oranges."

MARIE: Look, it's getting dark outside. I want to go home tonight.

SHLINK: I'll go with you, if I may.

GARGA: "Their hair-dos were bowls of black lacquer ware, very thin, their eyes were wiped clean by the winds of debauches in the drunken night, by sacrifices brought under the open sky."

MARIE: Please, don't ask me for that.

GARGA: "Their thin dresses, like iridescent snakeskins, clung to their eternally excited limbs as if soaked through by a continuous rain."

SHLINK: But I asked you, sincerely. I don't have any secrets to keep from anyone.

GARGA: "They wrap themselves in these garments from head to toe, their toes adorned with molten copper; and the virgin in the sky grows pale, seeing her sisters." (*Comes back, gives* SHLINK *a glass.*) Don't you want a drink? I find it very necessary.

SHLINK: Why do you drink? Drunk men are liars.

GARGA: It's great fun to have these conversations with you. And when I'm drinking, half my thoughts float away, downward, into the ground—and that makes it easier for me to be aware of them. Come on, have a drink!

SHLINK: I don't really want one. But, if it pleases you . . .

GARGA: I offer you a drink, and you refuse.

SHLINK: I don't refuse it. But my brain is all I have.

GARGA (*pause*): I'm sorry. Let's cut it this way: you'll lose some of that brain. And after you've had your drink, you'll have love.

SHLINK (*drinks, as if performing a ritual*): When I have had my drink, I will have love.

GARGA (*shouting, in the bedroom*): You have a glass too, Marie? No? Why don't you sit down, there's a chair?

THE BABOON: Shut up! I heard them talking all this time. But now they're quiet.

GARGA (*to* MARIE): Yes, this is the Black Hole. Now forty years will pass. I don't deny it. The ground gives, the sewers burst open, but their desires are too weak. Four hundred years I have dreamt of mornings at sea, and the salt wind in my eyes. How smooth it was! (*Drinks.*)

SHLINK (*submissively*): I ask you for your hand, Miss Garga. Do you want me to throw myself at your feet? Please, come with me. I love you.

MARIE (*runs out into the saloon*): Help me! They're selling me!

MANKY: Here I am, my lovely!

MARIE: I knew you would be here.

GARGA: A little gust of wind—like at the opera—blows openings into the screens. . . .

SHLINK: Miss Garga, please, don't go there, come back.

MARIE *comes out of the saloon.*

SHLINK: Please, Miss Garga, don't throw yourself away like that.

MARIE: I want to be in a room with nothing in it. . . . I don't want much of anything any more. I promise you, Pat, I'll never do it again.

GARGA: Watch it, Shlink—now speak up for yourself. . . .

SHLINK: Marie, Marie Garga, think of the slow years. . . . And remember, you're so tired now.

MANKY: Just you come with me: I got a thousand dollars, that's enough for a roof over our heads for the winter. And no more visions, excepting those in the vaude-ville theaters.

SHLINK: Please, Marie Garga, I ask you to come with me, if only you could make up your mind. I'll treat you as my wife, I'll serve you, and if ever I should offend you, I'll go and hang myself without further ado.

GARGA: He means it, too. I'm sure he means it. That's what you'll be getting from him, cent by cent. (*Exit to saloon.*)

MARIE: Tell me, Pat—even if I don't love you, do you love me?

MANKY: I believe I do. And it's been written nowhere twixt heaven and earth that you won't love me too, my beauty.

GARGA: So it's you, Jane. Still knocking them back? You don't look too much like your old self any more. You really sold out now?

JANE: Hey, Baboon, get that guy off my back. I don't like his face, and he's pestering me. Listen, Bab, even if my life isn't all milk and honey any more, I still don't have to take that kind of stuff from guys like him.

THE BABOON: Sure, Baby. If anyone ever comes along and says you're just an old shoe, if anyone ever says that, I'll bust his nose for sure.

GARGA: So they have been feeding you too? And now your face looks like what's left at the bottom of an ice-cream soda. All washed out; and you used to walk around in fine rags, like some opera singer, and now it's like a black powder covering your face. But still, I'll say that for you: you didn't give it away while it was only the flies that shit on you. . . . You're a stupid, boozy hen.

MARIE: We'll go, then—I am sorry I could not do you the favor, Shlink, but I just couldn't. And it isn't because I'm proud.

SHLINK: But why can't you stay, Marie—I won't repeat my proposal, if it displeases you. But don't go, don't let that great maw devour you. There are many places you can go, even away from a man.

GARGA: Not for a woman, there ain't. Leave her alone!
Don't you see what she's after? Yeah, Jane, if you'd
have chosen that roof for the winter, you'd still be
sitting there among your shirts. . . .

SHLINK: Marie, Marie Garga . . . Drink, before you make
love tonight.

MARIE: Let's go, Pat. This place is evil. Is that your wife,
George? Is she? I'm pleased to have met her, now.
(*Exit with* MANKY.)

SHLINK (*calls after them*): I won't desert you. Come back
to me, when you realize how it was!

THE BABOON: An old shoe, gentlemen, all trodden-down!
(*Laughs.*)

GARGA (*raising a candle to* SHLINK's *face*): Your face is
all there. And all I get from you is some good will.

SHLINK: The losses are heavy, on both sides. How many
ships do you need to get to Tahiti? Do you want
me to hoist my shirt for a sail, or your sister's petti-
coat? Here, how is this for a cargo—your sister's
fate. You have opened her eyes to the fact that she's
only an object among men, from here to eternity!
I hope I haven't spoiled anything for you. I came
close to getting her as a virgin, but you decided to let
me have what's left over. And don't forget your old
folks either, you're leaving them here! Now, you
have seen what you sacrifice.

GARGA: Yes, I'm going to slaughter them all now. I know
it. I'm ready to steal a march on you, there. And it's
clear to me now, why you've fattened and stuffed
yourself on the proceeds of your coal-carrying. . . . I
won't have that pleasure bargained off of me. So now
I'll even accept this little beast you've kept on ice
for me.

JANE: I won't let you insult me. I'm all alone in the world,
and I can take care of myself.

GARGA: And now, if I may ask, you'll give me the money

paid out in that crooked lumber deal: I hope you've been saving it for me, too—because now's the time to hand it over.

SHLINK *takes out the money and hands it over.*

Hey, I'm drunk. But even though I am drunk, I've got a pretty good plan, Shlink—a pretty damn good plan. (*Exit with* JANE.)

THE BABOON: That was all the loot you had, dear sir. . . . And where did it come from? They'll want to know, they'll want to know. Broost & Co. have put in a request for the lumber they paid for.

SHLINK (*without listening to him*): A chair.

The chairs are all taken, and no one gets up.

My bowl of rice and water.

THE WORM: No more rice for you, sir. You've overdrawn your account.

LAKE MICHIGAN
End of September

Woodland. SHLINK. MARIE.

MARIE: Those trees—they look as if they were covered
with human shit. . . . And the sky's so close you could
touch it, and what do I care for it. I'm cold. I feel
like a partridge half frozen to death; just about as
helpless. . . .

SHLINK: I don't know if it's any use telling you. But I
love you.

MARIE: I've thrown myself away. Yes, "bitter fruit"—
that's what my loving has turned out to be. . . . Others
have their good days and nights, loving; but I'm
shrinking and shriveling here, and worrying myself
like a bone. My body is full of stains.

SHLINK: Yes, say it, say how you're at the end of your
rope. It will help.

MARIE: I lay in bed with a man who is like a beast. I gave
myself to him though I was numb all over, gave
myself many times, and couldn't get any warmer.
The sailor; he smoked his cheroots in between times.
. . . And I loved you, every moment I spent there,
between those papered walls, and I got so wild thinking about it that he believed it was love, and wanted
to stop me. Then I made myself sleep, away into the
dark. I don't owe you anything, and yet my conscience is crying out to me, that I have wasted my
body, and that it belongs to you, though you didn't
want it.

SHLINK: I wish you wouldn't feel so cold. I thought, the
air is warm and dark. I don't know what men tell
their loves, in this country. But if it's any use to you:
I love you.

MARIE: I'm such a coward. I must have lost my courage,
too, with my innocence.

SHLINK: But you'll wash yourself; you'll feel clean again.

MARIE: Maybe I should go down, to the water, but I can't.
I'm not ready for that yet. Oh, this tearing thing, the
heart that won't leave me alone! I'm only half of
everything. I don't even love, it is just my vanity. I
can hear what you say, I'm not deaf, I have ears, but
what does it mean? Maybe I'm only sleeping, they'll
come and wake me; and maybe it's just that I'd do
anything, the most evil things, just to get under a roof;
that I'm telling lies to myself, closing my eyes. . . .

SHLINK: Come, it's getting cold.

MARIE: But the leaves are warm and good against the
sky—though the sky hangs down, too close. . . .

They walk away.

MANKY (*enters*): So this is where the trail takes us! You
sure need a great big sense of humor, this month of
September. The crawfish are mating—the red deer
are yelling for love in the thickets—and badgers are
in season. Yes, yes. But my goddamn fins are getting
cold, and I have to wrap my black socks in newspapers. Where the hell is she now, that's the worst
part! If she's laying around in that greasy flophouse,
like a dirty fishbone, she'll never change her petti-
coats again. Because *that* gives stains, it does! Oh,
Pat Mankyboddle, I'll court-martial you! I'm too
weak to defend myself, so I better start attacking.
The enemy will be devoured with feathers and skin,
digestion will be speeded up by prayers, the vultures
will be summarily executed and hung for display in
the Mankyboddle Museum! Pfffft, words! Toothless

phrases! (*Pulls a gun out of his pocket.*) That's the coldest solution! What d'you think you're doing, crashing through the undergrowth, looking for a skirt—you old hog. Down on all fours! This is a real suicide thicket! Hey, listen, Pat my buddy—where could she go, when she's all finished and done with? Leave it, lay off it, Pat m'boy, have a smoke, get something to eat, put that thing away. C'mon, let's go! (*Exit.*)

MARIE (*returns with* SHLINK): It is too disgusting, in the eyes of God and men. . . . I won't go with you.

SHLINK: Those are stuffy, rotten emotions. Your soul is suffocating—not enough air. . . .

MARIE: I can't do it. They all want to make me into a sacrifice.

SHLINK: But you always have to have your head under some man's shoulder, no matter who it is.

MARIE: I'm nothing to you.

SHLINK: You can't live alone.

MARIE: How quickly you took me—as if I were slipping away . . . And how like that other sacrifice it was.

SHLINK: Like a crazy bitch you ran into the woods, and like a crazy bitch you're running out again.

MARIE: Is it true, am I like that? I'm always like you say. I love you. Don't get confused about that: I love you. I love, like a crazy bitch, you said it. But now you want to pay for it. Yes, I like that too, I like to be paid. Give me your money, I'll live off it, I am a whore.

SHLINK: The water's running down your face—you, a whore!

MARIE: Give me that money. Don't make fun of me. Don't look at me. It isn't tears, on my face, it's the fog rising. . . .

SHLINK *gives her the money.*

I won't say thank you, Mr. Shlink from Yokohama.

It's a straightforward business transaction, no one has to say thanks.

SHLINK: No . . . Yes, get away from me. Get out of here, like they say. (*Exit.*)

7

THE GARGAS' LIVING ROOM
The 29th of September 1912

The room is full of new furniture. JOHN GARGA, MAE,
GEORGE, JANE, MANKY, *all dressed in new clothes, at the
wedding dinner.*

JOHN: Ever since that man, no one likes to say a word
about him here, the man whose skin is a different
color from ours, but he goes down to the coal district,
for a family he knows, and there he works for them,
day and night—ever since that man, with the different
skin, carrying coals, keeps us all here, I have to say
it: things have been improving day by day, in every
which way! Without knowing it, he's provided our
boy George with a wedding today, a wedding as
splendid as that of any real big shot in any big
business house. New neckties, black suits, a whiff of
good bourbon between our teeth—and all in these
festive, newly furnished surroundings!

MAE: Isn't it strange that he makes so much money, just
by carrying coals in the district?

GARGA: It's me who makes it.

MAE: You made up your mind to get married, overnight.
Wasn't it a little too much of a rush, what do you say,
Jane?

JANE: Well, the snow melts, too, and where's it gone?
And you pick the wrong one—that happens all the
time.

MAE: It's not whether it's the right one or the wrong one.
The thing is to keep on trying, trying.

JOHN: Aw, stop it. Eat your steak, shake hands with the bride!

GARGA (*takes her wrist*): It's a good hand. And I feel pretty good here. Let the wallpaper peel, I'll buy a new suit, I have steaks for dinner—I can taste the plaster dropping, I get covered in mortar, inches thick, I see a piano. Hang a wreath round the photograph of our beloved sister, Maria Garga, born twenty years ago in the flat country. And put everlasting flowers under the glass. It's good to sit here, it's good to lie here, the black wind doesn't get to blow in here.

JANE (*gets up*): What is it, George? You're raving!

GARGA: Yes, Jane. It makes me feel good, to rave.

JANE: I often wonder what it is you want to do to me, George.

GARGA: Why so pale, mother of mine? The prodigal son, don't you know, he's returned to sit here, under your roof. Why are you all standing around like chalky pictures on the wall?

MAE: I guess you were talking about the fight.

GARGA: Just flies buzzing in my brain—right? I can chase them away.

SHLINK *enters*.

GARGA: Hey, mother, a plate and a steak and a glass of whisky for our most welcome guest! You know, I got married this morning. Dearest wife, you tell him!

JANE: Me and my husband, we went to the Sheriff, quite early in the morning, straight from bed, and we asked him: can we get married here? And he said, I know you, Jane—do you think you'll stay with your husband? But I could tell he was a good man, with a beard, and he didn't have anything against me, so I said: Life isn't exactly the way you think it is. . . .

SHLINK: My congratulations, Garga. You're a revengeful man.

GARGA: That hideous fear in your smile, right now! And,

with reason. Don't hurry too much with your food, there's time enough. Where is Marie? I hope she is all right. Your satisfaction ought to be complete. I'm sorry, Shlink, there's no chair for you just now. We're one chair short. But otherwise the furnishings have been renewed and replenished. Just look at that piano! It's all so great, I sure hope to be able to spend my evenings here, with the family. I've turned over a new leaf. Tomorrow I'll go back to C. Maynes, to work in the lending library.

MAE: Oh, George, aren't you talking too much?

GARGA: There, you see, my family doesn't want me to go on with our acquaintance. It's all over, Mr. Shlink. It has been most profitable. The furniture speaks for itself. The clothes of all my dear relatives also. Cash isn't lacking either. So, I thank you.

A silence.

SHLINK: There's one more favor I'd like to ask you, a personal one. Here I have a letter from the firm of Broost & Co. I see the Seal of Justice of the State of Virginia on it, and I realize I haven't even opened it yet. Now, I would be most grateful if you could do that for me. Whatever the news is, even the worst will be easier to hear from your lips.

GARGA *reads*.

Now if you could give me a hint on how to proceed in this business—which is, certainly, my own, my private affair—it would make things much easier for me.

MAE: George, why don't you say anything? What is on your mind? Again your face looks the way it does when you're working out a new plan. And there's nothing I fear more than that. There you sit, screened by god knows what thoughts, they are like a cloud of smoke. And we wait, just wait, like cattle in the slaughterhouse. You say: wait a while, then you go away, you come back, and one can't recognize you any more, and we don't know what you have been doing with yourself. Tell me your plan—or even if you don't have one, tell me that, too, so I can arrange my life. Even I have to make plans for my years. Four years, in this city of iron and dirt! Oh, George!

GARGA: You know, the bad years were the best years, and now they're over and done with. Don't say anything to me. You, my parents, and you, Jane my wife: I've decided to go to jail.

JOHN: What's that you said? Was that where all your money came from? That you'd end up behind bars, well, I guess it was plain as writing on your forehead when you were five years old. I never asked what happened between the two of you. But I always knew it was some shady business. George, you've lost the ground under your feet. Buying pianos, going to jail, dragging home whole basketsful of steaks and ruining a family's livelihood, it's all the same to you. Where's Marie, your sister? (*He tears his jacket off and throws it on the floor.*) There's the jacket, and I didn't want to put it on in the first place. But I've gotten used to it, to whatever humiliations this city still may have in store for us.

JANE: How long will it be, George?

SHLINK (*to* JOHN): It was a crooked lumber deal, and someone will have to take the rap. The Sheriff doesn't care about the whys and hows. But as you know I'm your friend, and I could explain certain things to the Sheriff, I could make them sound just as convincing as the tax declaration of the Standard Oil Company. And I'm willing to listen to what your son may have to say, Mrs. Garga.

JANE: Don't let him soft-soap you, George. Do what you

think is right; don't care what they say. I'm your wife now, I'll run the house while you're away.

JOHN (*with a loud laugh*): She'll run the house! A girl who was picked off the streets only yesterday. So we'll feed on the wages of sin; is that it?

SHLINK (*to* GARGA): You just told me how attached you are to your family, how you wish to spend your evenings here, on these chairs, letting many a thought roam over to me, your friend, who is working to make life easy for you. So, I'm willing to save you for your family.

MAE: You can't go to jail now, George.

GARGA: I knew you wouldn't understand it. How hard it is to hurt anybody—and to destroy him, that's downright impossible. The world is too poor, we have to work like slaves to find weapons to attack it with. . . .

JANE (*to* GARGA): Now you're philosophizing, while the roof is caving in over our heads.

GARGA (*to* SHLINK): Look all over the world, you'll find ten evil men and not a single evil deed. Men are destroyed by almost irrelevant causes. No, that's enough of that for me. Now I'll draw a line under the reckoning, and then I'll go.

SHLINK: Your people want to know if you care for them. If you don't hold them, they'll fall. Only a word, Garga!

GARGA: I set them all free.

SHLINK: In other words, you let them rot away. There aren't that many of them any more, they might want to have a fresh start again, just like you—they might want to cut the tablecloth to shreds, to shake the cigar butts out of their clothes. Yes, all of them could decide to follow in your footsteps, to go free and unwashed in the world. . . .

MAE: Don't say anything, George. But it's all true, what he says.

GARGA: Now, at last, I'm able to see certain things—when I half close my eyes—to see them in a cold light. Not your face though, Mr. Shlink. Maybe you haven't got a face.

SHLINK: Forty years have been found dirty and wanting . . . and a time of great freedom is about to begin.

GARGA: Yes, that's the way it is. The snow was about to fall, but it got too cold. And again the leftovers will be eaten, again they won't be enough to still their hunger, and I, I will kill my enemy.

JOHN: Weakness and vice, that's all I see. Ever since I set eyes on you. Go, leave us alone. And let them take all that stuff away again.

GARGA: I once read, somewhere, that the weak waters can pick a fight with whole mountain ranges. . . . And I would like to see your face again, Shlink, your milk-glass face, your goddamn *invisible* face.

SHLINK: I have nothing to say to you any more. Three years—for a young man that's nothing, like opening and closing a door! But for me . . . Well, I got no profit out of you, if that's a consolation. Still, you don't leave a trace of sadness in me, now that I'll disappear back into this great, loud city—to go about my business like I did before you came. (*Exit.*)

GARGA: All I have to do now is phone the police. (*Exit.*)

JANE: Then I'll go to the Chinese Bar. I don't want to see any cops. . . . (*Exit.*)

MAE: Somet˙ ˙es I think even Marie won't come back again, ever.

JOHN: She's got only herself to blame. You're supposed to help them when they turn vicious?!

MAE: But when else should you help them?

JOHN: Aw, be quiet.

MAE (*goes over and sits down beside him*): What I wanted to know—what are you going to do now?

JOHN: Me? Nothing. It's all finished, for now.

MAE: But you did understand what George wants to do to himself?

JOHN: Well, yes. Just about. Well, the worse for us.

MAE: And what are we going to live on?

JOHN: The money we still have—and what we get for the piano when we've sold it.

MAE: But they'll take that away from us anyway. We bought it with crooked money. . . .

JOHN: Maybe we'll go back to Ohio. We'll find a way.

MAE (*gets up*): There was one other thing I wanted to tell you, John, but I can't do it now. I never believed it, but it is true: a human being can suddenly be damned, thrown into hell. They decide it, in heaven. It's a day like any other, nothing out of the ordinary, but from this day on you are one of the damned. . . .

JOHN: What's on your mind now?

MAE: John, I know exactly what I'm going to do. I want to do it, very much. Don't think it's for this or that reason. I'll put some more coal on the fire, and you'll find your supper in the kitchen. (*Exit.*)

JOHN: Listen, take care—that you don't get attacked by the ghost of a shark or something, out there on the staircase!

WAITER (*enters*): Mrs. Garga ordered this drink for you, sir. You want to have it here, in the dark, or shall I switch the light on?

JOHN: But no, of course, let's have some light.

Exit WAITER.

MARIE (*enters*): No speeches please! I've got some money.

JOHN: You dare come in here? What a family this is! And how do you look?

MARIE: Good is how I look. But where did you get all this new stuff from? Some kind of windfall? I got a windfall too.

JOHN: Where did you get the money?

MARIE: You really want to know?

JOHN: Let's have it . . . You've brought me pretty low down, with all these years of starvation.

MARIE: So you take the money, in spite of all that new furniture. Where's mother?

JOHN: Deserters go to the wall.

MARIE: Did you send her out to walk the streets?

JOHN: All right, be a cynic, wallow around in the gutter, drink and gloat. But I'm your father, and you can't let me die of hunger.

MARIE: Where's she gone?

JOHN: You can go, too. I'm used to being left alone.

MARIE: When did she leave?

JOHN: At the end of my life I've been condemned to poverty, to licking the spittle of my children. But I won't have nothing to do with vice. So, it's nothing to me—to chase you out of this house.

MARIE: Then give the money back. It wasn't meant for you.

JOHN: Not a hope. You can sew me up in a sack: I'll still ask for a pound of tobacco.

MARIE: Good-by. (*Exit.*)

JOHN: Five minutes' worth of words, that's all they ever have for anybody. Then they just run out of lies. (*Pause.*) Yeah, and it wouldn't take more than two minutes' silence, to think about all the things that could be said. . . .

GARGA (*coming back*): Where's mother? Has she gone away? Did she think I wouldn't come up here any more? (*Runs out, returns again.*) She's taken her other dress. She won't be back. (*He sits down at the table and writes a letter.*)

"To Police Headquarters: I direct your attention to the Malay lumber dealer, C. Shlink. This man assaulted and raped my sister, Marie Garga, while she was in his employ, and he has since made propositions of an immoral nature to my wife, Jane Garga. Signed,

George Garga." That's it—I'll leave my mother out of it.

JOHN: So that's how you'll liquidate your family.

GARGA: I've now written this letter, and I'll put it in my pocket, so that I can forget all about it. And in three years' time—because that's what I'll get—and eight days before I'm discharged I'll pass it on to the police, and the man will be wiped out, off the face of this city, he'll be gone and nowhere to be seen, when I come back again. But he'll know the day I'm free again: he'll recognize it by the howls of the lynching mob that will be out to get him.

8

C. SHLINK'S PRIVATE OFFICE
The 20th of October 1915, at 1 P.M.

SHLINK. *A young clerk.*

SHLINK (*dictates*): To Miss Marie Garga, who is applying
 for a secretary's job: tell her that I do not want to
 have any dealings with her any more, or with any
 member of her family. Then, the Standard Real Estate
 Brokers. Gentlemen: As of today, not a single share in
 our firm is held by any other company, and our business has achieved a stable position. Thus there is
 nothing to prevent us from accepting your offer of a
 five-year contract.

ANOTHER EMPLOYEE (*showing a* MAN *in*): This is Mr.
 Shlink.

THE MAN: I've got three minutes to give you some information, and you've got two minutes to act on it.
 This is it: half an hour ago, Police Headquarters
 received a letter from one of the state prisons. It is
 signed by a certain George Garga, and he incriminates
 you on several counts. The patrol wagon will be here
 in five minutes. You owe me a thousand bucks.

SHLINK *gives him the money. The* MAN *leaves.*

SHLINK (*beginning to pack a suitcase, carefully*): Go on
 with business as long as possible. Mail those letters.
 I'll be back. (*Exit quickly.*)

9

A BARROOM ACROSS THE STREET FROM THE STATE PRISON
The 28th of October 1915

THE WORM. THE BABOON. THE SNUBNOSE. SALOONKEEPER.
THE SALVATION ARMY OFFICER. JANE. MARIE GARGA.

Crowd noises from outside.

THE BABOON: You hear that mob howling? These are
  tough days for Chinatown. . . . A week ago they
  found out the crimes of a Malay lumber dealer. Three
  years ago he put a man into prison: three years that
  man kept it all to himself. But then, eight days before
  he was due to be discharged, he wrote a letter to the
  cops and spilled the beans.
THE SNUBNOSE: Ah yes, the ways of the human heart . . .
THE BABOON: The Malay fellow's cleared out of course,
  how else. But it's the end of him, anyway.
THE WORM: How can you say that about anybody. Just
  consider life on this here planet: a man doesn't get
  finished off at once, ever—they want to have at least
  a hundred goes at him! Everybody's got far too many
  chances. For example, just listen to this story about
  G. Wishoo, the Bulldog Man. But I'll want the
  nickelodeon on for that.

(*Nickelodeon starts playing.*)

This is the life of George Wishoo, the dog: George
Wishoo was born in Ireland, that emerald isle. At the
age of eighteen months he traveled tó the great city

of London, in the company of a fat man. Like a stranger he left his native land. And in the great city he soon fell into the hands of a cruel woman, and she forced him to submit to incredible tortures. After much suffering George escaped and arrived in a region where people chased him down the green country lanes. He was shot at, with big and dangerous firearms, and often he was chased by other dogs. He lost a leg during this period of his life and walked henceforth with a limp. He tried this and he tried that, and after many failures, discouraged and half-starved, he found refuge with an old man who shared his bread with him. And there he died, at the age of seven and a half years, after a life full of disappointments and adventures, but nevertheless with great composure and peace. He lies buried in Wales. . . . And I'd like to know what you make of all that, dear sir.

THE SNUBNOSE: Who is that man whose picture they have there on the search warrant?

THE WORM: That's the Malay fellow they're looking for. He went bankrupt once already, but in three years he built the whole lumber business up again, by hook and crook—and made a lot of enemies in his part of town. But there's nothing the law could have got him for, if that guy in prison hadn't come up with those sex crimes. (*To* JANE:) When's your man getting out of the clink?

JANE: Oh, but that's just it, I still knew it a moment ago. Please, gentlemen, don't think I don't know it—it's on the twenty-eighth, yesterday or today.

THE BABOON: Lay off it, Jane.

THE SNUBNOSE: And who is that, that bird with the indecent dress?

THE BABOON: She's the victim—the man's sister.

JANE: Yes, that's my sister-in-law. She's pretending not

to know me, but when we were married and living together, she didn't come home a single night.

THE BABOON: See, the Malay ruined her.

THE SNUBNOSE: What is she putting into the bucket over there?

THE WORM: I can't see. She's talking to herself, too. Hey, be quiet, Jane!

MARIE (*lets a bank note flutter into the oak bucket used for rinsing glasses*): When I held the notes in my hand, that time, I could see God's eye watching me. I said: I did it all for him. And God turned away, with a sound like tobacco leaves rustling in the fields. Yet I kept them. A note! And another! See, I'm shedding myself, giving away my purity. . . . Now it's gone, that money! But I don't feel any easier. . . .

GARGA (*enters with* C. MAYNES *and three other men*): I asked you to accompany me, to have you see with your own eyes the injustice I've been made to suffer. I brought you along, Mr. Maynes, to have a witness— to testify that I find my wife in a place like this, coming back after three years in prison. (*He takes the men to the table where* JANE *is sitting.*) How d'you do, Jane. How is life with you?

JANE: George! Is it the twenty-eighth today? I didn't know, I would have stayed home. Did you notice how cold it is there, at home? Did you think I'd be sitting here, just to keep warm?

GARGA: This is Mr. Maynes, you'll remember him. I will go back to work for him again. And these gentlemen have been kind enough to take an interest in my story; they also live on our street.

JANE: Good evening, gentlemen. But, oh George, how awful for me, to forget your day! And what you all think of me, to be sure! Ken See, please come and serve these gentlemen.

SALOONKEEPER (*to* THE SNUBNOSE): That's the jailbird who ratted on the Malay fellow.

GARGA: Hello, Marie; have you been waiting for me? As you can see, my sister is here too.

MARIE: Hello, George. Are you all right?

GARGA: Jane, let's go home now.

JANE: Oh George, you just say it, like that. But if I go with you, you'll be mad at me when we get home, and I better tell you right away: I haven't cleaned the place up at all.

GARGA: I know you haven't.

JANE: That is an unkind thing to say.

GARGA: I'm not accusing you. Jane, listen: we'll make a new start. My fight is over. What else could it be—see for yourself: I've hounded my enemy out of town.

JANE: No, George, it can't be, it has to get worse again. . . . They say things are looking up, but they're not, they're getting worse, because they *can* still get worse. I hope you like it here, gentlemen? We could always move on, someplace else . . .

GARGA: But what's the matter with you, Jane? Aren't you pleased that I came to get you?

JANE: But you know that George. And if you don't, I can't tell you, either.

GARGA: What do you mean by that?

JANE: Just that people aren't as simple as you think, George, even when they're almost dead and buried. Why did you bring these gentlemen along? I always knew I would end up like this: when they told us in confirmation school what happens to those who are weak, I knew, I knew it right away: that's what will happen to me. But why?—you didn't have to prove it to anybody else.

GARGA: So you don't want to come home with me?

JANE: George, please don't ask me.

GARGA: But I am asking you, dear Jane.

JANE: Then I have to be plainer about it: you see, I've been living with this gentleman here. (*She points to*

THE BABOON.) I admit it, gentlemen, what else could I do, and it won't make things any easier.

THE BABOON: She's raving mad.

MAYNES: How terrible!

GARGA: Jane, listen to me. This will be your last chance in this city. I'm willing to draw a line under all of this, these gentlemen can be my witnesses. And I ask you to come home with me.

JANE: That is handsome of you, George. I'm sure it is my last chance. But I don't want it. Things aren't what they ought to be, between the two of us, and you know it. I'm going now, George. (*To* THE BABOON:) Come on!

THE BABOON: And a good evening to you all. (*Exit with* JANE.)

ONE OF THE MEN: He's in a tough spot, that guy.

GARGA: I'll leave the front door open for you, Jane. You can always ring the bell, at night.

THE WORM (*comes over to the table*): Maybe you've already noticed: there's a family here, or rather, the remnants of a family; and this, let's say, pretty moth-eaten family would gladly pay their last cent, if you could tell them where their mother is now, the mainstay of the old household. You know, I've actually seen her: saw her one morning round about seven, cleaning the floor in a fruit dealer's warehouse. She's forty years old, she has taken on a new job, and her old face looked pretty good and serene. . . .

GARGA: But listen, you, weren't you at one time working for the lumber business owned by that man all of Chicago's gunning for now?

THE WORM: Me? I never saw the man. (*Exit.*)

Passing the nickelodeon, THE WORM *puts a coin in, and it starts playing the "Ave Maria" by Gounod.*

SALVATION ARMY OFFICER (*at a small corner table, reading*

the fancy drinks list in a metallic voice, yet savoring each word): Cherry Flip, Cherry Brandy, Gin Fizz, Whisky Sour, Golden Slipper, Manhattan Cocktail, Curacao Extra Sec, Orange, Maraschino Cusinier, and, the specialty of this bar: Eggnog. This alone consists of the following: egg—raw egg, sugar, brandy, Jamaica Rum, milk.

THE SNUBNOSE: You really know all those fancy drinks, sir?

SALVATION ARMY OFFICER: No!

Laughter.

GARGA (*to his companions*): You'll understand that I find it humiliating to exhibit my broken-up family this way, though it's necessary for me to do so. But you'll also realize that this evil, yellow fungus must never again be allowed to spread in this city! As you know, my sister Marie worked for this man Shlink for some time. And now, when I talk to her, I have to be as gentle as I can manage, because I know that she still has some of her natural delicacy of mind, even in this state of abject misery! (*He sits down at Marie's table.*) To see your face again . . .

MARIE: It isn't a face any more. It isn't me.

GARGA: No. But I remember, once, you were only nine, we went to church and you said: let him come to me, let him come tomorrow. And we supposed you meant God.

MARIE: Did I say that?

GARGA: I still love you. You have neglected yourself, you're soiled and worn, but even if I knew that you know it, that you can do anything at all with yourself, if I tell you: I'll always love you—even then I'd say it.

MARIE: And as you're saying it, you're looking at me? At this face?

GARGA: Yes, at that face. People remain what they are, even when their faces fall to pieces.

MARIE (*gets up*): But I don't want that. I don't want you to love me that way. I love myself the way I was, once. Don't tell me I have never been different.

GARGA (*in a loud voice*): Are you earning money? Or just living off men, what they pay you?

MARIE: I see—have you brought people here who ought to know that? Can I get a whisky? With plenty of ice? Let's bring it all out into the open. Well then: at first, I wasted myself: but then I started asking money for it, right away, so that everybody would know what I am, and that I can make a living out of it. And now, it's an easy enough racket—I have a good body, I don't let anyone take any liberties, like smoking without asking for permission first. . . . Yet I'm not a stupid little virgin any more, I know what loving is about. And so, I've got money. But I want to make more, and I want to spend it, spend it— when I've earned some, I don't want to save up, here it is, you see, I throw it into that bucket over there. That's how it is with me.

MAYNES: Terrible.

ANOTHER MAN: It ain't no laughing matter.

SALVATION ARMY OFFICER: People are too durable, that's their main trouble. They can do too much to themselves, they last too long. (*Exit.*)

MAYNES *and the three men get up.*

MAYNES: Garga, we're satisfied that you have suffered great injustice.

THE SNUBNOSE (*sidling up to* MARIE): Whores! (*He whinnies like a horse.*) Vice—it's perfume for the ladies.

MARIE: Yes, us whores! Powder on our faces, so you can't see the eyes that were blue once. But the men who make their money on crooked deals, they get their loving from us: we sell our sleep, we live off our bruises.

A shot is heard.

SALOONKEEPER: That gentleman has shot himself, in the throat!

The men drag the SALVATION ARMY OFFICER *back in, lay him out on the table among the glasses.*

FIRST MAN: Don't touch him. Hands off.

SECOND MAN: He's saying something.

FIRST MAN (*leaning over him, loud*): Is there anything we can do for you? Any relatives? Where d'you want us to take you?

SALVATION ARMY OFFICER (*murmurs*): "La montagne est passée: nous irons mieux."

GARGA (*leaning over the* SALVATION ARMY OFFICER, *laughing*): He's missed it, and in more ways than one. He thought those would be his last words, but they're the last words of someone else; and besides, they aren't his last words anyway, because he's a bad shot and it's only a little scratch.

FIRST MAN: Hey! Such shitty luck! Well, he did it in the dark—he should've done it in the light. . . .

MARIE: His head is hanging down, why don't you prop him up a little! How lean he is. Now I know who it is: he's the one Shlink spit in the face, that time.

Exeunt all, with the wounded man, except MARIE *and* GARGA.

GARGA: His skin is too thick. It bends and deflects everything you thrust at him. There aren't enough spears.

MARIE: Is he always in your mind?

GARGA: Yes, he is. And I don't care if you know it.

MARIE: Loving, hating: how they bend us down, how low they make us!

GARGA: They do. You still love him?

MARIE: Yes—yes, I do.

GARGA: And no hope of more favorable winds?

MARIE: Well, yes, sometimes.

GARGA: I wanted to help you. (*Silence.*) This fight has been such a tremendous debauch that I need all of Chicago today, to keep me from going on with it. Sure, it's possible that he'd decided to quit, already. Didn't he tell me himself that three years, at his age, could be as long as thirty. . . . I've taken it all into consideration, and I have destroyed him, without having to put in an appearance—and with a very crude weapon. And I've prevented him from meeting me again. So this last blow can't be argued any more: he won't get a chance to speak to me. At every street corner of this city the cab drivers are watching out for him, they'll see to it, he won't make it into the ring any more. He's been k.o.'d without a fight, just like that. The city of Chicago has thrown the towel in for him. I don't know where he's hiding out: but he'll know it, just the same.

SALOONKEEPER: There's a fire in the lumber yard on Mulberry Street.

MARIE: It's a good thing, that you've shaken him off. But I have to go now.

GARGA: I'll stay here, right in the dead center of the whirlpool. But I'll be back home tonight, and we'll live together again.

Exit MARIE.

In the mornings I'll drink that hot black coffee again, splash cold water on my face, put on fresh clothes, starting with the shirt. There's a lot of things I'll comb out of my hair tomorrow morning; there will be a lot of new sounds, new happenings all around me in this city—now that the craze has left me that was going to take me down, all the way down. But there's still a lot to do.

Opens the door wide and listens, laughing silently,

*to the howls of the lynching parties; they have grown
stronger.*

SHLINK *has entered. He wears an American-style suit.*

SHLINK: You're alone? It wasn't easy to get here. I knew
you were coming out today. I've already been to look
for you at your house. . . . They're following me here.
Come on, Garga, let us go now!

GARGA: Are you out of your mind? I denounced you—
to get rid of you.

SHLINK: I'm not a brave man. I died three times on my
way here.

GARGA: Yes . . . They tell me they're stringing the Chinks
up like colored washing on the Milwaukee Bridge!

SHLINK: The more reason for us to hurry. You know that
you have to come with me. We haven't settled yet.

GARGA (*very slowly, as he's aware of* SHLINK's *despera-
tion*): I am sorry, but you're asking me for a favor
at a most unfavorable hour. You see, I have company,
I'm not alone. There's my sister, Marie Garga: gone
to the dogs in September three years ago, all of a
sudden. . . . My wife, Jane Garga: gone to the dogs
at the same time. And finally, a gentleman from the
Salvation Army, we don't know his name: he, too,
got ruined, spit on, finished off, though he doesn't
matter all that much. But, first and foremost, my
mother Mae Garga: born in the year 1872 down
South, disappeared in October three years ago, disappeared even from memory, gone without a face.
It has fallen off her, like a yellow leaf . . . (*Listens.*)
Incredible yelling!

SHLINK (*also lost in listening*): Yes. But it isn't the right
kind of yelling yet; not the white kind. When we
hear that, they'll be here. So we still have a minute
to go. There, now, listen! Now it is the right kind—
the white yell! Come on!

Exit quickly with GARGA.

10

DESERTED R.R. WORKERS' TENT IN THE GRAVEL PITS BY LAKE MICHIGAN
The 19th of November 1915, about 2 o'clock in the morning.

SHLINK. GARGA.

SHLINK: The everlasting roar of Chicago has faded away. Seven times three days the skies have grown pale, and the air gray-blue, like a smoky drink. Now it's here, at last: the silence that can't conceal anything.

GARGA (*smoking*): You're a born fighter. What a stomach you have for it! I was just thinking of the times when I was a kid; seeing the oil fields, with the blue rapeseed growing, and the polecats in the dry gulches, and the shallow rapids shooting by. . . .

SHLINK: Right, all those things were in your face. But now it's hard like amber: sometimes you can find dead creatures encased in it, you can see them there.

GARGA: You always stayed alone?

SHLINK: Forty years.

GARGA: And now, as the end draws near, you've become a victim to the black addiction of this planet: you want to touch others.

SHLINK: By hating them?

GARGA: By hating.

SHLINK: So you have understood it. We're companions, comrades in a metaphysical action! We didn't know each other long, but for a while it was the most important thing. And the time has passed quickly. The stations of life are not the same as those of memory.

The end is not the final aim: the last installment is no more important than any other. Twice in my life I owned a lumber business: two weeks ago I made it over to your name.

GARGA: Premonitions of death?

SHLINK: Here, this is the ledger of your firm. It starts from where ink was once spilled over the accounts.

GARGA: You've been carrying it around with you? Why don't you open it yourself. I'm sure it's dirty. (*He reads.*) A tidy calculation; nothing but subtractions. On the seventeenth: the lumber business, twenty-five thousand dollars for Garga. Just before that, ten dollars for clothes. Then a sum of twenty-two dollars for Marie Garga, "our" sister. And at the very end: the whole business burned down once again. I can't find sleep any more, Shlink. I'll be glad when the lime will cover you, at last.

SHLINK: But don't try to back out from what there was, Garga! Don't just look at the figures. Remember the question that was put to us. Get a grip on yourself, Garga: I love you.

GARGA (*looks at him*): You're pretty disgusting! You know, you disgust and frighten me—and an old man, like you.

SHLINK: So maybe I won't get an answer. But when you, Garga, get an answer sometime—think of me, and of my mouth, stuffed with rotting earth. What are you listening for?

GARGA (*lazily*): You show some traces of feeling. You're old.

SHLINK: Is it such a great thing, always to show your fangs?

GARGA: If they're good fangs.

SHLINK: People are so impossibly alone—you can never arrive at real hatred. . . . But even with animals you can't make yourself understood.

GARGA: You can't make yourself understood by speaking.

SHLINK: I've been watching animals: and love, or the warmth given off by bodies moving in close to each other, that is the only mercy shown to us in the darkness. But the coupling of organs is all, it doesn't make up for the divisions caused by speech. And yet they go on coupling to create others that might help them in their hopeless loneliness. . . . And the generations stare coldly into each other's eyes. If you cram a ship's hold full of human bodies, so it almost bursts —there will be such loneliness in that ship that they'll all freeze to death. Are you listening, Garga? Yes, loneliness is so powerful, there cannot even be a fight. The forest! That's where mankind comes from, from right here. Hairy, with ape's mouths, good animals who knew how to live. It was all so easy. They just tore each other to pieces. I can see them now—how they stared into the whites of each other's eyes, how they stood there, panting, then buried their teeth in the jugular vein, rolling down on the ground: and the one who bled to death down there among the tree roots, he was the loser, and the one who had trampled down most of the undergrowth, he was the winner. Do you hear something, Garga?

GARGA: Shlink . . . For three weeks I've been listening to you. And all this time I've been waiting for a rage to come into me, for any excuse, however small. But now, looking at you, I realize it's all so much hot air: and your voice sickens me. Isn't it Thursday night, tonight? How far is it to New York? Why am I sitting here, wasting my time? Haven't we been lying about here for three weeks already? We thought the planet would be thrown out of orbit, but what happened? Three times it's been raining, and one night there was a storm. (*Gets up.*) Shlink, I think the time has come for you to take off your shoes. Take off your shoes, Shlink, and give them to me. Because you won't have much left in the way of money.

Shlink, now I declare our fight has come to an end, in its third year, in the woods by Lake Michigan: it has used up all its fuel, it ceases to exist, this very moment. I can't finish it off with a knife, and I see no big words that need to be said. But my shoes are full of holes, and your speeches don't keep my toes warm. It's as simple as that, Shlink: the younger man wins.

SHLINK: Today I could sometimes hear the shovels of the railroad people, all the way down here. And I noticed you were listening, too. You're leaving, Garga? You're going to them, to betray me?

GARGA (*lies down, lazily*): Exactly, yes, that is what I am going to do.

SHLINK: And never, George Garga, there will never be an outcome to this fight—never an understanding?

GARGA: No, there won't.

SHLINK: But you'll get away, with nothing but your life?

GARGA: It's better to have that life than any other.

SHLINK: Tahiti?

GARGA: New York. (*With an ironic laugh.*) "I'll go there, and I'll return, with limbs of iron, with a dark skin, with a rage in my eye. When they look at my face, they'll have to believe that I belong to a strong race. I will have gold, I will be lazy and brutal. Women like to take care of such wild patients returning from the hot countries. I will swim, tread the grass down, hunt and smoke my pipe, smoke my pipe more than anything else, and enjoy drinks as hot as boiling metal. I will throw myself into life, I will be saved." Such idiocies! Words, on a planet that is no longer in the center! When you'll lie covered in lime, Shlink, the lime that is your own natural excretion of old age, I'll still be able to choose my own amusements.

SHLINK: What pose is it you're striking now? And please, take that pipe out of your mouth. If all you want to

say is that you've become impotent, then you'd better
do it in another tone of voice.

GARGA: Whatever you say.

SHLINK: That gesture proves it to me. You're not worth
the fight.

GARGA: I only complained that you bore me.

SHLINK: Complained, you said? You! A hired bruiser! A
drunken sales clerk! I bought you for ten bucks—
a blue-eyed boy who couldn't tell his right leg from
his left, a nothing!

GARGA: Don't kid yourself: a young man.

SHLINK: A white-faced creature, hired to ruin me, to stuff
my mouth with a little slime or rot, to give me a
taste of death on my tongue! Six hundred feet
through that wood I'll find myself as many lynchers
as I wish.

GARGA: Well, yes, maybe I am a leper, but what's it
matter. You're a suicide. What do you have to offer
me? You hired me all right, but you haven't paid.

SHLINK: You got what your kind needs. I bought you
some furniture.

GARGA: That's right; a piano—that's what I got out of you,
a piano. And we had to sell it. And a good meal,
with a meat dish. And a suit I bought, and gave up
my sleep, for your blabbing!

SHLINK: Your sleep, your mother, your sister, and your
wife. Three years of your stupid life. But what a
shame! Now it ends in this slime. You never understood what it was. You just wanted to finish me off,
but I wanted the fight: and it wasn't the body, it
was the soul.

GARGA: And the soul, you know, the soul is nothing. It
isn't important to come out on top, what matters
is to be the one who comes out alive. I can't win:
I can just stamp you into the ground. I'll take my
own raw meat out there, into the icy rain: Chicago

is a cold place. I'll go there. Maybe I'm doing the wrong thing. But what the hell, I still have plenty of time. (*Exit.*)

SHLINK *falls to the ground.*

SHLINK (*rising*): Now, after the last thrusts have been delivered, and the last words, whatever words came into our heads, I want to thank you for the interest you have taken in my person. A lot has been shed off us, there's hardly even the naked bodies left now. In four minutes' time the moon will rise, and your lynching party may arrive. (*Only now he realizes that* GARGA *has left; he sets out to follow him.*) Don't go away, George Garga! Don't give up, just because you're young. The forests have been cut down, the vultures have stuffed their bellies, and the golden answer will be buried in the ground. . . . (*Turns. A milky light begins to glow in the thicket.*) The nineteenth of November! Three miles south of Chicago. A westerly wind. Drowned, four minutes before moonrise, while catching fish.

MARIE (*enters*): Please, don't chase me away again. I am so wretched.

The light grows stronger in the thicket.

SHLINK: But it all adds up. Fish that swim into your maw . . . Where's that crazy light coming from? I have a lot to consider. . . .

MARIE (*takes her hat off*): I don't look good any more. Don't look at me: the rats have had their first nibble. But I've dragged to you what's left.

SHLINK: Strange milky light . . . Oh, I see! The luminosity of decay . . . What?

MARIE: Has my face swollen up already, do you think?

SHLINK: Do you know that you'll swing from a branch, if the mob gets hold of you here?

MARIE: As if I would care!

SHLINK: I ask you to leave me alone now, for the last minute of my life.

MARIE: Come, you can hide in the thicket. And there's a hide-out in the quarry.

SHLINK: Oh, damn you! Are you crazy? Can't you see that I have to take a last look across the treetops? That's what the moon is rising for. . . . (*Goes to the entrance.*)

MARIE: I can only see that you've lost the ground from under your feet. Have mercy on yourself!

SHLINK: So you really can't do me this last favor?

MARIE: I only want to look at you. I know that this is where I have to be.

SHLINK: Maybe. All right, stay!

A signal, from far off.

Two o'clock. I have to get going, I'm not safe here anymore.

MARIE: Where is George?

SHLINK: George? He ran away! What a mistake—safety! (*He tears his scarf off.*) The barrels are stinking already. Good, fat, caught-by-hand fish! Well dried, nailed up in crates! Salted down! After having been planted in ponds, bought, overpaid, overfed! Death-loving fish, suicidal fish, swallowing bait and hook like holy wafers! Oh, hell! And now, fast. (*He goes over to the table, sits down. Takes a drink from a small bottle.*) I, Wang Yen, known as Shlink, begotten and born in Yokohama in the Northern Province of Pei-Ho, under the constellation of the Tortoise: I have run a lumber business, I have nourished myself on rice, I have had dealings with many sorts of people. I, Wang Yen, known as Shlink, fifty-four years of age, ended three miles south of Chicago, leaving no inheritors.

MARIE: What is it with you, now?

SHLINK (*still sitting on the chair*): You're here? My legs

are growing cold. Throw a piece of cloth on my face, have pity on me! (*He sags, chin dropping to his chest.*)

Groans, footsteps, hoarse curses from the thickets and in back of the tent.

MARIE: What are you listening for? Answer me! Are you asleep? Do you still feel cold? I'm quite close to you now! What do you want the cloth for?

At this moment knife-blades cut entrances into the tent. The men of the lynching posse appear soundlessly in these openings.

MARIE (*rises, goes to meet them*): Go away. He has just died. He doesn't want anyone to look at him.

11

PRIVATE OFFICE OF THE DECEASED C. SHLINK
Eight days later

The premises of the lumber business are a burned-down lot. There are signs hanging here and there: "This Business For Sale."

GARGA. JOHN GARGA. MARIE GARGA.

JOHN: What a fool you were, to let the place burn down like this. Now all you have is some charred old beams, and who's going to pay a cent for those?

GARGA (*laughs*): They're cheap enough. But what are you planning to do?

JOHN: I thought we'd stick together now.

GARGA (*laughs again*): No, I'm clearing out. You going to get a job?

MARIE: I'll work, all right. But I won't go scrubbing staircases like my mother.

JOHN: I've been a soldier. We used to sleep nights in well troughs, and the rats on our faces were at least seven-pounders, never any less. And when it was all over and they took my rifle off my shoulder, I said: from now on each one of us will keep his cap on forever when he goes to bed.

GARGA: What you meant was: each one of us will sleep, will sleep.

MARIE: We have to go now, father. It is getting late, and I haven't found a room yet.

JOHN: Yes, let's go. (*Looks around.*) Let's go! A soldier by your side. Onward, into the jungle of the city!

GARGA: I've left that behind me. Hey, hello!

MANKY (*enters, radiant, hands in pockets*): It's me, all right, I saw your ad in the paper. And if your lumber business isn't too damn expensive, I'll buy it.

GARGA: What's your offer?

MANKY: Why are you selling out?

GARGA: I'm going to New York.

MANKY: And I'll move in here.

GARGA: How much can you give me?

MANKY: I've got to keep some cash to get the business started.

GARGA: All right, six thousand: if you take her into the bargain.

MANKY: It's a deal.

MARIE: This is my father. He has to stay with me.

MANKY: And your mother?

MARIE: She isn't here anymore.

MANKY (*after a while*): It's a deal.

MARIE: Now you draw up an agreement!

The men sign it.

MANKY: I guess we're going to treat ourselves to a little something. You joining us, George?

GARGA: No.

MANKY: But you'll still be here when we come back?

GARGA: No.

JOHN: Good-by, George. Have a look round New York. And you know you can always come back to old Chicago, if the going gets too rough. (*Exeunt.*)

GARGA (*pocketing the money*): To be alone—that's a good thing to be. The chaos has been used up. And it was the best time.

———◆———

Cities and people
as in the first decades of this century.

DRUMS IN THE NIGHT

TRANSLATOR'S NOTE

This is the story of a man trapped between his past and what other people think is his future. For various reasons these others try to take away his present: his love for a woman who loves him; but he fights them off and wins.

Put baldly like that, the play sounds like romantic guff. Its author regretted its openness to that view. He thought that at the time of writing it he had, or should have, overcome individualism. But the play presents, with seeming approval, a man who has a chance to join a radical revolution and deliberately turns his back on it. In later years Brecht was so ashamed of having pleased the public and even won a prize by such a work that he thought of burning it. Instead he revised it, taking out some of the wilder language and adding, by way of counterpart to his non-joining hero, references to a young nephew of Glubb the tavernkeeper, who does fight in the Spartacist ranks and is killed.

But the changes were useless. The work still stands, and will stand for a long time, as a vindication of integrity against powers that think it stupid. Kragler's only consistent defenders in the play, a waiter and a prostitute, are exploited by those same powers; but they accept their situation, and he doesn't. That is why they admire him. Against his prospective in-laws and his girl's fiancé, who think him an archaic nuisance; their friend, the journalist Babusch, who thinks he will join the uprising to drown his worries about Anna; and Glubb, who wants him to get drunk *and* join the revolution—against all these he reacts as an insistently singular person. At first, believing Anna has turned him down, he thinks of killing himself by drink or the knife. Then, as a man of military discipline and skill, he decides he prefers death in action to passive extinction by alcohol. Finally, on learning that the girl still loves him, he drops everything to get her back. His last long speech, a blistering attack on the forces that have tried to hold him down, stands on the words *Jeder Mann ist der beste in seiner Haut:* "Every man for himself" or "To each his own," a slogan which, as if to counteract his other changes, Brecht transposed in the revised text from the middle of the last act to the end, where it is even more striking.

The poet, however, took comfort for his apparently reactionary success in the thought that this play, like his other early works, such as *Baal* and *Jungle of Cities,* shows, as he put it in 1954, "how the great flood breaks upon the bourgeois world." Certainly his portrait of Papa and Mama Balicke is among the most brilliantly savage comments in modern drama on crassly undialectical materialism. It bears comparison with the contemporary cartoons of George Grosz, to whom Brecht wrote in an open letter that his own attack on the middle class in *Drums in the Night* was "by no means as effective, but no less serious" than the painter's.

Also of value in the play are certain approaches to Brecht's later technique of estrangement. Manke's speeches in the second act, especially his report to the man off-stage just before it ends, frame the action in a manner that, had Brecht maintained it, might have helped to alienate the audience from Kragler as a tragic or at least serious character. Here, briefly, he appears as comic or absurd. These passages, with the "winged, musical" and detachable third act, and some of Glubb's remarks in the fourth, suggest that the playwright was already considering better means of distancing than the signboards described in his note on staging.

From the author's standpoint, then, and perhaps also from that of Brecht's ideal spectator, this is very much a period piece. But it is liberated from the crises of its time by the ludicrous and moving persistence of its sometimes inarticulate, sometimes imaginative hero. Much the same might be said of Brecht himself. As he grew he became, like so many German writers, an institution: an "anti-romantic institution," to adapt Babusch's epithet for Manke. But in *Drums in the Night* we may discern the bitter roots from which that formidable system sprang. Despite Brecht's later opinion that Kragler is a proto-Nazi and his girl a morbid seeker after sexual thrills, this Anna and her ghost from Africa haunt us more vividly than anything they can be made to stand for. Once more Brecht puts it best: "The thing is, I don't know what will come out when I do my job as best I can." Perhaps his audiences know.

NOTES ON THE PRODUCTION

The action takes place in Berlin during the winter of 1918, when the Spartacist movement, led by Karl Liebknecht and Rosa Luxemburg, was in conflict with the Social-Democratic Party over the speed with which Germany should be socialized. The Spartacists were crushed, and Liebknecht and Luxemburg killed, after attempting a coup in January 1919—not November 1918, as implied in Brecht's note, at which time there were similar revolts in other German cities. Brecht corrected the date in his revised version of the play, first published in 1953.

"Raspberry" (literally, "damask raisin") Manke, the waiter at Glubb's gin mill, is not so nicknamed in the body of the play, as he is in the list of characters—presumably to distinguish him from his brother who works at the Piccadilly Bar. To avoid further confusion, a director might discard the kinship (which seems to have little, if any, relevance to the action) and give the waiters different names.

This translation follows the text published by Propyläen Verlag, Berlin, 1922, and copyright by Drei Masken Verlag in Munich, where the play was first performed on September 30, 1922.

—Frank Jones

—For *Bie Bahnholzer 1918*

CHARACTERS

Andrew Kragler
Anna Balicke
Carl Balicke ⎫
Emily Balicke ⎬ *her parents*
Frederick Murk, *her fiancé*
Babusch, *a journalist*
Glubb, *a liquor dealer*
Piccadilly Bar Manke
Raspberry Manke, *his brother*
A drunk
Bulltrotter, *a newspaper vendor*
Laar
Augusta ⎫
Marie ⎬ *prostitutes*
A maid
A woman who sells newspapers

The Manke brothers are played by the same actor.

The action takes place during a night in November, from the twilight of evening to that of dawn.

A NOTE ON STAGING

This play was performed in Munich with the following backdrop: Behind pasteboard screens, about six feet high, which represented the walls of a room, there stood a childish painting of the big city. A few seconds before each time Kragler appeared, the moon gave off a red glow. Noises were faintly indicated and in the last act the "Marseillaise" was played on a phonograph. If the third act lacks a winged, musical effect and does not speed up the tempo it may be omitted. It is recommended that several signboards be hung in the auditorium, bearing pronouncements such as EVERY MAN FOR HIMSELF and NO ROMANTIC GAPING.

ACT ONE
Africa

In Balicke's house. A gloomy room with muslin curtains.
Evening.

BALICKE (*shaving by the window*): He's been missing for
four years. He'll never come back now. Damn uncertain times. Any man's worth his weight in gold. I'd
have given my blessing two years ago, but your
blasted sentimentality loused things up. Right now
I'd stop at nothing.

MRS. BALICKE (*looking at a photograph, on the wall, of
Kragler as an artilleryman*): Such a good fellow he
was, such a nice boy.

BALICKE: He's rotten now.

MRS. BALICKE: Supposing he came back!

BALICKE: Nobody ever comes back from heaven.

MRS. BALICKE: By all the hosts of heaven! Anna would
drown herself!

BALICKE: If she says that, she's a goose, and I never saw
a goose drown.

MRS. BALICKE: All the same, she's just sick about it.

BALICKE: Then tell her to lay off blackberries and pickled
herrings. That Murk's a fine fellow, we can thank
God on our knees for him.

MRS. BALICKE: Sure, he earns money. But compared to
the other! It brings tears to my eyes.

BALICKE: Compared to the corpse! Listen, I'm telling you:
now or never! Is she waiting for the Pope? Does she
want a black man? I'm sick of these fantasies.

MRS. BALICKE: And if he comes, the corpse you say is
rotting—from heaven or from hell—"My name is

99

Kragler . . ." Who's to tell him he's stone cold and
his girl's been sleeping with another man?

BALICKE: I'll tell him! And now you tell the silly creature I've had enough and it's Wedding March time
and Murk's the man. If I told her she'd drown us.
Say, how about some light?

MRS. BALICKE: I'll get the adhesive tape. You always nick
yourself when there's no light.

BALICKE: Light costs money. Nicks don't. (*Calling:*)
Anna!

ANNA (*at door*): What is it, Father?

BALICKE: Be so kind as to listen to your mother and not
blubber on your happy day!

MRS. BALICKE: Come here, Anna. Father thinks you
look as pale as if you weren't getting any sleep.

ANNA: But I do sleep.

MRS. BALICKE: Look, it can't go on like this for ever.
He'll never come back now. (*Lights candles.*)

BALICKE: Look at her! Cry-baby!

MRS. BALICKE: I know it hasn't been easy for you. He
was a good man. But now he's dead.

BALICKE: And buried and rotten!

MRS. BALICKE: Carl!—As for Murk, he has ability, he's
getting on.

BALICKE: See?

MRS. BALICKE: So say yes, for heaven's sake.

BALICKE: And no dramatics!

MRS. BALICKE: For heaven's sake, take the man.

BALICKE (*struggling with the adhesive tape*): Goddamn
it, do you think men grow on trees? Yes or no, now!
Don't be an idiot! Quit reaching for the stars!

ANNA: Y-yes, daddy.

BALICKE (*tenderly*): All right, start bawling. The flood-
gates are open. Just give me time to get my trunks on.

MRS. BALICKE: Don't you love Murk at all?

BALICKE: It's immoral, that's what it is!

MRS. BALICKE: Carl! Come now, Annie, how are things
with Freddy?

ANNA: Oh, all right. But you know . . . and I feel so awful.

BALICKE: I know nothing! I tell you the guy's moldy
rotten! His bones have fallen apart! Three years and
not a sign of him! And his whole battery blown up!
sky high! in pieces! Missing! Tell me, pretty one, tell
me where he's gone. It's just that you're so damn
scared of ghosts. Get yourself a man, and you'll have
no ghosts to fear at night. (*Bearing down on* ANNA.)
Tell me: are you a healthy piece, or not? Well, then!

The bell rings.

ANNA (*terrified*): It's him!

BALICKE: Keep him outside and stuff him!

MRS. BALICKE (*at door with laundry basket*): Anything
for the wash?

ANNA: Yes. No. No, I don't think there's anything.

MRS. BALICKE: It's the eighth already.

ANNA: The eighth? So soon?

MRS. BALICKE: That's what I said. The eighth.

ANNA: What if it was the eighteenth?

BALICKE: What's all that chatter at the door? Why don't
you come in?

MRS. BALICKE: Better make sure you get something in the
wash. (*Goes out.*)

BALICKE (*sits down, takes* ANNA *on his knee*): See here
now. A woman without a man is a god-awful mess.
You miss the one they put in the great big army.
Sure. But do you still know him? Not a bit, my
sweet! His death has made a freak of him. He's had
a three-year beauty treatment. If only he wasn't
as dead as a doornail, and not the way you think
he is! Anyhow, he's rotten. He don't look so good
no more. His nose is gone. But you miss him! So get

yourself another man! It's nature, you know. You'll perk up like a rabbit in a cabbage patch! You still have healthy limbs and appetites. Nothing god-awful about that!

ANNA: But I can't forget him, ever. You both keep nagging me about it, but I can't!

BALICKE: Take Murk. He'll help you get over him.

ANNA: I do love him, and some day I'll love him more, but it hasn't happened yet.

BALICKE: Oh, he'll bring you round. All he needs is certain rights. Marriage is best for hammering them home. I can't explain it to you, really; you're too young. (*Tickling her.*) So it's a deal?

ANNA (*with a dainty laugh*): But I don't know if Freddy wants to.

BALICKE: Get in here, wife!

MRS. BALICKE: Please come into the parlor. Do step in, Mr. Murk.

BALICKE: Evening, Murk. Say, you look like a drowned corpse.

MURK: Miss Anna!

BALICKE: What's wrong with you? Somebody let you down? Why so cheesy-looking, man? Is it the shots in the night air? (*A silence.*) Better take care of him, Anna. (*Struts off with* MRS. BALICKE.)

ANNA: What's up, Fred? You really are pale.

MURK (*sniffing*): What's the red wine for? An engagement party? (*A silence.*) Has somebody been here? (*Going up to* ANNA.) Was a man here? You're white as a sheet. How come? Who was he?

ANNA: Nobody! Nobody's been here! What's the matter with you?

MURK: Then what's the rush? Don't give me that. . . . Well, he's welcome to it. But I'm not getting engaged in this shack.

ANNA: Who's talking about getting engaged?

MURK: Your old lady is. The eye of the Lord maketh the cattle fat. (*Walks around restlessly.*) Well, what if we did?

ANNA: You keep acting as if my parents cared. But they don't, I tell you! Not a rap!

MURK: Oh, come on. When did you take your first Communion?

ANNA: I just think you take things sort of easy.

MURK: Do I, now! And the other man?

ANNA: I didn't say a word about the other man.

MURK: But he hangs around, he's here, he haunts you!

ANNA: That was something very different . . . something you could never understand, because it was . . . spiritual. That was it.

MURK: And our affair is physical?

ANNA: What's between us is nothing.

MURK: It's something now!

ANNA: You can't be sure.

MURK: They'll be singing another song here pretty soon.

ANNA: Believe it if you want.

MURK: I propose.

ANNA: Is that your declaration?

MURK: No, that comes later.

ANNA: And there's a box factory at the end of the road.

MURK: My, you're a sharp one! Didn't they smell a rat last night?

ANNA: Oh, Freddy, they sleep like logs. (*Snuggles up to him.*)

MURK: But we don't!

ANNA: Rascal!

MURK (*hugging her but his kiss is casual*): Smart-ass!

ANNA: Shhh. I hear a train passing in the night. Don't you? Sometimes I'm afraid he's coming. It sends cold shivers down my back.

MURK: The mummy? I'll take care of him. I tell you he's got to get his walking papers. I want no cold meat between us in bed. I won't stand for anyone else but me!

ANNA: Don't be mean, Freddy. Please forgive me.

MURK: Old Saint Andrew? A phantom! It can't live any longer after we're married than it did after it was buried. Wanna bet? (*Laughs.*) I'll bet: a baby.

ANNA (*burying her face in his chest*): Oh, you shouldn't say such things.

MURK (*heartily*): That's what you think! (*Toward door:*) Do drop in, Mother! Hi, Dad!

MRS. BALICKE (*close behind door*): Oh, children! (*Starts to sob.*) Out of a clear sky like that!

BALICKE: A difficult birth, eh? (*General embrace, with feeling.*)

MURK: Twins! When's the wedding? Time is money!

BALICKE: Three weeks from now, if you ask me. Both beds are in good shape. Supper, Mother!

MRS. BALICKE: Right away, husband, just let me get my breath back. (*Runs out.*) Out of a clear sky like that!

MURK: Allow me to invite you to the Piccadilly Bar for a drink tonight. I favor an immediate engagement. Don't you, Anna?

ANNA: If it must be.

BALICKE: Why the Piccadilly Bar? Why not here? Got rocks in your head?

MURK (*nervously*): Not here. Absolutely not.

BALICKE: Now what?

ANNA: He's so funny. Let's go to the Piccadilly Bar, then.

BALICKE: On a night like this? It'd be taking your life in your hands!

MRS. BALICKE *enters with* MAID. *Supper is served.*

MRS. BALICKE: Yes, children, life is full of surprises. To the table, folks!

They pitch in.

BALICKE (*raising glass*): Here's health to the couple!
   (*Clinks glasses.*) These are shaky times. The war's
   over. The pork's too fat, Emily. Demobilization is
   flooding the oases of peaceful toil with disorder, greed,
   and bestial inhumanity.

MURK: Here's to ammunition boxes! Drink to them, Anna!

BALICKE: Uncertain livelihoods are on the increase: respectable but shady. The government is too soft in
   combating the vultures of cataclysm. (*Unfolds a newspaper.*) The agitated masses lack ideals. But worst of
   all—I may say it here—are the soldiers back from
   the front: spoiled adventurers run wild, who've forgotten how to work and hold nothing sacred. Hard
   times indeed; a man's worth his weight in gold. Get
   a good grip on him, Annie. Make sure you come
   through, but stick together. Always onward and upward! Your health! (*Winds a phonograph.*)

MURK (*wiping off sweat*): You bet! If you're a man you
   can make it. What you need are elbows and hob-
   nailed boots and a square jaw and no looking down.
   That's the way it goes, Annie! I'm an underdog too.
   Errand boy, machine-shop, a deal or two, live and
   learn. That's how all Germany got where it is today!
   With gloves? No, sir—hard work, day in, day out!
   Now we're on top! Cheers, Anna!

The phonograph plays a love song.

BALICKE: That's great! What's wrong now, Anna?

ANNA (*has stood up and partly turned away*): I don't
   know. It's all happening so fast. Maybe that's not
   good, is it, Mother?

MRS. BALICKE: What's this, child? Such a goose! You
   should be glad! What could be wrong?

BALICKE: Sit down. Or else wind the phonograph, now
   that you're up.

ANNA *sits down. A pause.*

MURK: Your very good health! (*Clinks glasses with* ANNA.) What's the matter with you?

BALICKE: Now to business, Freddy. Ammunition boxes will soon be dead ducks. A couple more weeks of civil war and that'll be it. I'm thinking of baby buggies. Seriously! Whichever way you look at it, the factory's riding high. (*Takes* MURK'S *arm and moves upstage with him; pulls curtains back.*) New Building One, New Building Two. All solid and up-to-date. Anna, wind the phonograph! This gets me where I live.

Phonograph plays "Deutschland, Deutschland uber Alles."

MURK: Say, folks, there's a man standing in the factory yard. What's up?

ANNA: Oh, I'm scared. I think he's looking up here!

BALICKE: Probably the night watchman. Why are you laughing, Fred? Something stuck in your throat? The women are all pale.

MURK: I have a funny feeling. . . . Spartacus . . .

BALICKE: Nonsense. Nothing like that at our place! (*He turns away, disturbed.*) Well, that's the factory. (*Goes to table.*)

ANNA *draws the curtains.*

The war laid a golden egg in my lap. There it was, right on the street! Why not pick it up? I'd have been crazy not to. Someone else would have grabbed it. End of pig, start of sausage. If you look at it right, the war was a bit of luck for us. We live securely now: our days are round and full and cozy. So we'll go ahead and make baby buggies. No hurry! Are you with me?

MURK: You bet, Dad! Here's to it!

BALICKE: And you go ahead and make babies. Ha ha ha ha ha!

MAID: Mr. Balicke, Mr. Babusch is here.

BABUSCH (*trotting in*): Well, boys and girls, the Reds are running wild, but you're snug enough here. Spartacus mobilizing, negotiations broken off, artillery fire expected on Berlin in twenty-four hours!

BALICKE (*napkin round his neck*): Damn it, aren't those fellows ever satisfied?

MRS. BALICKE: Artillery? Oh, my God! What a night we're in for! The basement for me, Balicke!

BABUSCH: So far all's quiet in the center of the city. Revolutionary activity is apparently confined to the outskirts. I hear they're trying to take over the newspapers.

BALICKE: But we're celebrating an engagement. To do a thing like that deliberately, on this day of all days! Madmen!

MURK: Shoot 'em!

BALICKE: Shoot all malcontents!

BABUSCH: You getting engaged, Balicke?

MURK: Babusch, meet my fiancée.

MRS. BALICKE: Right out of a clear sky. When did the shooting start?

BABUSCH (*shaking hands with* ANNA *and* MURK): Spartacus has been hoarding vast numbers of weapons. What a bunch of creeps! That's the girl, Anna, don't be put off. No trouble will get this far. This is a peaceful hearthside. The family! The German family! "My home is my castle."*

BALICKE: At a time like this, at a time like this! Your happy day, Anna!

BABUSCH: All the same, boys and girls, it's damn interesting.

BALICKE: Not in my book. Absolutely not. (*Wipes mouth with napkin.*)

MURK: Know something? Come with us to the Piccadilly Bar. Engagement party!

---

* In English in the original.—*Tr.*

BABUSCH: And Spartacus?

BALICKE: They'll wait, Babusch! They'll shoot others in the belly, Babusch. Come along to the Piccadilly Bar! Get dressed, girls!

MRS. BALICKE: The Piccadilly, on a night like this? (*Sits on a chair.*)

BALICKE: It used to be called that. Now it's the Fatherland Café. Frederick's invited us! So it's a night like this. What are cabs for? Get moving, old girl. Put on the glad rags!

MRS. BALICKE: I will not step out of this house. Are you crazy, Freddy?

ANNA: Man proposes, man disposes! Frederick wants to go.

All look at MURK.

MURK: Not here, no sir, not here. I want music and bright lights. That's a fine place, you know—and here it's so gloomy. I put on my best suit just for tonight. So how's about it, Mother-in-law?

MRS. BALICKE: It's beyond me. (*Goes out.*)

ANNA: Wait for me, Fred. I'll be ready in a jiffy.

BABUSCH: Terrific goings-on. It beats the band. Babes and sucklings, organize! Do you realize that a pound of apricots—soft as butter, flesh colored, juicy—costs five whole marks? Idlers, don't let anyone provoke you! There are mobs of shady characters all over the place, shrilly whistling into cafés in broad daylight! Their flag's a skull and lazybones! And high society waltzes in the dance halls! Oh well, a toast to the happy pair!

MURK: The ladies will please not change. Equality's the watchword now. People will stare if your skin's glossy.

BALICKE: Quite right. These are trying times. Any old rag will do for the mob. Anna: come down at once!

MURK: We'll go on ahead. Don't change!

ANNA: How crude! (*Goes out.*)

BALICKE: Forward march! Off to heaven with a bugle blast! But I've got to change my shirt.

MURK: You'll follow us with Mother, won't you? And we'll take Babusch along as chaperone, won't we? (*Singing.*) "Babusch, Babusch, Babusch, prancing through the ballroom . . ."

BABUSCH: That wretched doggerel, written by a mad young man . . . can't you get it out of your head? (*Takes his arm, goes out.*)

MURK (*still singing, outside*): "Thumbs out of your mouths, kids, we're off to a bacchanal." Anna!

BALICKE (*alone, lighting a cigar*): Everything taken care of, thank God! The girl's so full of tricks, you have to drive her into bed! And still crazy about that corpse! I've soaked a clean shirt with sweat. Now come what may! Password: baby buggies. (*Calling.*) Wife! A shirt!

ANNA (*outside*): Fred! Fred! (*Rushing in.*) Fred!

MURK (*at door*): Anna! (*Drily, restless, arms hanging down like a monkey's.*) Are you coming?

ANNA: Say, what's the matter with you? You look weird.

MURK: Are you coming? Look, I know what I'm asking you. No faking, now. Out with it!

ANNA: Yes, yes, yes! Surprise!

MURK: Fine, fine . . . I'm not so sure. For twenty years I hung around in garrets, chilled to the bone. Now I wear button shoes. Take a look at them, please. I sweated by gaslight in the gloom, it spoiled my eyes, and now I have a tailor. But I'm still shaky. There's a wind blowing under me, an icy breeze blowing, a man's feet turn cold under him. (*Moves toward ANNA, does not embrace her, stands unsteadily before her.*) Now the body waxes, now the red wine flows. Now I'm here! Bathed in sweat, eyes shut, fists clenched so that my fingernails pierce the flesh. Enough! Security! Warmth! Overalls off! A bed that's white

and wide and soft! (*Passes to window, glances out.*)
Come to me. I open my fists. I sit in the sun in
my shirt sleeves. I have you.

ANNA (*rushing over to him*): Darling!

MURK: Hot pants!

ANNA: But now I'm yours.

MURK: Isn't she down yet?

BABUSCH (*from outside*): Don't be long, kids. I'm your
chaperone!

MURK (*winds the phonograph again and joins in the love
song*): "I'm the best fellow in the world, if they'd
only let me be."

The lovers go out, entwined.

MRS. BALICKE (*in black, scurries in, looks in mirror, fixes
her hat*): The moon, so big, so red . . . and the
children! Ah, God! Yes indeed! Say what you will,
tonight's a night to be thankful for.

*At this point a man in a dirty dark-blue artillery
uniform, with a small pipe in his mouth, appears in
the doorway.*

KRAGLER: My name is Kragler.

MRS. BALICKE (*supporting herself, weak-kneed, on the
dressing table*): Oh, Lord . . .

KRAGLER: Why the unearthly look? Been wasting money
on wreaths? What a shame! I wish to report that I
set up as a ghost in Algiers. But now the stiff has a
hell of an appetite. I could eat worms! What's the
matter, Mother Balicke? A stupid song! (*Shuts off
phonograph.*)

MRS. BALICKE, *still speechless, can only stare at him.*

Don't collapse right away. Here's a chair. We can
get you a glass of water. (*Goes to cupboard, hum-
ming.*) I still know my way around here pretty well.
(*Pours a glass of wine.*) Wine! Nierensteiner! Say,

I'm sort of lively for a ghost! (*Looks after* MRS. BALICKE.)

BALICKE (*from outside*): Come on, old girl! Let's go! Angel mine, how fair thou art! (*Enters, looks, loses heart.*) Now what?

KRAGLER: Evening, Mr. Balicke. Your wife isn't feeling too good. (*Tries to pour wine down her throat but she turns her head away in horror.*)

BALICKE *looks on for a moment, upset.*

Come on, have a little. Eh? You'll feel better right away. I didn't think I'd be so well remembered. I've just come from Africa, you know. Spain, skulduggery, passport, all that. Tell me: where's Anna?

BALICKE: For God's sake leave my wife alone. You'll get her drunk.

KRAGLER: Oh, no.

MRS. BALICKE (*fleeing to* BALICKE, *who stands rigid*): Carl!

BALICKE: Mr. Kragler, if you are the person you claim to be, may I ask you to inform us what you want here?

KRAGLER (*is struck dumb for a moment, then*): Listen: I was a prisoner of war, in Africa.

BALICKE: Hell! (*Goes to a small cabinet, takes a drink of brandy.*) That's great. You sure look like it. What a goddam mess! What do you want, anyhow? What do you want? This evening, less than half an hour ago, my daughter got engaged.

KRAGLER (*sways, unsteadily*): What do you mean?

BALICKE: You were gone four years, she waited four years. We waited four years. It's all over now, and you have no prospects in that quarter—none whatever.

KRAGLER *sits down.*

(*Unsteadily, but striving to keep his dignity.*) Mr. Kragler, I have obligations this evening.

KRAGLER (*looking up*): Obligations? (*Distraught.*) Yes . . .

(*Slumps back in chair.*)

MRS. BALICKE: Don't take it so hard, Mr. Kragler. There's lots of fish in the sea, you know. Learn to suffer without complaining.

KRAGLER: Anna . . .

BALICKE (*harshly*): Wife!

She goes up to him, hesistantly.

(*With sudden firmness.*) Down with sentimentality! Let's go! (*Leaves with wife.*)

MAID *appears at door.*

KRAGLER: Hmmm . . . (*Shakes his head.*)

MAID: The ladies and gentlemen have left. (*A silence.*) They went to the Piccadilly Bar, to celebrate an engagement.

A silence; wind.

KRAGLER (*looking up at* MAID): Hmmm! (*Rises slowly, heavily, surveys the room. Walks around silently, head bowed, looks out window, turns, ambles slowly out, whistling, without his cap.*)

MAID: Hey! Your cap! You forgot your cap!

ACT TWO
Pepper

The Piccadilly Bar. Large window in rear. Music. Red moon in window. Wind when door opens.

BALICE: All the way to the Zoo District, kiddies! The moon's bright enough. Three cheers for Spartacus! What crap! Red wine, ho!

MURK (*enters arm in arm with* ANNA; *they disengage*): A storybook night! Storm over the dailies! A cab ride with your fiancée!

ANNA: I feel sort of sick. Can't help it. I'm all shook up.

BALICKE: Here's to it, Fred!

MURK: This is where I feel at home. It'd be a damn bore in the long run, but it's swellegant. Babusch, look after the older generation!

BABUSCH: Fine. (*Going out.*) And you look after the next! (*Drinks.*)

ANNA: Kiss me.

MURK: You're nuts. Half Berlin is looking.

ANNA: Who cares? If there's something I want, nothing else matters. Aren't you that way, too?

MURK: Certainly not. And you're not either.

ANNA: You're mean.

MURK: Am I, now!

ANNA: Coward!

MURK *rings, a* WAITER *enters.*

MURK: Ten-SHUN! (*Leans across table, knocking over glasses, and kisses* ANNA *violently.*)

ANNA: Darling!

MURK: Dis-MISS!

113

WAITER *leaves.*

A coward, eh? (*Looking under table.*) Now you can quit playing footsie with me.

ANNA: What's got into you?

MURK: And he shall be thy lord and master.

BALICKE *enters with* BABUSCH *and* MRS. BALICKE.

BALICKE: Here they are! Where's the waiter?

ANNA: Where have you been?

MRS. BALICKE: It's so red, the moon out there. A moon like that upsets me. And there's shouting around the newspaper offices.

BALICKE: Wolves!

MRS. BALICKE: You two, just be sure you get together.

BABUSCH: In bed, eh, Freddy?

ANNA: Don't you feel well, Mother?

MRS. BALICKE: Just when do you plan to get married?

MURK: Three weeks from today, Mom.

MRS. BALICKE: Shouldn't we have invited more people to the engagement party? This way, nobody knows about it. And people ought to know about it.

BALICKE: Blah, blah, blah. Just because the wolf is howling? Let him howl—till his tongue hangs red between his knees! I'll fix his wagon. Bang, he's dead!

BABUSCH: Murk, help me open this bottle. (*In a lower tone.*) He's here. He's come with the moon. The wolf with the moon. From Africa.

MURK: Andy Kragler?

BABUSCH: The wolf. A nuisance, eh?

MURK: He's in his grave. Kindly draw the curtains.

MRS. BALICKE: Your father's been rolling into every other tavern. He's really tying one on. There's a man for you! What a man! He'd drink himself to death for his children!

ANNA: Yes, but why?

MRS. BALICKE: Don't ask, child. Not me, anyhow. Everything's upside down, it's the end of the world. Daughter, I need some brandy right away.

BALICKE: It's those raspberries you ate, Mother. Draw the curtain!

WAITER *does so.*

BABUSCH: You had an inkling of it?

MURK: I'm good and ready. Was he at your place?

BABUSCH: Yes, earlier.

MURK: Then he'll be here next.

BALICKE: What's that plotting behind the wine bottles? Come and join the party.

All take places at table.

Let's get going! I've no time to be tired.

ANNA: Wow, that horse! How funny he was! Right in the street he stood stock still. "Get out, Fred, the horse is balking." Right in the street, there he stood. Shivering. And his eyeballs were like gooseberries, all white, and Fred poked him in the eye with a stick, and then he jumped! It was like the circus.

BALICKE: Time is money. Damn hot in here. I'm sweating again. Soaked one shirt today already.

MRS. BALICKE: You'll end up selling pencils if you use so many shirts.

BABUSCH (*eating prunes out of his pocket*): A pound of apricots costs ten marks now. So I'll write an article about prices. Then I can afford apricots. If the world comes to an end, I'll write about that. But what will the others do? If the Zoo District is blown sky high I'll be sitting pretty. But you people—!

MURK: Shirts, apricots, Zoo District . . . When's the wedding?

BALICKE: In three weeks. Wedding in three weeks. Harrumph. The news has been heard in heaven. Are we together? United on the wedding? All right, lovebirds, full speed ahead!

They clink glasses. The door has opened. KRAGLER *is there. The candles flicker in the wind.*

BALICKE: Why is your glass shaking, Anna? Are you like your mother?

ANNA *who sits facing the door, has seen* KRAGLER. *She slumps, and looks at him fixedly.*

MRS. BALICKE: Lord save us, child, what flattened you?
MURK: What a draft!
KRAGLER (*hoarsely*): Anna!

ANNA *gives a low-pitched scream. Now all look round and leap up. Simultaneous outbursts.*

BALICKE: Hell! (*Gulps some wine.*) Mother, it's the ghost!
MRS. BALICKE: Jesus! Kra . . .
MURK: Throw him out! Throw him out!

KRAGLER *has stood, swaying, in the doorway for some time. He looks grim. During the outbursts he moves, rather fast but heavily, toward* ANNA, *who still sits alone, her glass trembling before her. He takes the glass, leans on the table, stares at her.*

BALICKE: He's stinko, that's what.
MURK: Waiter, this fellow's disturbing the peace. Throw him out. (*Runs to wall, draws curtain back. Moon.*)
BABUSCH: Watch out—he still has raw meat in his belly! It's giving him the itch! Don't go near him! (*Bangs on table with cane.*) Don't start anything. Just go quietly. Leave in good order!
ANNA (*has run from table, clings to her mother*): Mother! Help!

KRAGLER *goes around table, sways up to* ANNA.

MRS. BALICKE (*about simultaneously with following*): Spare my child! You'll go to jail! Jesus, he'll kill her!
BALICKE (*raging at a safe distance*): Are you stoned, you

bum? Pauper! Anarchist! Trench fighter! Pirate!
Nightmare! Where's your sheet, you ghost?

BABUSCH: If you have a stroke, he'll marry her. Shut up,
all of you. He's the victim here. You must let him
have his say. It's his right. (*To* MRS. BALICKE:) Have
you no heart? He was gone four years. It's a matter
of heart.

MRS. BALICKE: She can barely stand up! She's white as
a sheet!

BABUSCH (*to* MURK): Just look at his face. She's seen it.
Once he had a peaches-and-cream complexion; now
he looks like a moldy fig. You have nothing to fear.
(*They go out.*)

MURK: If you're talking about jealousy, that's not my dish.
Ha ha!

BALICKE (*still standing between table and door, somewhat
drunk, legs bent, glass in hand*): A black wreck. A
face like a bankrupt elephant. A total loss. What in-
solence! (*Bumbles off.*)

Now only the WAITER *stands in front of door at right,
holding tray. Gounod's "Ave Maria" is played. The
light fades.*

KRAGLER (*after a pause*): I feel like everything's been
wiped out of my head and nothing's left in it but
sweat. I can't seem to follow what's going on.

ANNA (*picks up a candle, stands loosely, shines it in his
face*): Didn't the fish eat you up?

KRAGLER: I don't know what you mean.

ANNA: Didn't you burst?

KRAGLER: I don't understand.

ANNA: Didn't a shell go through your face?

KRAGLER: What makes you look at me like that? Do I look
that bad? (*A silence. He looks out the window.*) I've
come to you like some old beast. (*A silence.*) My
skin is like a shark's—black. (*A silence.*) And I used

to be pink and white. (*A silence.*) And I keep bleeding, too, it just pours out of me. . . .

ANNA: Andy!

KRAGLER: Yes.

ANNA (*hesitantly approaching him*): Oh, Andy, why were you gone so long? Did they keep you from me with guns and sabers? I can't come to you now.

KRAGLER: Was I really away?

ANNA: In the first days you were with me for a long time, and then your voice was clear. When I walked along the path I brushed against you, and in the meadow you called me behind the maple tree. The message said you'd been shot through the face and buried after two days. But things had changed anyway. When I walked along the path it was empty and the maple tree was still. When I stood up at the washtub I could still see your face, but when I spread the laundry in the meadow I couldn't any more, and all that long time I didn't know what you looked like. But I should have waited.

KRAGLER: You should have had a photo.

ANNA: I was afraid. I should have waited with my fear, but I'm bad. Let go my hand, I'm bad all over.

KRAGLER (*looking at the window*): I don't know what you're saying. Maybe it's the red moon. I'll have to try and think what it means. I have swollen hands and webby fingers, I have no manners, I break glasses when I drink. I can't even talk nicely with you. My voice is as hoarse as a black's.

ANNA: Yes.

KRAGLER: Give me your hand. Do you think I'm a ghost? Come here: give me your hand. Won't you come to me?

ANNA: Do you want it?

KRAGLER: Let me hold it. I'm not a ghost now. Are you looking at my face again? Is it like crocodile skin? I

look awful. I've been in salt water. It's only the red
moon. . . .

ANNA: Yes.

KRAGLER: Take my hand too. Why don't you hold it?
Let me touch your face. Does that upset you?

ANNA: No, no.

KRAGLER (*embracing her*): I'm a dirty old wreck, that's
what I am! A throatful of mud! Four years! Do you
want me? Anna! (*Whirls her around and sees the*
WAITER; *leans forward, grins, stares at him.*)

WAITER (*disconcerted, drops tray, stammers*): The main
question is: does she still have her . . . lily . . . her
lily . . .

KRAGLER (*holding* ANNA, *guffaws*): What was that he said?
Lily?

WAITER *runs out.*

Don't go, you novel-reader! Something got loose from
him! Lily! Something's happened to him! Lily! Did
you hear? He was so deeply moved!

ANNA: Andy!

KRAGLER (*he's let her go; looks at her, head down*): Say
that again. That was your voice! (*Runs toward right.*)
Waiter! Come here, fellow!

BABUSCH (*at door*): Man, there's body in that laugh! It has
the color of flesh! How do you feel?

MRS. BALICKE (*behind him*): Anna! Child! You had us
worried!

*"The Lady from Peru" has been playing in the next
room for some time.*

BALICKE (*runs in, somewhat sobered*): Sit down! (*He
draws the curtain. A rattle of metal is heard.*) Over
by Babusch's paper they have a red moon at their

side and guns at their backs. We're going to have to settle accounts with you. (*He relights all the candles.*) Sit down!

MRS. BALICKE: What a face you're making! There go my legs again! Waiter! Waiter!

BALICKE: Where's Murk?

BABUSCH: Freddy Murk is cheating at whist.

BALICKE (*in an undertone*): Just get him a chair. If he's sitting he's half tamed. A man can't strut sitting down. (*Aloud.*) Be seated, everybody! Quiet! Pull yourself together, Emily! (*To* KRAGLER:) And you sit down too, for God's sake!

MRS. BALICKE (*takes a bottle of brandy from the* WAITER'S *tray*): I've got to have some brandy or I'll die. (*She brings it to the table.*)

MRS. BALICKE, BALICKE, ANNA *are seated.* BABUSCH *has edged around the table and made* ANNA *sit down. He now pushes* KRAGLER, *who has been standing helplessly, onto a chair.*

BABUSCH: Sit down. Your knees aren't too firm. Want some brandy? Why do you guffaw like that?

KRAGLER *stands up again.* BABUSCH *pushes him down. He stays put.*

BALICKE: What do you want, Andrew Kragler?

MRS. BALICKE: Mr. Kragler, our Emperor bids us: "Learn to suffer without complaining."

ANNA: Keep your seat.

BALICKE: Shut up. Let him talk. What do you want?

BABUSCH (*standing up*): How about a drop of brandy? Say something, man!

ANNA: Think first, Andy!

MRS. BALICKE: You'll put me under early. Can't you shut up? You know nothing about anything.

KRAGLER (*tries to get up but is pushed down by* BABUSCH. *Very seriously*): If you ask me, it's not simple. And I

don't want any brandy to drink. Because that might
start something.

BALICKE: No tricks now. Tell us what you want. Then I'll
throw you out.

ANNA: No, no!

BABUSCH: You really should have a drink. You look so
dry. It'll make you feel better, believe me.

At this moment MURK *slips in, left, with a prostitute
named* MARIE.

MRS. BALICKE: Murk!

BABUSCH: Even genius has its limits. Have a seat!

BALICKE: Good going, Freddy! Show this guy what a man
is. Freddy's no coward, he's having fun! (*Claps
hands.*)

MURK (*grimly—he has been drinking—leaves* MARIE *and
comes to the table*): Isn't this low farce over yet?

BALICKE (*drags him to a chair*): Shut up!

BABUSCH: Go right on, Kragler. Never mind him.

KRAGLER: His ears are damaged.

ANNA: He used to grease cars.

MURK: There's an egg in his head.

KRAGLER: He should get out of here!

MURK: And they hit him on the head.

KRAGLER: I must pay close attention to what I say.

MURK: So he has egg sauce in his head.

KRAGLER: That's true: they hit me on the head. I was gone
for four years. I couldn't write a letter. There was no
egg in my brain. (*Silence.*) It was four years ago. I
must pay close attention. You didn't recognize me.
You're still not sure it's me; you don't feel it that
way. Oh, I'm talking too much.

MRS. BALICKE: His brain's all dried up. (*Shakes her head.*)

BALICKE: So you had a bad time, fighting for Emperor
and Empire? My heart bleeds for you. Is there anything you want?

MRS. BALICKE: The Emperor said "Be strong in pain."

Have a drop of this! (*Pushes brandy bottle toward him.*)

BALICKE (*drinking; rubbing it in*): You stood firm in the hail of bullets? Like steel? Stout fella! Our army did a terrific job. Went laughing to a hero's death. Have a drink! What'll it be? (*Offers him cigar box.*)

ANNA: Didn't you get a new uniform, Andy? Still wearing the old blue one? It's out of date!

MRS. BALICKE: So many women, aren't there? Another brandy, waiter! (*Passes brandy to* KRAGLER.)

BALICKE: We weren't idle on the home front, either. See here: what do you want? Not got a red cent? Sleeping on the pavement? Fatherland hand you a barrel organ? Absolutely not. Such conditions must not recur. What do you want?

MRS. BALICKE: Don't worry. No barrel organ for you!

ANNA: "The night is stormy and the waves are high." Whoo!

KRAGLER (*has got up*): Since I feel that I have no rights here, I beg you, from the depths of my heart, to go with me at my side.

BALICKE: What's he jabbering about? What did he say? Depths of my heart! At my side! What kind of talk is that?

The others laugh.

KRAGLER: Because no man has a right . . . because I can't live without you . . . from the depths of my heart.

Loud laughter.

MURK (*puts feet on table. Cold, malevolent, drunk*): All the way to the bottom. Fished up. Mud in his mouth. Look at my shoes! I used to have boots like yours! Get yourself some like mine! Come back later! Do you know what you are?

MARIE (*suddenly*): Were you in the service?

MURK: Shut your trap! (*To* KRAGLER:) So the steam roller

got you, did it? That happened to lots of fellows.
Well, some of us didn't let it roll. Your face has gone,
has it? Would you like a new one, as a gift? Do you
want the three of us to give you a beauty treatment?
Did you crawl down here to find us? Don't you know
what you are yet?

BABUSCH: All right now, that's enough.

WAITER (*coming forward*): Were you in the service?

MURK: Nah. I'm one of the guys that are supposed to pay
for your heroic deeds. The steam roller broke down!

BABUSCH: Oh, knock off the act. It's disgusting. You know
damn well you got something out of it. And why drag
your boots into this?

BALICKE: See here: I'll tell you what it all boils down
to. Here's' the rub. No dramatics now, just practical
politics—something we lack in Germany. It's very
simple. Have you the means to support a wife? Or
are there webs between your fingers?

MRS. BALICKE: Hear that, Anna? He hasn't got a dime!

MURK: If he has, I'll marry his mother. (*Jumps up.*) He's
trying to con you into marrying him, the cheap crook!

WAITER (*to* KRAGLER): Say something! Tell 'em something!

KRAGLER (*has got up, shaking. To* ANNA): I don't know
what I ought to say. When we were down to skin
and bones and had to keep boozing so we could pave
the roads, we often had nothing left but the evening
sky. That's very important, because in April I slept
with you in the bushes. I told the others about that,
too. But they were dropping like flies.

ANNA: Like horses, eh?

KRAGLER: Because it was so hot, and we kept on drinking.
But why am I going on about the evening sky? I didn't
mean to. I don't know . . .

ANNA: Did you keep thinking about me?

MRS. BALICKE: How childishly he talks! It makes you
ashamed for him.

MURK: Why don't you sell me your boots, for the Army Museum? I'll give you forty marks.

BABUSCH: Keep talking, Kragler. You're on the right track.

KRAGLER: We had no shirts left, either. Believe me, that was the worst part. Would you think a thing like that could be the worst?

ANNA: We're listening, Andy!

MURK: All right, sixty marks. Sell 'em!

KRAGLER (*to* ANNA): Are you ashamed of me now? We're surrounded, you know, like in the circus, when the elephant pisses in fear. And they don't know a thing!

MURK: Eighty marks!

KRAGLER: I'm no pirate, either. That red moon is nothing to me. My trouble is, I can't get my eyes open. I'm a hunk of flesh and I'm wearing a clean shirt. I tell you I'm not a ghost!

MURK: All right, a hundred marks!

MARIE: You should be thoroughly ashamed of yourself.

MURK: Now the son of a bitch won't sell me his old boots for a hundred marks!

KRAGLER: Anna, I hear words. What voice is speaking them?

MURK: You've got sunstroke. Can you still leave by yourself?

KRAGLER: Anna, it thinks no one's going to squash it.

MURK: Can anyone see your face now?

KRAGLER: Anna, it's one of God's creatures.

MURK: Is this you? What do you want, anyway? You're nothing but a stiff! You stink already! (*Holds his nose.*) Don't you like being clean? Do you think you should be worshiped because you swallowed the African sun? I worked! I slaved till my boots were bloody! Look at my hands! You have all the sympathy because you got beat up, but I didn't beat you up! You're a hero, and I'm a worker, and this is the girl I'm going to marry.

BABUSCH: Keep your seat, Murk! You're just as much a

worker when you're sitting down. Kragler, world history would be different if humanity did more sitting on its rear.

KRAGLER: I can see nothing in him. He's like a latrine wall, with filth scrawled over it. The wall can't help it. Anna, is he the one you love? Is he the one you love?

ANNA *laughs and takes a drink.*

BABUSCH: You're taking your life in your hands, Kragler.

KRAGLER: No, just chewing him out. (*To* ANNA:) Do you love that prune-face? Are you going to throw me over for him? He has an English suit and a chest stuffed with paper and blood in his shoes, and I have nothing but my old suit with moths in it. Say you can't marry me because of my suit! Say it——I'd rather hear that!

BABUSCH: Sit down, damn it. Now they're off!

MARIE (*claps hands*): That's him, all right——the one that danced with me and shoved his knees in my belly until I felt ashamed.

MURK: None of your lip! (*To* KRAGLER:) God, what a look you have. I guess there's a knife in one of those boots, to cut my throat with, because you blistered your brain in Africa? Pull it, I've had enough now, hack me to pieces!

MRS. BALICKE: Anna! Can you stay here and listen to this?

BALICKE: Waiter, bring me four glasses of brandy. The hell with it all.

MURK: Watch out, don't pull that knife on me. Control yourself: no heroics here or you'll end up in jail.

MARIE: Were you in the service?

MURK (*furious, throws a glass at her*): Why weren't you?

KRAGLER: I've come now.

MURK: Was anybody yelling at you?

KRAGLER: Here I am.

MURK: Bastard!

ANNA: Shut up, honey.

KRAGLER *ducks.*

MURK: Robber!

KRAGLER (*soundlessly*): Thief!

MURK: Ghost!

KRAGLER: Watch your language!

MURK: Watch your knife! Did that get under your skin? Ghost? Ghost! Ghost!

MARIE: You bastard! you bastard!

KRAGLER: Anna, Anna, what am I doing? Seasick on a sea that swarms with corpses but doesn't suck me down. Rolling southward in the dark cattle cars: nothing can happen to me. Burning in the fiery oven: I burn hotter myself. A man goes mad in the sun: not me. Two men fall into a water hole: I go on sleeping. I shoot blacks. I eat grass. I'm a ghost.

At this point the WAITER *rushes to the window and yanks it open. The music stops suddenly. Excited shouts are heard: "They're coming!" "Keep still!" The* WAITER *blows out the candle. Then, outside, a measured stamping, slowly growing louder. Yells, whistles, singing, drumming. The stamping and yelling continue.*

A MAN (*enters doorway from left*): Please be calm, ladies and gentlemen. You are requested not to leave the premises. Disturbances have broken out. Fighting is going on around the newspaper offices. The situation is still unsettled.

BALICKE (*sits down heavily*): Spartacus! Your pals, Mr. Andrew Kragler! Your partners in crime! Your comrades, yelling around the papers and whistling into cafés. Reeking with murder and arson. Brutes! (*Silence.*) Brutes, brutes, brutes! Everybody knows it! You're cannibals! You'll have to be wiped out!

WAITER: And you gluttons are the ones to do it.

MURK: You got a knife, too? Let's see it!

MARIE (*moving in on him with* WAITER): Will you shut up?

WAITER: This thing isn't human, it's a brute!

MURK: Draw the curtain, you ghosts!

WAITER: Are we to be stood against the wall we built ourselves—the one you people hide behind when you guzzle your brandy?

KRAGLER: Here's my hand. There's the artery. Slash it! It'll bleed plenty if I croak.

MURK: Ghost! ghost! What are you, anyhow? Am I supposed to sneak away because you're wearing an African skin? And beat drums in the streets? And yell around the papers? Can I help it if you were in Africa? Can I help it if I wasn't?

WAITER: He's got to have his woman back. It's cruel.

MRS. BALICKE (*in front of* ANNA, *raging*): Listen: they're all sick! They all have something! Syphilis, syphilis, they all have syphilis!

BABUSCH (*pounding table with cane*): Now you've shot the works!

MRS. BALICKE: Leave my child alone, I tell you! Leave her alone, you swine!

ANNA: Andy, I don't want to. You're all driving me crazy.

MARIE: You're the swine in this bunch.

WAITER: It's not decent. There must be justice somewhere.

MRS. BALICKE: Hold your tongue, flunky. I'm ordering brandy, you wretch. Do you hear me? You'll be fired!

WAITER: It's a matter of common decency! It concerns us all! He simply must have his . . .

KRAGLER: You stay out of this. That's enough. Decency, my eye. What does this drunken cow want? I've been alone and I want my wife. What's this weepy angel after? Are you haggling over her belly as if it was a pound of coffee? If you drag her away from me with steel hooks you'll only tear her apart!

WAITER: You're tearing her apart!

MARIE: Like a pound of coffee!

BALICKE: And he hasn't a red cent!

BABUSCH: You're knocking his teeth in and he's spitting them in your face!

MURK (*to* ANNA): Why is your complexion like thrown-up milk? Why do you let him lick you with his eyes? Your face looks as if you'd been peeing in nettles!

BALICKE: A fine way to talk about your fiancée!

MURK: Fiancée? Is that what she is? She's running out on me already! Has he come back? Do you love him? Has the spider caught the fly? Got the itch for African thighs? Is that the way the wind is blowing?

BABUSCH: You wouldn't have said that sitting down.

ANNA (*moves closer to* KRAGLER, *looks offendedly at* MURK. *In an undertone*): Listen, you're drunk.

MURK (*grabbing her*): Let's see your face. Blacken your teeth, you whore!

KRAGLER (*without a word, lifts* MURK *up. Glasses rattle on the table.* MARIE *applauds throughout*): You're not too steady on your feet. Get out of here and vomit. You've drunk too much. You're falling over. (*Kicks him.*)

MARIE: Let him have it! Oh boy, let him have it!

KRAGLER: Leave him lay. Come to me, Anna. I want you now. He tried to buy my boots, but I took off my coat instead. My skin was drenched in icy rain, so it's red and it cracks in sunlight. My pack is empty, I haven't got a red cent, I want you, I'm not handsome. Up to now I've been down and out but now I'll have a drink. (*Takes a drink.*) And then we'll go. Come!

MURK (*all in a heap, shoulders slumped, says almost calmly to* KRAGLER): No drinking. You don't know the whole story. Take it easy. I was drunk. But you don't know the whole story. Anna, (*quite soberly*) tell him! What'll you do? The way you are?

KRAGLER (*not hearing him*): Don't worry, Anna. (*Hold-*

ing the brandy.) Nothing will happen to you. Don't be afraid! We'll get married. I've always been lucky.

WAITER: Hurrah!

MRS. BALICKE: Wretch!

KRAGLER: If you have a conscience, the birds shit on your roof. If you have patience, the vultures will get you in the end. Everybody works too hard.

ANNA (*suddenly lets go, collapses over table*): Andy, help me! Help, Andy!

MARIE: What's wrong with you? What's the matter?

KRAGLER (*looks at her, amazed*): What's up?

ANNA: I don't know, Andy. Oh, Andy, I'm so miserable. I can't tell you why, you mustn't ask. (*Looks up.*) I can't be yours, so help me God.

KRAGLER's *glass falls from his hand.*

And so, Andy, I'm asking you to leave.

A silence. From the next room the man who came in before is heard asking "What is it now?"

WAITER (*answering toward door at left*): The crocodile-skinned lover from Africa has waited four years and the girl he wants to marry still has her lily in her hand. But the other lover, a fellow with button shoes, won't let her go, and the girl who still has her lily in her hand doesn't know which side to take.

VOICE: Is that all?

WAITER: The revolt in the newspaper quarter has a part in all this, too, and besides the girl has a secret: something the lover from Africa, who has waited four years, doesn't know. The entire matter is undecided.

VOICE: No decision has been reached?

WAITER: It's still entirely undecided.

BALICKE: Waiter! What sort of riff-raff is that? Must we share our wine with bedbugs? (*Leaning over toward* KRAGLER.) Did you get the message? Are you satis-

fied? Shut up! The sun was hot, eh? Well, that's
what Africa is for. It's in the geography book. And
you were a hero? That'll be in the history book. But
there's nothing in the bankbook, and therefore the
hero will return to Africa. That's that. Waiter: take
this thing away.

The WAITER *takes* KRAGLER *in tow. He goes along,
slowly, clumsily. But on his left goes the prostitute*
MARIE.

BALICKE: What a farce! (*Shouts after* KRAGLER, *because
it has turned too quiet*): Were you looking for meat?
This is no meat auction. Pack up your red moon and
sing songs to your chimpanzees. I don't give a damn
for your date palms. You're something out of a novel,
anyhow. Where's your birth certificate?

KRAGLER *has gone.*

MRS. BALICKE: That's right, yell your fill. (*To* ANNA:)
Now what's wrong with you? Are you trying to drink
yourself under the table with that brandy?
BALICKE: What's happened to her face? It's white as paper!
MRS. BALICKE: Yes, just look at the child! What's got into
your head now? This is the limit!

ANNA *sits silently behind the table, almost wrapped
in the curtain. Has a wicked look. A glass is in front
of her.*

MURK (*crosses to her, smells glass*): Ugh! Pepper!

She takes it back from him, contemptuously.

Oho! What the devil is the pepper for? Would you
like a scalding hot bath, too? You need some sense
knocked into you, that's what. I'm shocked! (*Spits,
and throws glass on floor.*)

ANNA *smiles.*

Machine-gun fire is heard.

BABUSCH (*at window*): We're off. The masses are in revolt. Spartacus is rising. Murder goes on.

All stand rigid, listening to the noise outside.

ACT THREE
Ride of the Valkyries

A road leading to the suburbs.
Red brick barracks wall, from top left to bottom right.
Behind it, in faded starlight, the city. Night. Wind.

MARIE: Where are you rushing off to?

KRAGLER (*hatless, coat collar turned up, hands in pants pockets, has entered, whistling*): Who's this red-haired slut?

MARIE: Don't run so fast!

KRAGLER: Aren't you following me?

MARIE: Do you think somebody's after you?

KRAGLER: Do you want to go to bed? Where's your room?

MARIE: That's not a good idea.

KRAGLER: All right then. (*Wants to keep on going.*)

MARIE: I have lung trouble.

KRAGLER: Must you keep following me, like a dog?

MARIE: What about your wife?

KRAGLER: Ah, that's finished. Washed up. Cancelled.

MARIE: And what will you do with yourself till tomorrow morning?

KRAGLER: God! There's sleep. There's booze. There's tobacco. There's knives.

MARIE: Jesus Christ!

KRAGLER: Take it easy. I don't like you to scream like that. There's tobacco too. What do you want? I can try laughing, if you'd get a kick out of that. Tell me, did they lay you on the steps before you were confirmed? Oh, forget it. Do you smoke? (*He laughs.*) Let's go on down.

MARIE: They'll be floating in booze down there tonight.

132

KRAGLER: Maybe they can use us!

Both leave.
Wind. Two men enter, going in the same direction.

FIRST MAN: Let's do it here.
SECOND MAN: Who knows if we could down there?

They pee.

FIRST MAN: They sure are beating those drums.
SECOND MAN: Hell! In our part of town, too!
FIRST MAN: Where you blended that phony alcohol!
SECOND MAN: The moon alone can drive you crazy.
FIRST MAN: Yes, if you've been peddling phony tobacco.
SECOND MAN: All right, so I peddled phony tobacco. But you shoved people down ratholes.
FIRST MAN: Feel better now?
SECOND MAN: I won't swing alone.
FIRST MAN: Getting dizzy?
SECOND MAN: Getting short of breath?
FIRST MAN: You smell already.
SECOND MAN: Oh, God!
FIRST MAN: A fine thing, to have you along, with that bowler of yours.
SECOND MAN: You have one too.
FIRST MAN: It has a cleft.
SECOND MAN: I can split mine.
FIRST MAN: Your stiff collar's worse than a hangman's rope.
SECOND MAN: It's sweaty, though. And you have button shoes.
FIRST MAN: Your paunch!
SECOND MAN: Your voice!
FIRST MAN: Your look, your walk, your appearance!
SECOND MAN: I know all that means the gallows for me, but you have an educated face.

FIRST MAN: I have a banged-up ear with a bullet hole in it, my dear sir.

SECOND MAN: Oh, damn!

Both go out. Wind. From left the Valkyries ride in: ANNA, *as if in flight; beside her, in dress cloak but hatless, the waiter* MANKE, *from the Piccadilly Bar, pretending to be tight. Behind them comes* BABUSCH, *dragging* MURK, *who is drunk, pale and puffy.*

MANKE: Put him out of your minds! He's vanished without a trace. Maybe the suburbs have swallowed him up. There's shooting all over, all kinds of stuff is going on around the papers, this very night. He might even have been shot. (*To* ANNA, *with "drunken" insistence:*) A man may run away if there is shooting, but a man may also not run away. In any case, an hour from now nobody will be able to find him. He's melting like paper in water. He's got the moon on the brain. He's running after every drum. Go! Save the man who was, no, is your lover.

BABUSCH (*thrusting himself in* ANNA'S *way*): This Valkyrie ride has got to stop. Where are you off to? It's cold and windy and he's landed in some tavern. (*Mimicking* WAITER.) The one who has waited four years. But now nobody will find him.

MURK: Nobody. Not a soul. (*Sits down on a stone.*)

BABUSCH: Look at that, would you? Now it's drunk, but a while ago it had button shoes and followed its own sweet will. At present, however, it feels cold, I'd have you know, and is not too sure of itself. And it shouldn't be left lying there.

MANKE: What's that to me? Give him a coat! You've no time to lose! The one who has waited four years is moving faster than those clouds up there! He's out-running the wind!

MURK (*dully*): There was dye in that punch. Just now,

when everything's ready—the laundry in, the rooms rented. Come to me, Bab!

MANKE: Why do you stand there like Lot's wife? This is no Gomorrah. Are you shaken by the sight of drunken misery? Can't you step over it? Is it the laundry? Is it that drunk heap over there? Will the clouds hang back for that?

BABUSCH: What business is this of yours, anyhow? What have you to do with the clouds? You're a waiter.

MANKE: What it has to do with me? If a man's indifferent to a dirty deal, the stars fall clean out of their courses! (*Grabs himself by the throat.*) It burns *me* up, too! It grabs *my* throat, too! People shouldn't be petty when a man's down and out.

BABUSCH: Down and out, did you say? Where did you get that idea? Believe me, something will be roaring like a bull down by the papers before tomorrow dawns, and that'll be the one that's down and out. I've known him since he was a kid.

MANKE: He'll go to the dogs and into Glubb's dive. If he's in luck they'll shoot him.

BABUSCH: He'll prefer the dive, or he'll lead them all a chase, and if toward morning you hear a hullabaloo around the papers and drumming in the night—that's him.

MURK (*has got up, whines*): Why are you dragging me around in this wind? I feel terrible. Why are you running away? What's wrong? I need you. It's not the laundry.

ANNA: I can't.

MURK: Don't you see me?

ANNA: I see you.

MURK: My legs are wobbly.

MANKE: Sit down! You're not the only one! Things are moving now. The Father's had a stroke and the drunk kangaroo's in tears, but Daughter's going down to

Skid Road, to her lover who has waited four years.

MURK (*somewhat sobered, to* ANNA): The linen's bought and the rent's paid. Where are you going?

MANKE: Hark, hark, the dogs do bark. You want to know where she's going? I'll tell you. We want to enter the small and greasy houses. You know, the kind so full of vomit a man can slip on the steps. Dark, wormy rooms with the wind whistling through.

ANNA: That's where I want to go.

MANKE: Are we downhearted? No. It rains on the ancient beds and nobody can get warm in the wind that whistles through. Maybe it's worse there! That's where you must go! You can get lost there. Those are the houses where drumming is heard today. They're packed with heaps like this one, but down there they have no shirts, and it'll go on that way for twenty years, maybe thirty, the last years of this world. You can't count them. And still you feel better in your soul down there than any other place.

MURK: Your father and mother have us married.

ANNA: I can't go through with it.

MURK: The linen's all in the closet, the furniture's all in the rooms.

MANKE: The sheets are folded but the bride will not be there.

ANNA: My linen is bought, I put it in the chest, piece by piece, but I don't need it now. We've paid the rent and the curtains are up and there's no lack of carpets. But the one who waited four years has come.

MURK: The one without a clean shirt to his name . . .

MANKE: And a skin like a crocodile's!

MURK: The one you didn't recognize, because he looked so bad.

MANKE: But she still had her lily when he came.

ANNA: The man who hasn't a shoe, and only one coat, and that has moths in it.

MANKE: And shantytown swallows him up! The gin mill awaits him! Night! Misery! Rejection! Save him!

BABUSCH: This play is called The Angel in the Waterfront Dives.

MANKE: That's it, the angel!

MURK: You want to go down there? Shantytown, darkness, nothing?

ANNA: Yes, I want to go to nothing.

MURK: Nothing but a drunken frenzy! Nothing but a movie serial! Nothing but the snows of yesteryear!

ANNA: Nothing else . . .

MANKE: That's right, nothing else! Now she knows. For nothing!

MURK: And nothing holds you back?

ANNA: I know of nothing.

MURK: Nothing? Not even that lily? When no wind touches you, when you've sunk right down to the bottom, won't you still be thinking of "the other"?

ANNA: No. I don't want it any more.

MURK: You don't want "the other"?

ANNA: It's my halter.

MURK: And it isn't holding you?

ANNA: It's untied.

MURK: Is your child like you?

ANNA: It's like me.

MURK: Because the coatless man arrived?

ANNA: I didn't know who he was.

MURK: Then he's not the one! You didn't know who he was!

ANNA: He stood among us like an animal.

MURK: We took care of him, but good!

ANNA: And they beat him like an animal.

MURK: And he yelled like an old woman!

ANNA: He yelled like a woman.

MURK: And he pulled out and left you in the lurch!

ANNA: He went away and left me in the lurch.

MURK: It was all up with him. He was done for.

ANNA: It was all up with him.

MURK: He went away . . .

ANNA: But when he went away and it was all up with him . . .

MURK: There was nothing. Nothing at all.

ANNA: There was a flurry behind him and a little breeze and then it was very strong and stronger than anything and now I'm going away and now I'm here and now it's all over between me and him. Because . . . where has he gone? Does even God know where he is? It's a big world, and where is he? (*Looks calmly at* MURK *and says lightly to* MANKE:) Please go back to your bar, and take him along, he's drunk. Bab: come with me. (*Runs off to right.*)

MURK (*fretfully*): Where's she gone? Into the wind—and me so drunk. I can't even see my hands. And she takes off!

BABUSCH: Now I see the light, old man. We've been fishing the wrong river. The Valkyrie ride's a flop, my boy, and the tale of the ghost in the pond is turning deadly serious.

MANKE: The lover is missing, but the beloved races after him on wings of love. The hero has taken a fall, but the ascent to heaven is already prepared.

BABUSCH: Yes, but the lover will kick the beloved into the gutter and prefer a descent to hell. Oh, you romantic monument!

MANKE: Behold her vanish as she rushes toward the suburbs. Like a white sail she remains in sight, like an idea, like the last verse of a poem, like a maddened swan flying over the waters. . . .

BABUSCH: What shall we do with the drunken sailor?

MURK: I'm staying right here. It's chilly. She'll come back when it gets cold. You people know nothing at all. Because you don't know the other thing. Let her go!

He can't take two! He's left one, and two are on his tail! (*Laughs.*)

BABUSCH: Take this home. Do something for your salvation. Now, by God, she's vanishing like that last verse. (*Trudges after* ANNA.)

MANKE (*pulls* MURK *to his feet, stretches both arms wide, proclaims*): The suburbs are gulping them down. Will they find each other?

ACT FOUR
The Booze Dance

A small gin mill.
GLUBB, *the tavernkeeper, in white, is singing the "Ballad of the Dead Soldier," accompanying himself on the guitar.* LAAR *and a dim drunk are staring at his fingers. A little square man named* BULLTROTTER *is reading the paper.* MANKE, *the waiter, is drinking with* AUGUSTA, *the prostitute. All present are smoking.*

BULLTROTTER: I don't want a dead soldier, I want a drink!
I want to read the paper, and I can't understand a goddam word in it without a drink.
GLUBB (*in a cold, flat voice*): Don't you like it here?
BULLTROTTER: Sure, but there's a revolution going on.
GLUBB: What for? Thieves and poor men sit in my place and sing.
DRUNK: You're the poor man, I'm the thief.

BABUSCH *enters with* ANNA *behind him.*

BABUSCH: Has an artilleryman been here, by any chance?
GLUBB (*pouring a drink*): Nope. Nobody's been here.
BABUSCH (*to someone behind him*): He hasn't been here.
GLUBB: Should someone be coming here?

BABUSCH *shrugs.*

Should I give him a message?
BABUSCH (*looking at* ANNA, *who is shaking her head*): No. We'll be back.

Both leave.

MANKE: If they ask for anything, it's a drink. If they share anything, it's beds. If they make anything, it's kids.

140

Oh, Lord! (*To* GLUBB:) My dear old soul, if you had a drink inside you, and pale faces and shaky knees, (*acting it out*) and your nose in the air in the rain, there'd be rain right enough, my dear old soul —a rain of bullets. And with sticks in your hands and an itch in your fingers—man, there'd be hell to pay!

BULLTROTTER: Freedom! Space! Air! (*Takes his collar and coat off.*)

GLUBB: Drinking without your coat on is against the law.

BULLTROTTER: Reaction!

MANKE: They're rehearsing the "Marseillaise," for four voices and falsetto, you bourgeois!

BULLTROTTER (*throws a newspaper at him*): Birds of a feather . . .

The two throw papers at each other.

Freedom!

MANKE: Freedom! Should a man with clean shirt-cuffs clean the toilet?

GLUBB: Watch out, you're cracking that wooden marble.

AUGUSTA: Keep your ugly mug out of this. Why shouldn't guys with white cuffs clean the toilet?

BULLTROTTER: You'll be shot at dawn, boy!

AUGUSTA: If they won't clean the toilet they should have their asses tied.

MANKE: Augusta! You're vulgar.

AUGUSTA: Ah, you pigs, you oughta be ashamed. They oughta hang you, rip your guts out, string up those white-collar fellows from lampposts. Feet on the floor, please. There're ladies present. Why should I have to smell your sweaty feet, you jerk?

GLUBB: His collar isn't white, and that's a fact.

DRUNK: What's that rumble out there?

MANKE: Cannon!

DRUNK (*grinning palely at the others*): What's that clatter out there?

GLUBB *runs to window, yanks it open. They hear artillery pieces speeding down the alley. All to the window.*

BULLTROTTER: Revolt! Strike! Revolution!

AUGUSTA: Holy smoke! Where are they off to?

GLUBB: The papers, girl! They're the readers! (*Shuts window.*)

BULLTROTTER: Who let the wind in?

AUGUSTA: Holy smoke! Who's that by the door?

KRAGLER *at door, teetering as if drunk, enters with* MARIE.

BULLTROTTER: This is great. He's in artillery uniform.

MANKE: A peculiar covering. I assume you are about to lay an egg?

AUGUSTA: Who are you, coming with the guns like that?

KRAGLER (*with a wicked grin*): Nobody.

AUGUSTA (*drying him off*): Why, there's water all down his neck.

MANKE (*crossing to him*): Come on, fellow, tell us what you've been up to. I know the characters that come in here. Barroom troubles, eh?

AUGUSTA: Did you run away like that?

MARIE: They took away his girl that he waited four years for. They drove to the Piccadilly Bar and he ran all the way there, following their cab.

DRUNK: Like a calf! Man, what a story!

AUGUSTA: Is it romantic?

KRAGLER: I don't know any stories.

BULLTROTTER (*to* MARIE): Are you mixed up in this? Do you belong to him?

MARIE: I only ran away with him.

MANKE: So why are you running like a calf?

DRUNK: Got the trots?

KRAGLER: No, I don't have the trots.

DRUNK: But is it a story?

BULLTROTTER: What do you mean, story?

DRUNK: Or maybe it's a gospel? Give him a shot of brandy and a smoke, then he can tell us all.

The door is shut. KRAGLER *leans against the wall. The others smoke and stare at his mouth.* GLUBB, *detached, wipes glasses.*

DRUNK: Keep the door shut. It's only the wind, brother, but there's more to come. There's more to come.

KRAGLER (*blustering, with bitter humor*): I was in Africa . . . Lots of sunshine there. We knocked off niggers, you know, and . . . that kind of thing. Paved roads, too. Went down there in cattle cars.

MANKE: Prisoner?

MARIE: Missing, too.

AUGUSTA: Missing, too?

MARIE: Yeah. Prisoner, too.

AUGUSTA: Tell us about Africa!

KRAGLER: Africa. Yes, indeed. (*Silence.*) The sun scorched your head like a date, our brains felt like dates, we shot blacks, always in the belly, and paved roads, and I got a fly in my head, fellows, when my brain was gone. They often beat me on the head, too.

BULLTROTTER: That's a gripping story, all right. Well-thought out. Have another drink. What happened before?

KRAGLER: Before? I was lying in a clay pit. Like garbage in filthy water. We pumped water. We watched the time. It didn't move. And then we gaped at the sky; it was like a big umbrella, and pitch black all day long. But we had the dropsy anyhow, because the ditch was always full. (*Drinks.*)

GLUBB: A great set-up for goofing off.

AUGUSTA: More about Africa, more about Africa!

KRAGLER: Well, the time wouldn't move and all we could do was stink. We were defending our homeland, the stones and the rest of it, and I was defending everything—the sky, and the ground, and the water, and —everything.

MARIE: Andy! That's his name, Andy.

KRAGLER: Andy! That's my name. That was my name. Thick green trees, way up in the air. I saw that. But not for all four years.

GLUBB: You didn't see them, but it doesn't matter.

KRAGLER: I was defending and all the time people kept falling and I had a fly in my head, a fly—it was my wife, only she wasn't yet. She was innocent, and (*drinks*) then came Africa.

BULLTROTTER (*smiling broadly*): How about the broads down there? What are the broads like?

KRAGLER: It was an island, or something like that. We got no letters and the nights were cold. (*Opens eyes wide.*) Be sure to throw cats off a wall. (*Drinks.*)

MARIE: How long did it last? how long?

KRAGLER: Three years. Three years: that's more than a thousand days. They kept us underwater, you see, like cats in leather bags. They don't want to die either. (*Counts on fingers.*) I might have died on the second day, or the tenth, or after twenty days, or forty. . . . But there is Anna: morning after morning she stands behind the barracks, among the dogs.

DRUNK: Didn't you run away then?

KRAGLER (*more calmly*): The third time I ran away I was lucky and I sang when things got tough and I was lucky and I made it. (*Sits down, starts having a lot to drink, speaks more and more slowly and heavily; pauses now and says very calmly:*) Don't think I was greedy or anything like that, and supposed she'd go to the barracks every morning and never do anything else. I had worked out a way to help her get used to me again, because I'd become a ghost. That's how it was. (*Drinks.*)

The wind is heard; the DRUNK *groans with fascination.*

KRAGLER (*calmly*): She wasn't home when I got there.

GLUBB: That she wasn't. No, indeed.

BULLTROTTER: And then?

DRUNK: Was she away? Where was she?

KRAGLER: The liquor was all drunk up and the blacks were
dead and the umbrella snapped shut and the fly . . .
the fly . . . it flew away. (*Gazing before him.*) I was
defending *him*. He sent the liquor for the beasts of
burden, and the umbrella. He let the fly live to
keep us from getting bored. (*Points as if seeing him.*)
And now he's running loose, that other guy. Now he
lies in bed and you take your hat off when you see
him and he takes your skin off and my wife is in
his bed.

BULLTROTTER (*holding paper*): Somebody stole her, eh?

GLUBB: They stole my bicycle.

MANKE (*with a motion of cutting his throat*): What patience you have, boy!

AUGUSTA: And you didn't choke her like a cat?

MARIE: They hustled her off and he came trotting after.

KRAGLER (*drinks*): When they told me that I turned cold
all over and couldn't think of anything. And when
I think of it now, my pulse stays normal. You can
feel it for yourselves. (*Stretches a hand out, holds
bottle with other.*) I was looking for her, and she
knew who I was, too, even if I did have a fresh complexion once. And she said something to me. Give
me back that glass.

DRUNK: Go on! What did she say?

KRAGLER: Well, she said (*drinks*) "It's all over." (*Silence;
he keeps feeling his pulse, absently.*)

GLUBB: That's old stuff.

DRUNK: And then what did you do?

KRAGLER: Oh, go on and booze! I'm off. Keep at it, I
won't be around. Dance and drink and kick the
bucket, all in good time. (*Turning tearful.*) Take me,
for instance. I've got Africa in my blood—a terrible

sickness. A fly in my head, a gadfly, keep dancing, gimme some booze, not everything is known yet. Louder, nickelodeon! It'll all come out some day!

MANKE: You've had a real rough time, man. Better tie one on.

BULLTROTTER: Yeah, get good and drunk. He has the feel of a corpse—he's dead but he won't lie down. Just like the story we ran last week from Merseburg. . . .

DRUNK: Is she still alive? (*Has started the nickelodeon.*) That kind of thing just doesn't happen.

KRAGLER (*hums the tune, grabs* AUGUSTA, *whirls around with her*): March, march, march on!

GLUBB: Better not break my glasses, gunner boy!

MARIE: He's drunk now. He's taking it easier.

KRAGLER (*at rear, as* AUGUSTA *gives him a drink*): He is, is he? No meat on his bones, eh? Made of paper, eh? Never mind, brother, say things like that don't happen. Hear that, Brother Brandy Bottle? Hear that wind? Jump, Sister Whore! Jump, Brother Red! Don't hang back, I tell you. What's a pig to God? Nothing! Get good and drunk, the pig counts for nothing, you won't feel it.

GLUBB: Why are you yelling so loud?

KRAGLER: Who's paying here? Who's making that thing play? It keeps on playing! There's a fly in my head! I must have booze to drown it! Can you get rid of soldiers or the good Lord? Can you get rid of the troubles there are, and the torments that men have taught the devil? No, you can't get rid of them, but you can drink. Drink, and sleep on stones, too. For them that sleep, I tell you, all things shall be for the best. It's in the catechism, you'd better believe it. So drink and shut the door and don't let the wind in, it feels cold too. Block it with wood. Don't let the ghosts in. They're cold.

GLUBB: Dear me, Brother Gunner, you have been somewhat wronged.

KRAGLER: Wronged, did you say, Brother Red? What kind of a word is that? Wronged! Make yourselves at home on this star, it's cold here and sort of gloomy, Mr. Red, there's no time for wrong, the world's too old for better days and liquor's cheaper and heaven's full up, my friends. (*Goes to rear, singing. Shoves coins into nickelodeon. It plays fast, short pieces.*)

BULLTROTTER (*has been drinking in silence*): What'll we say to that? Handcuffs! Handcuffs!

MANKE (*getting up*): Damn it, man, your wife is looking for you.

KRAGLER: Trot, trot! On the double! (*Sings.*) "A dog went in the kitchen / An egg from Cook to swipe . . ."

MANKE (*smoking*): Now he's jumping around with his gadfly.

AUGUSTA: How do you like your smoke?

GLUBB: Listen, you guys, in here you're supposed to drink and that's all.

MANKE: But we're smoking, too.

DRUNK: Yeah, you're the revolutionary. We know you and your speeches. They poured your stuff down the toilet. You were the liquor dealer.

GLUBB (*keeping busy with glasses; coldly*): I had more under the floor. And it's not because the booze was gone, but because there are human hands that pour it down the toilet.

KRAGLER (*blinking, and as if he were waking up*): Anna! Anna!

BULLTROTTER (*screeching*): Handcuffs! If only you'd snitched some handcuffs!

GLUBB: I was standing in the yard. It was night. It happened to be raining, I was looking around, most likely that was when I got the idea. And now I'm all for drinking. But I sing hymns too.

KRAGLER: "And Cook picked up his cleaver/ And hacked the dog to tripe."

MARIE: What are we supposed to do? We're little folks. Many are saying "Go to the papers." That's the place to go. But what's in the papers?

KRAGLER: A cab is driving to the Piccadilly Bar.

AUGUSTA: Is she in it?

KRAGLER: She's in it.

MANKE: Your wife is bound to be looking for you, man.

DRUNK (*who has climbed on the table and is looking at the city night*): Keep on drinking, everybody!

LAAR: Small potatoes, it was small potatoes. . . .

GLUBB: Another country heard from.

LAAR: And one guy had some money in his pocket.

BULLTROTTER: And then you went and sold, you dumb cluck!

LAAR *ambles toward rear.*

GLUBB (*to* KRAGLER, *who has calmed down again*): Go ahead and drink. Some of the fellows outside are drumming, and now they've started shooting. You can hear it very clearly. What matters now is to keep quiet. They're shooting for your sake. Heaven and hell are up in arms, my man, so why shouldn't you have your booze? You were somewhat wronged. Say yes and take a swig. Keep still when they rip your skin off, or it'll split. It's the only one you've got. (*Puts down a glass toward rear; calmly:*) Man the machine guns!

SEVERAL PEOPLE: To the papers!

GLUBB: Yes, you'll have to get a paper out.

KRAGLER: It's a long, long way to the Piccadilly Bar!

MANKE (*chewing a cigar and taking his coat off*): What goes too far need not be allowed to trample on one's stomach.

GLUBB (*looking at* MANKE *standing there in shirt sleeves*): That's right, put a clean shirt on your rotten skin so nobody will see it! Are stories something to feed

on? God, a bit of a wrong! Eat your salad and drink
your brandy! (*Starts nickelodeon.*) Let's face it, you
fellows are sort of tight on brandy, they've sort of
kicked you around and also sort of clobbered you with
guns and sabers, and sort of shit on you, and spit on
you a bit.

AUGUSTA: You cowards let us starve and then pray over
us. Gimme a drink and take a look at me! I'm a rotten
girl and I've had a rotten time. Just look at me, would
you? Augusta is my name.

GLUBB: You've got syphilis, too.

NEWSGIRLS (*in back*): Extra, extra! Spartacus takes over
newspapers! Red Rosa speaks in Zoo District, in open
air. State of siege. Revolution!

BULLTROTTER: Paper here! This is for us!

NEWSGIRLS (*shrilly*): The mob is raising hell. Where's the
army? Only twenty pfennigs. Where's the army? Come
on, Gunner Boy!

KRAGLER: Has hell broken loose again? (*Ducks.*) Is this
a joke? Man the barricades, you ghost! (*Stands
steady, takes a deep breath.*) Making an end is better
than getting drunk. No, it's no joke. To vanish is
better than to sleep.

BULLTROTTER (*jumping onto table*): I was at Skagerrak,
and that was no picnic either.

GLUBB *closes cupboard and wipes hands.*

MANKE: Let's go, Augusta! With my shield or on it!

BULLTROTTER: And what of your gin mill, whisky baron?

GLUBB: Let the rats have it.

KRAGLER (*on chair, struggling with lamp, an old relic*):
Hell has broken loose again, my friends. Over the top
at dawn, or drown like cats in the alley!

THE OTHERS (*yelling*): Over the top at dawn, Andy!

KRAGLER (*turns lamp off*): Or drown like cats in the alley!

MANKE: Augusta: forward!

DRUNK (*pointing at* MARIE): "A slut angelically good/ Swam with him through the tearful flood."

KRAGLER (*sliding down*): A corpse, that's what I am! It's all yours! (*Evilly.*) Come one, come all, for a great big hug, and let's go off to the papers! (*The others follow him.*)

DRUNK (*hard on their heels*): Jesus, wash me white as snow!

LAAR *reels to nickelodeon, takes drum from it and goes swaying and twisting after the procession.*

ACT FIVE
The Bed

A wooden bridge.
Shouting. Big red moon.

BABUSCH: They stormed the barracks after two o'clock.

ANNA: He won't come now.

BABUSCH: Now they're marching into the newspaper offices. You really ought to go home.

ANNA: I can't, now.

BABUSCH: The last time, about four, it seemed to me he'd gone under. He was swimming hard but he didn't come up.

ANNA: What's the use? I waited with my photo for four years, and then I took another man. The nights were so scary!

BABUSCH: I'm out of cigars. Aren't you going home at all?

ANNA: How the year draws in, how red the moon is! As if in sleep. I sit here on a stone, and there's the red moon, and it's late in the year.

BABUSCH: There they go, beating those drums again. They tear up papers and throw 'em into puddles, yell at machine guns, shoot themselves in the ear, think they're making a new world. Here comes another bunch.

ANNA: It's him!

Deep unrest invades the alleys as the group approaches. Shots ring out from several directions.

The alleys are on the watch for them. Fever breaks through the roofs. The houses are troubled. Now I'll tell him!

BABUSCH: I'll shut you up!

151

ANNA: I'm no animal! I'm going to scream!

BABUSCH: Fever has broken out and I have no cigars!

> *From among the houses emerge* GLUBB, LAAR, *the* DRUNK, *the two tarts and* KRAGLER.

KRAGLER: I'm hoarse. I'm up to my neck in Africa. I'm going to hang myself.

GLUBB: Couldn't you do it tomorrow, and go to the papers with us today?

KRAGLER (*staring at* ANNA): Yes.

AUGUSTA: Seen a ghost?

MANKE: Man, your hair's on end!

GLUBB: Is she the one?

KRAGLER: What's the matter? Got stuck? You'll be shot at dawn! Forward march! Keep going!

ANNA(*goes up to him*): Andy!

DRUNK: Love beckons. Get a move on!

ANNA: Andy, stand still. It's me. I wanted to tell you something. (*Silence.*) I wanted to call your attention to something. Stand still a little, I'm not drunk. (*Silence.*) You have to go, though, I guess. But you have no cap, it's cold. I've got to whisper something in your ear, I've forgotten what. Maybe it shouldn't have happened.

KRAGLER: Are you drunk?

AUGUSTA: His girl's after him. She's drunk!

ANNA: What will you say to this? (*Takes a few steps after him.*) I'm going to have a baby.

> AUGUSTA *laughs shrilly.*
> KRAGLER *sways, looks toward bridge, sidles as if thinking of leaving.*

AUGUSTA: You're gasping for air like a fish.

MARIE: Maybe you think you're asleep.

KRAGLER (*at attention*): Yes, sir!

MANKE: She's with child. That's what she's for. Come along now!

KRAGLER (*stiffly*): Yes, sir! Where to?

MANKE: He's lost his wits.

GLUBB: Weren't you in Africa one time?

KRAGLER: Morocco. Casablanca. Hut number ten.

ANNA: Andy!

KRAGLER (*listening*): Listen! My wife, the whore! She's come, she's here, she has a big belly!

GLUBB: She's somewhat anemic.

KRAGLER: Shhh! It wasn't me, I wasn't the one.

ANNA: Andy, there are people here.

KRAGLER: Are you gassy, or have you turned whore? I was away, I couldn't watch you. I was lying in the dirt. Where did you lie while I lay in the dirt?

MARIE: You shouldn't talk like that. What do you know about it?

KRAGLER: And I wanted to see you! I'd be lying where I belong now, with the wind on my temples and dirt in my mouth, and I wouldn't know a thing. But I wanted to see this. I wouldn't settle for less. I ate grape skins. They were bitter. I crawled out of the clay pit. Smart, eh? What a clod! (*Opens eyes wide.*) Are you all watching? Do you have passes? (*Picks up handfuls of dirt and throws them around.*)

AUGUSTA: Hold him down!

ANNA (*has got up*): Keep throwing, Andy! Keep throwing! This way!

MANKE: Get that woman out of here. He'll stone her to death!

KRAGLER: Go to hell. You'll have all you need down there. Open your mouths, there's nothing else to do.

AUGUSTA: Shove his head down! Shove it into the dirt!

The men hold KRAGLER *down on the ground.*

GLUBB: She's made of earth too, boy. Look at her from below!

AUGUSTA: Better fade, miss.

GLUBB: Yes, go home now. Early morning air is bad
    for the ovaries.

BABUSCH (*rushes across the battlefield to* KRAGLER *and
    announces to him, chewing his beat-up cigar*): Now
    you know where the shoe pinches. Thou art the
    Lord, thou hast thundered. As for the lady, she's
    pregnant. She can't just sit there: the nights are turn-
    ing cold. Perhaps you have something to say?

GLUBB: Yes. Say something, man!

The men let KRAGLER *up. A silence. The wind blows.
Two men in a hurry pass by.*

FIRST MAN: Now they've got to the papers.

SECOND MAN: And the artillery's coming up.

FIRST MAN: Everything will change now.

SECOND MAN: It's going far too slowly. There aren't nearly
    enough of them.

FIRST MAN: Many are on the way.

SECOND MAN: Much too late.

*They have gone, but in the background many men
are marching on the newspapers.*

AUGUSTA: You heard them. Let's get this over with!

MANKE: Fling the answer in his face—that bourgeois and
    his whore.

AUGUSTA (*trying to drag* KRAGLER *along*): Come with us
    to the papers, boy! Now you've got hair on your teeth!

GLUBB: Let her sit on her stone in peace. The next train
    leaves at seven.

AUGUSTA: No subways today. Are his hands still stuck
    in his pockets?

DRUNK: Forward! On to the land of milk and honey!

ANNA *has got up again.*

MARIE (*looking at her*): White as a sheet.

GLUBB: Somewhat pale, somewhat thin.

BABUSCH: She's going to the dogs.

GLUBB: The light's bad, of course. (*Looks at sky.*)

AUGUSTA: They're marching! They're shouting! They're hailing us!

GLUBB (*rubbing his hands*): You came with the guns. Maybe you belong with them.

KRAGLER *is silent.*

You have nothing to say. That's wise. (*Walks around him.*) Your uniform is a bit shot up and the bad light makes it look as if your hair had fallen out. On the whole you're somewhat faded, somewhat worn. Your fingers have turned black, too. Let's see them! But that makes little difference. Maybe it's just that your shoes are rather uncomfortable. They creak. But you can grease them. (*Sniffs air.*) I've only known you for four hours. It's true that since then the starry heavens have been flooded and the sparrows have eaten several Messiahs, but luckily you're still with us. Only your digestion gives me any reason to complain. All the same, the light does not go through you yet. At least you are visible.

KRAGLER: Come here, Anna!

MANKE: Come here, Anna!

ANNA: Is it seven yet?

KRAGLER: Come here to me, Anna.

ANNA: Please tell me how to reach the subway.

AUGUSTA: No subway today. Today there's no subway, no elevated, no streetcars, all day long. Today there's peace and quiet everywhere. The trains are at a standstill on all the tracks, and we walk around like human beings, until nightfall, my love.

KRAGLER: Come to me, Anna!

ANNA: Are you so kind?

GLUBB: Wouldn't you rather have a drink?

KRAGLER: To me!

ANNA: Is it because of the catechism?

KRAGLER: Anna!

AUGUSTA: Aren't you a soldier, boy?

ANNA: Oh, lay off him.

GLUBB: A cow should be milked while she's warm.

MANKE: You're still in uniform!

KRAGLER: My throat's worn out with yelling, but watch out, my knife's still good.

> GLUBB *stands in front of* ANNA. *The marchers in the background cast long shadows on the houses, and snatches of the "Marseillaise" float by on the wind.*

GLUBB: She does look like thrown-up milk. It's unpleasant.

> KRAGLER *says nothing.*

> A few of us would have liked a few more shots of whisky, but you were against it. Several would have liked to sleep in a bed once more, but you had no bed, so nothing came of cigar-smoking either. Too bad.

> KRAGLER *says nothing.*

> Won't you come a ways with us, Brother Gunner?

> KRAGLER *says nothing.*

MANKE: Why is he staring so strangely? Is he laying another egg?

ANNA: Don't you want to go, Andy?

MANKE: Quit dragging your feet, man.

ANNA: You can go. Go on, Andy.

AUGUSTA: Now he's lighting his pipe!

ANNA: Go on, go on. I'm through with you. Your face is black. I'll be glad to see the last of you.

KRAGLER: You can stone me but I'll stand right here. I'll give you the shirt off my back, but not my neck for the knife.

DRUNK: Heavens to Betsy and oh, my ass!

AUGUSTA: The papers? the papers? the papers?

> KRAGLER *shakes his head.* AUGUSTA *gives a whinnying laugh.*

GLUBB: The eternal feminine draws him upward.

KRAGLER (*looking straight ahead*): Come, Anna.

GLUBB: Can't you go into the water a ways, and take a bath?

KRAGLER: No, I've got cold feet.

AUGUSTA (*at rear*): There's only a handful left. They're moving faster. They've gone. On to the papers, fellows!

GLUBB (*to* ANNA): Can't *you* get this tiger to the papers?

KRAGLER: It's no good. I won't be dragged to the papers in my shirt. I'm no lamb now, I don't want to die. Every man for himself. (*Takes pipe from trouser pocket again.*)

GLUBB: So you have no pity on these people?

KRAGLER: So help me God, and stone me if you want: No. Why the face, Anna? Must I defend myself to you, too? (*To* GLUBB:) They poured your brandy down the toilet, but I have my wife back. Come, Anna.

GLUBB: And if they saddled me with six brandy distilleries I'd spit in their faces for the brandy, I'd tear their guts out for it, I'd burn their houses down for two barrels of it, and I'd keep on smoking all the time.

KRAGLER: Anna! (*To* GLUBB:) You're risking your neck and smoking all the time! I see you lined up to be shot at dawn. (*To the others*:) Don't you see him, back to the wall, gray-faced and glassy-eyed? Can't you smell it on him? What will become of you all? Go home.

> AUGUSTA *laughs.*

GLUBB: Oh, they'll get little wounds in the neck or the breast, as the rules prescribe, and when they're stiff

they'll have numbered tickets stuck on their chests—
not like drowned cats, but more like people who have
been somewhat wronged.

KRAGLER: Stop that.

GLUBB: Sort of beggarly, in fact.

KRAGLER: Listen, man, they'll shoot your chest till it's
nothing but a black hole! What'll happen to it then?

GLUBB (*looks at him coolly*): The rats will live in it.

A fancily dressed female comes over the bridge.

AUGUSTA: Did you come from the newspaper district?

WOMAN: Yes, I did.

MANKE: Are they fighting there? How's it going?

WOMAN: Nobody knows.

AUGUSTA: Have they taken over the papers yet?

WOMAN (*raises her arm. Shouting starts in the distance*):
Is that the gunner the fellows from Friedrichstadt are
waiting for?

AUGUSTA: Waiting, are they?

WOMAN: Oh, there'll be plenty knocked off today. (*Hurries
off.*)

AUGUSTA: Listen! The attack!

KRAGLER: Anna.

AUGUSTA: Will the gentleman please come along now?

KRAGLER (*to* ANNA): Why the hell are you looking at me
like that?

AUGUSTA: So it was all lies—Africa and all?

KRAGLER: No, it was true. Anna!

MANKE: The gentleman has been roaring like a broker,
and now he wants to go to bed.

KRAGLER: I have the woman now.

MANKE: You think so?

KRAGLER: Come here, Anna! She's damaged goods, she's
not innocent. Were you a good girl or are you carrying a brat?

ANNA: A brat . . . Yes, I've got one.

KRAGLER: You've got one.

ANNA: He's here, inside. The pepper didn't help and my hips will be no good for weeks.

KRAGLER: See? That's how she is.

MANKE: What about us? Up to our necks in booze, up to our bellies in talk, and these knives in our paws—where did they come from?

KRAGLER: From me. (*To* ANNA:) So that's the kind you are.

ANNA: That's the kind I am.

GLUBB: So you didn't yell "To the papers," eh?

KRAGLER: Yes, I did. (*To* ANNA:) Come on!

MANKE: You did that? You yelled "To the papers"? That'll be your neck, boy.

KRAGLER: And I'm going home. (*To* ANNA:) Come on, damn it!

AUGUSTA: Son of a bitch!

ANNA: Leave me alone. I fooled my folks and slept with a bachelor.

AUGUSTA: Bitch!

KRAGLER: What's wrong with you now?

ANNA: I bought the curtains with him. And slept in the bed with him.

KRAGLER: Shut up!

MANKE: Listen, I'm going to hang myself if you change your mind.

Distant shouting in background.

AUGUSTA: Now the attack is on.

ANNA: I clean forgot you, every bit of you, photo or no photo.

KRAGLER: Shut up!

ANNA: Forgot! forgot!

KRAGLER: I love you. Shall I take you away with my knife?

ANNA: Yes, get me out of here. With your knife!

MANKE: Now they're at the boiling point. (*Moves toward* ANNA.) Throw this garbage into the drink.

The men rush ANNA.

AUGUSTA: That's it! Get the bitch off his back!
MANKE: Grab her by the neck!
AUGUSTA: Drown the crooked slut!
ANNA: Andy!
KRAGLER: Hands off!

Now only panting is heard. Far away, at irregular intervals, muffled cannon shots.

MANKE: What's that?
AUGUSTA: Artillery.
MANKE: Cannon.
AUGUSTA: May God have mercy on them all.
KRAGLER: Anna!

AUGUSTA *ducks and runs to rear.*

BULLTROTTER (*appears at rear, on bridge*): Artillery! Damn it, Kragler, where are you?
GLUBB: He's gone to the can.
MANKE: The fink! (*Leaves.*)
KRAGLER: And now, my dear old soul, I'm going home.
GLUBB (*on bridge*): Yeah, the moon's turning pale and you still have your balls.
KRAGLER: Hell's broken loose again. Hold on tight, Anna.
ANNA: I'll make myself thin as a rail.
GLUBB: Just the same, you'll hang yourself tomorrow morning, in the can.

AUGUSTA *has disappeared with the others.*

KRAGLER: You're risking your neck, you know.
GLUBB: My boy: there's a strong smell of morning. The night is fading like black smoke. But there are some who will reach safety. (*He disappears.*)
KRAGLER: You nearly drowned in the tears you shed for me, but I used them to wash my shirt. Is my flesh

supposed to rot in the gutter so that your idea can
get to heaven? Are you plastered?

ANNA: Andy, it makes no difference now.

KRAGLER (*looks away from her face, weaves round,
reaches for his throat*): I've got it up to here.
(*Laughs angrily.*) Cheap theatricals, that's all it is.
There's some boards and a paper moon and a butcher
shop in back—that's the only real part. (*Runs round
again, arms low, and fishes up the drum from the
tavern.*) They left their drum. (*Pummels it.*) "The
Half-Rotten Lover, or, A Night of Love!" "Blood
Bath among the Newspapers, or, The Man who
Justified himself!" "Stake in the Flesh, or, Tiger in
the Gloaming!" (*Looks up, blinks.*) With your shield
—or else without it. (*Drumming.*) The bagpipes
play, the poor die among newspapers, houses fall
down on them, morning dawns, they lie like drowned
cats on the pavement, I'm a louse and the louse is
going home. (*Takes a deep breath.*) I'll put on a clean
shirt, I've still got my skin, I'll take off my uniform,
I'll grease my boots. (*With a wicked laugh.*) The
shouting will be over tomorrow morning but I'll be
lying in bed tomorrow morning and multiplying myself so as not to perish from the earth. (*Drumming.*)
Stop that romantic gaping, you profiteers! (*Drumming.*) Cutthroats! (*Roars with laughter, nearly
chokes on it.*) Bloodthirsty cowards! (*The laughter
sticks in his throat. He has reached the end of his
rope. He whips round and hurls the drum at the
moon, which was a street lamp. Drum and moon fall
into the river, which has no water in it. But the man
goes to the woman and goes home.*) Drunkenness
and kid stuff. Now for bed—the big, white, wide
bed. Come!

ANNA: Oh, Andy!

KRAGLER (*leading her toward rear*): Are you warm, too?

ANNA: But you have no coat on. (*She helps him into it.*)

KRAGLER: It's turning chilly; it's early in the year. (*Wraps her shawl around her.*) Come. Now!

A little streamer of cloud. The pink of dawn in the twilit, smoky sky. The pair walk together, without excitement, ANNA *a little behind* KRAGLER. *In the air, high up, very far off, a white, wild outcry. It is in the newspaper district.*

KRAGLER *stops, listens, puts his arm around* ANNA *as he stands there.*

It's been four years now.

The outcry continues. They leave.

ROUNDHEADS AND PEAKHEADS

Rich and Rich
make
good company

CHARACTERS

CZUCHS
(Roundheads)

The Regent

Missena, *his privy councilor*

Angelo Iberin

Callas, *tenant farmer*

Nanna, *his daughter, waitress at Madame Cornamontis'
café*

Mistress Callas and her four children

Parr, *tenant farmer*

The Mother Superior of San Barabas

The Abbot of San Stefano

Alfonso Saz ⎤
Juan Duarte ⎬ *landowners*
De Hoz ⎦

Madame Cornamontis, manager and owner of a café

Family lawyer of the De Guzmans

Lord Chief Justice

Police Inspector

Callamassi, *owner of house property*

A fat woman, *owner of grocery shop*

Palmosa, *tobacconist*

A writer, Iberin soldiers, tenant farmers, small townsmen

CZICHS
(Peakheads)

Emanuele de Guzman, *a landowner*

Isabella, *his sister*

Lopez, *a tenant farmer*

Mistress Lopez and her three small children

Ignatio Peruiner, *a landowner*

A second lawyer

A grocer

A tenant farmer

An office worker

The inhabitants of the land of Yahoo, in which the action takes place, consist of Czuchs and Czichs, two races, of which the first have round and the second peak heads.

PROLOGUE

Seven players come before the curtain: The manager of the theater, the viceroy, the rebel farmer, the landlord, his sister, the farmer Callas and his daughter. The latter four are in ordinary clothes. The viceroy, who is in costume but without a mask, is holding a pair of scales with two models of round heads in one pan, and two of peak heads in the other. The rebel farmer holds a pair of scales with two pieces of fine clothing in one pan and two in rags in the other. He, too, is in costume but without a mask.

STAGE MANAGER:

Good people all, we'll now begin our play.
The author is a man who's traveled in his day
(We do not say he always traveled at his will) but still
He'll tell you in this play
What he noticed on his way.
And now to put you wise without undue verbosity
He saw his fill of hatred and ferocity.
He saw the white man wrestling with the black,
A yellow dwarf with a yellow giant on his back;
A Finn took up a stone and flung it at a Swede,
And a snub nose hit a hook nose and made it bleed.
Our playwright inquired as to how
The quarrel arose and was told that now
Through all lands stalks the great skull-classifier,
The great, panmundane pacifier,
His pockets filled with all shapes of noses, all colors
    of skin,
And with them separating friends and kin;
Insisting that it matters quite a lot
What kind of a skull you've got.
And so wherever the great skull-classifier goes

People examine your skin and hair and nose;
And anyone whose physiognomy won't do
Is beaten brown and black and blue.
Everywhere the head problem—
People asked the playwright: Didn't it trouble him;
Were all men the same in his sight?
And he said: There's a difference all right,
Deeper than any line on his face
That decides a man's fate on this earthly bit of space:
The difference which
Divides the poor and the rich.
Without more ado
I write a parable for you
In which I hope to make it clear
The difference we're concerned with here.
And now, good people, we are going to act this
    parable before you,
And for that purpose we have put on the stage a land
    called Yahoo.
Here the great skull-classifier will sort out his pates
And one or two people will be hurried to their fates.
But the playwright will so arrange that you'll be sure
To pick the rich man from the poor.
He will distribute clothes
By purse, not by nose.
Shut the doors now
And let the skull-classifier make his bow.

DEPUTY REGENT (*comes forward to the sound of stage
    thunder and shows his scales*):
I've two kinds of skulls, and a world between
By the wise can be seen.
One is pointed and the other round.
One is spoiled but the other's sound.
When justice blinks and things go wrong
To this one the blame belongs.
In deformity or fatty degeneration

—Here's the explanation!
(*He presses down the pan on which the round heads are lying.*)

STAGE MANAGER (*bringing the* REBEL TENANT *forward*):
  Now clothes-classifier, it's your turn
  The audience waits your tricks to learn.
  Show us the clothes you use for weights
  That balance men in all their states.

REBEL TENANT (*showing his clothes scales*):
  Which is the fine and which the shoddy—
  That can be seen by anybody.
  To fine clothes all doors open wide
  But in rags a man must stand aside.
  Who weighs with my scales
  Will know who wins, who fails.
  (*He presses down the pan on which the fine pieces of clothing are lying.*)

STAGE MANAGER:
  The playwright his two scales before you places.
  On one he weighs apparel, poor and grand,
  And on the other different kinds of faces.
  Then comes the joker and takes *both* scales in-hand.

  (*He has taken first one pair of scales and then the other and has them weighed one against the other. He now gives them back and turns to his players.*)

  Now you whose job it is to act this play
  Choose, here in public, cranium and array,
  According as the author has laid down.
  And if, as I believe, his theory is right
  Best choose your lot by picking out a gown
  And not a cranium. Now for the fight!

REBEL TENANT (*reaching for two round heads*):
  We'll take round heads, daughter.

LANDOWNER:

    With peaks we'll be bedecked.

LANDOWNER'S SISTER:

    True to the will of Bertolt Brecht . . .

TENANT'S DAUGHTER:

    The daughter of a Roundhead is a Roundhead,
    I am a Roundhead of the female sex.

STAGE MANAGER:

    And now for the costumes.

LANDOWNER:

    I am a landlord.

REBEL TENANT:

    A tenant, I—no more.

LANDOWNER'S SISTER:

    I, the landlord's sister.

TENANT'S DAUGHTER:

    I, the whore.

STAGE MANAGER (*to the players*):

    Now I hope everything is clear.

PLAYERS:

    Quite.

I

REGENT S PALACE

Night. The REGENT *of Yahoo and his privy councilor* MISSENA *are in the royal chamber with newspapers and champagne bottles before them. The privy councilor, wielding a large red pencil, is underlining certain unpleasant passages in the newspaper for the* REGENT. *In the antechamber next door a ragged clerk is sitting working by candlelight. Near him a man is standing, his back to the audience.*

REGENT:

    Enough Missena.
    Morning is near and all our counseling
    Has brought us to the same conclusion—
    What we wish is not—
    But what, however we avert our heads,
    Is bound to come: civil commotion
    And the state's collapse.

MISSENA:

    Sh! Don't say it out loud.

REGENT:

    Bankruptcy—stronger hands than mine are needed.

    MISSENA *is silent.*

REGENT (*glancing at papers*):

    Perhaps your figures are a little out.

MISSENA:

    Not to that extent.

REGENT:

    I should read the papers more often.
    I'd know what's happening in the country.

MISSENA:

>Milord, it is abundance that destroys us.
>Our native land Yahoo is one that lives by corn.
>And likewise dies by corn. And now is dying,—
>Dying from surfeit. For our fertile lands
>Have brought forth corn in such abundance,
>We're crushed by the overheavy gift.
>It's forced down prices, down so low,
>They do not cover cartage nor the grinding.
>I tell you, corn has risen against mankind.
>Abundance has brought want. Farmers hold back
>>their rent.
>The pillars of the state are tottering. The landlords
>Waving their contracts clamor that we collect their
>>rents
>While in the south the tenants mass
>And on their flag a sickle flashes—

(*The* REGENT *sighs. A chord has been touched in his own heart, for he is a landowner himself.*)

REGENT:

>Shouldn't we pawn the railways?

MISSENA:

>Already pawned, Milord—twice over.

REGENT:

>And the Customs?

MISSENA:

>They too.

REGENT:

>The Big Five? Perhaps
>They'll help us with a loan.
>More than a third of all the fertile land
>Is in their hands. I'm sure they can. . . .

MISSENA:

>Undoubtedly
>They can, but they demand
>That first we crush the Sickle League.

REGENT:
>   That would be splendid!

MISSENA:
>   The Big Five, Milord,
>   Have lost their patience with us.
>   We've not shown zeal in rent collecting.

REGENT:
>   Have they no faith in me?

MISSENA:
>   Now, between ourselves, you,
>   After all, are our biggest landlord.

>   (*He has made this remark inadvertently.*)

REGENT (*aroused*):
>   Yes, and I can trust myself no longer,
>   I suppose, and must say as landlord
>   To myself as regent: look here, my friend,
>   Not a peso more, do you understand. . . .

MISSENA:
>   There's a way out, but dangerous
>   And bloody. . . .

REGENT:
>   Not that, . . . sh. . . .

MISSENA:
>   No one can hear us. War
>   Could bring us new markets,
>   Purge our surfeits, gain us
>   Mines, and all we lack.

REGENT:
>   No! War's no good.
>   The first tank you send through Yahoo
>   Would make such an almighty stir that. . . .

MISSENA:
>   The enemy in our midst it is
>   That ties our legs when we would hunt abroad.
>   What evil times when well-armed men
>   Must creep about in fear, and generals

Must stay at home by day;
Like murderers, must lie low.
A different tale we'd tell
If the Sickle fell—

REGENT:

The Sickle!

MISSENA:

It must be crushed!

REGENT:

But how?
By whom? I cannot do it. If I knew a man
Who could, right here
I'd give him full authority.

MISSENA:

I told you once about a man who could.

REGENT (*firmly*):

I won't have *him!* Once and for all I say, I *won't* have
him.
(*Pause.*)
Bah—you've got that Sickle on your brain.

MISSENA:

I fear I have displeased you. Perhaps you wish to be
alone?

REGENT:

Yes, leave me. I'll see you tomorrow.

MISSENA (*taking his leave*):

I hope I haven't displeased you.
(*To the audience:*)
If the devil will not prompt his wit
A little trick may encompass it.

(*He stops at the door and hastily sketches something
red on the wall with his red pencil.*)

Hello, what's this?

REGENT:

What's the matter?

MISSENA:
  Nothing.
REGENT:
  Why did you start?
MISSENA:
  I didn't start.
REGENT:
  You did. (*Half rises.*)
MISSENA:
  It's all right, there's nothing here.

  (*The* REGENT *comes up to him.*)

REGENT:
  Step aside, please.
  (*He fetches a lamp from the table.*)
MISSENA:
  Milord, I cannot think how that sign came here.

  (*The* REGENT *starts back as he sees a huge sickle drawn on the wall.*)

REGENT:
  What? Has it come to this? There are hands even here. . . .
  (*Pause.*)
  I must retire now. I have to consider everything. . . .
  (*Suddenly.*)
  I'll delegate my power.
MISSENA:
  You should not. . . .
  (*Pause.*)
  To whom?
REGENT:
  I must then?
  Well? To whom?
MISSENA:
  It must be one who first of all
  Will crush the tenants. While the Sickle stands

There'll be no war. These Sickle men, I tell you,
Are scum who will not pay their rent.
Liberals say the farmers *cannot* pay their rent.
They're on the side of property,
But fear to face stark hunger.
The farmers' rising can be curbed
Only by a man of quite different views,
Whose only thought is of the state's first need.
Unmoved by selfish aims—at least as such
    renowned—
There's only one. . . .

REGENT (*sulkily*):
Name him. Iberin?

MISSENA:
He's of the middle class by birth,
Not landlord nor farmer; not rich, nor poor.
The unending quarrel of the rich and poor
Enrages him, for it rocks the land and shakes
His class that holds itself the core of all.
Both rich and poor alike he does condemn
As money grubbers; for him the state's decline
Is spiritual and reflects corrupted souls.

REGENT:
Ah ha, spiritual I see, and what about . . . ?
(*Makes the gesture of counting money.*)

MISSENA:
It all has the same cause.

REGENT:
And what is that?

MISSENA:
That's Iberin's great discovery.

REGENT:
Columbus' egg, eh?

MISSENA:
As a matter of fact, it is two-legged.

REGENT:
Eh?

MISSENA:

Milord, this Iberin knows the people well.
He knows an abstraction must be given face
And form ere they can recognize it.
Therefore he's given the spiritual ill a shape.

REGENT:

A human shape?

MISSENA:

Yes.

REGENT:

And it isn't us?

MISSENA:

Certainly not.

REGENT (*ironically*):

Show me the creature.

MISSENA:

Iberin has discovered that in Yahoo
There are two peoples living side by side
Of quite a different racial origin.
You tell them by the contour of their skull.
One race has peaked heads, the other round.
Each shape betokens quite a different soul.
The domed skull frames nobility and worth,
The peaked a crafty mind conceals.
The Roundhead race
Is called by Iberin the race of Czuchs.
'Twas they who first inhabited
Our soil, and are of pure descent.
The peak-skulled race
Is foreign to our native land,
A homeless and a hearth-profaning race—
These are the Czichs.
And Iberin's teaching is that all the ills
That plague our land come from the Czichish soul.
This is his great discovery.

REGENT:

Most entertaining, but then—?

MISSENA:

>Instead of the war of rich and poor,
>He'll have the Czuchs and Czichs fighting—

REGENT:

>Ah, ha! not a bad idea!

MISSENA:

>He's for justice—
>If the rich are overgrasping, he calls them Czichs.

REGENT:

>He calls them Czichs, does he? . . .
>What about the rent?

MISSENA:

>He does not talk about such things; or if
>He does, no one can understand—
>All the same, he's on the side of property,
>The "Czuchish joy of ownership's" his favorite phrase.

(*The* REGENT *smiles.* MISSENA *also smiles.*)

REGENT:

>That's good. The overgrasping men are Czichs,
>The graspers, Czuchish.. Who supports the man?

MISSENA:

>He chiefly has the middle class behind him,
>Tradesmen, artisans and clerks,
>The poorer, "better educated" kind,
>The small depositor, in short the ruined burgher type.
>These he has gathered in his Iberin League,
>Which, I may add, is very nicely armed.
>If anyone can crush the Sickle men, it's he.

REGENT:

>However, arms had better not be shown. . . .
>Tin hats and tanks have no admirers now.

MISSENA:

>Iberin can do without an army.

REGENT:

>Very good, I'll make the man dictator.
>I'll try the man. Tell him to come.

MISSENA (*rings*):

>He's here. He's waited seven hours
>In the antechamber.

REGENT:

>Oh, I quite forgot.
>How thoughtful of you. But wait!
>The Big Five!
>Are they for him?

MISSENA:

>One of them brought him here.

REGENT (*signing the commission while putting hat and coat on, and placing his walking stick over his arm*):

>All this I willingly shake off awhile—
>I'll take some traveler's checks
>And a few books which before
>I never had time to read. I'll go away
>To nowhere in particular—out into the street
>To watch the crowds.
>And from some peaceful corner
>I'll see this month pass quietly away.

MISSENA:

>With the Sickle men storming Yahoo
>Unless of course. . . .
>(*He makes a magnificent gesture toward the door.*)
>Mr. Iberin!

(*The waiting man in the antechamber, at a sign from the ragged clerk, has risen. Coming through the door he makes a deep bow.*)

2

A STREET IN YAHOO

GIRLS *are hanging a large white banner with Iberin's head imprinted on it out of the window of Madame Cornamontis' café.* MADAME CORNAMONTIS *is below, directing operations. Beside her are a* POLICE INSPECTOR *and a* CLERK, *both barefoot and in rags. The provision shop is closed with roller blinds. The tobacconist* PALMOSA *is standing in front of his shop reading a newspaper. Through the window of this house is seen a man shaving. It is* CALLAMASSI, *owner of the house. In front of the grocer's shop to the right stand a* FAT WOMAN *and a* SOLDIER *of the Iberin militia with a white band and a large straw hat, armed to the teeth. All watch the hanging out of the banner. The sound of passing troops and the cries of newsboys can be heard indistinctly in the distance.*

MADAME CORNAMONTIS: Put the flag pole further out so that the wind can catch the cloth, and a little further to the side.

ONE OF THE GIRLS: First to the left, and then to the right. But have it as you please.

POLICE INSPECTOR: Madame Cornamontis, what do you as a housewife think of the new turn of affairs?

MADAME CORNAMONTIS: I'm hanging my flag out as you see. I should think that says enough. And you may be quite sure I won't employ any more Czichish girls in my café. (*She sits down in a wicker chair and opens out a newspaper.*)

CALLAMASSI (*still to be seen shaving, through the window*): Today, the eleventh of September, will go

180

down in history. (*Looks at his flag.*) It cost a good sum of money, that flag.

HOUSE LANDLORD MUNGOSI: Do you think there'll be a war? My Gabrielle was twenty the other day.

IBERIN SOLDIER: What are you thinking about? Nobody wants war. Iberin is a friend of peace, just as he is a friend of the people. Early this morning, the last troops of the regular army were evacuated at Iberin's orders. Have you seen a tin hat anywhere? The streets have been put completely in the hands of us Iberin men.

PALMOSA: It says here in the paper that Iberin is the people's best friend. He has seized power, it says, "in order to put a check on the oppression of the poorer sections of the community."

IBERIN SOLDIER: That's the truth.

FAT WOMAN: I say he must first see to it that in such a small street there should not be two grocers' shops when there's barely enough trade for one. That shop over there is not needed on this block.

CLERK: If the new government doesn't make things easier for us office workers, Inspector, I'll not venture home next rent day.

POLICE INSPECTOR: My truncheon has become so rotten that I'm afraid it will break into splinters if I hit a Peakhead with it. And my whistle's rusted. (*He tries the whistle.*) Do you hear anything?

CLERK (*shakes his head*): I had to borrow some chalk out of a whitewasher's tub the other day to whiten my collar. Officer, do you think we'll get our salaries on the first?

POLICE INSPECTOR: I'm so certain of it that I'm going to treat myself to a cigar this morning at Palmosa's.

They both enter the tobacconist's.

CALLAMASSI (*pointing to the* CLERK): One of the best

things that could be done would be to get rid of these penpushers altogether. There are too many of them and their salaries are too high.

MADAME CORNAMONTIS: And what will become of your good tenant if you get rid of her last customers!

IBERIN SOLDIER: What do you think of my new books? We're all being supplied with them! (*Reads aloud to the* HOUSE LANDLORD *and the* FAT WOMAN.) "The manner in which Iberin seized power is itself the best testimony one could have of the man he is. In the middle of the night when everyone in Government House was asleep, he marched in with his fearless followers and demanded at the point of a pistol to see the regent. It is reported that at the sight of such determination, the regent capitulated, allowed himself to be deposed, and was glad to make his escape."

FAT WOMAN: It is really most remarkable that while every other house on this street has hung out a flag there is one house whose inmates do not consider it worth-while to do so. (*She points to the grocer's shop opposite.*)

IBERIN SOLDIER: That's right—they haven't put out a flag. (*He looks at each in turn and they all shake their heads.*) We can help him, though, can't we?

FAT WOMAN: He doesn't need a flag. The man's a Czich.

IBERIN SOLDIER: Then it's the height of impudence. I tell you, Madame Tomaso, we'll show the damned swine how one celebrates Iberin's inauguration. Ah, there's some of our boys, the dreaded, hat-tipping Huas of the bloody Zazarante, camp commander of the Holy Cross. Don't be alarmed. They just peep under hats; and if they don't find a peak head they apologize and act like perfect gentlemen.

Shouts are heard, "Hats off! Head checking!" Three HUAS, *or hat-tippers, appear at the end of the street. They knock a passer-by's hat off.*

FIRST HUA: Your hat has fallen off, Sir.

SECOND HUA: Rather a strong wind today.

PASSER-BY: Excuse me.

THREE HUAS: Don't mention it.

FAT WOMAN: If you want to see a real peak head, Sirs, you've only got to knock at the door of that grocer's shop opposite.

IBERIN SOLDIER (*announces*): Czichish grocer. Shows his disapproval of the Iberin government by refusing to hang out the flag.

A Peakhead appears in front of the shop door, looking very pale, with a ladder and a flag. Everyone looks at him.

FIRST HUA: I can hardly believe my eyes. He's hanging up a flag!

SECOND HUA: How disgusting, the Iberin banner in the greasy paws of a Czich.

The HUA looks at each in turn. They all shake their heads.

IBERIN SOLDIER: That is the height of impudence.

The three HUAS go up to the Peakhead.

THIRD HUA: Dirty swine of a Czich. Put your hat on. Do you think anybody wants to look at your filthy peak head?

FAT WOMAN: The Czich thinks that Iberin is for the Czichs, I suppose! His hanging out a flag is an insult to the government—a deliberate insult, making out that the government is for the Czichs!

The Peakhead goes in to fetch his hat.

FIRST HUA: He's trying to escape.

They drag him back and start beating him.

FIRST HUA: Thinks he can resist, so that's the game, is it!
   I strike at his eyes and he lifts his hand!

SECOND HUA (*still hitting out at the Peakhead*): We'll put
   him in protective custody, rush him to the concentra-
   tion camp where we put all people who must be pro-
   tected against our righteous indignation.

FAT WOMAN: Hail Iberin!

The third HUA *hangs up a poster on the provision
shop with the words:* "Czichish Shop."

THIRD HUA (*to the* FAT WOMAN *while he pulls a poster out
   of his pocket*): Dear madame and fellow race-mem-
   ber, it is just as well nowadays for people that the
   right kind of blood should have it down in black and
   white. This poster costs thirty pesos, but you'll find
   it will pay for itself over and over again!

FAT WOMAN: Couldn't you let me have it for ten? Trade's
   pretty bad, you know.

IBERIN SOLDIER (*meaningfully*): There's some people who
   have a secret sympathy for the Peakheads.

FAT WOMAN: Very good, I'll take one. (*She takes out the
   money in some agitation.*) Have you change for fifty
   pesos? (*Hangs up the poster which bears the words:*
   "Czuchish Shop.")

THIRD HUA: Twenty pesos change. Nothing like honesty
   in trifles. (*He goes away, however, without giving
   change.*)

FAT WOMAN: He hasn't given me my change!

The IBERIN SOLDIER *looks at her threateningly.*

Anyway that Czich over there will have to be got rid
of. A fortnight ago he said that Iberin wouldn't make
bananas grow on a thornbush.

MADAME CORNAMONTIS: A typically Czichish remark. A
   nation is awakening and he talks about bananas.

IBERIN SOLDIER: The Czich is always guided by the most
   abject materialism. For his own selfish advantage he

denies his fatherland which isn't *his* fatherland anyway. The Czich never knows who is his father and
mother. That's probably because he hasn't got any
sense of humor. You've just had an opportunity of
seeing it for yourselves. They live promiscuously and
the only curb on their sensuality is their miserliness.

PALMOSA (*calls up to the man who can be seen shaving on
the first floor*): No more materialism now, Mr. Callamassi. I hope you realize you needn't come for the
rent any longer. Shopkeepers won't be required to
pay rent.

IBERIN SOLDIER: Quite right!

CALLAMASSI: On the contrary, my good fellow. In the
future it will be possible to mortgage shop rents.
Listen to the battalions on the march. Those are the
fighters of the Iberin League. They are marching off
to put down the rebel farmers who refuse to pay their
rents. Put that in one of your pipes, Mr. Tobacconist,
and smoke it!

IBERIN SOLDIER: Quite true.

PALMOSA: You seem to have forgotten, Mr. Callamassi,
that my son is marching with those troops. (*To the*
FAT WOMAN:) I said to him this morning as they
marched off for the south: "My son, bring back a
Sickle flag and I'll let you start smoking." They say
the bankers are helping the small tradesmen who are
in debt, they're giving new credits.

IBERIN SOLDIER: Hail Iberin!

FAT WOMAN (*to her landlady,* MADAME CORNAMONTIS):
Have you heard? Rents are going to be lowered.

IBERIN SOLDIER: Yes, that's right.

MADAME CORNAMONTIS: No, I've heard that they are going
to be raised; they certainly ought to be.

IBERIN SOLDIER: Quite true.

FAT WOMAN: It can't be. Perhaps the Czichs' rents will be
raised. Anyway I won't pay any more.

MADAME CORNAMONTIS: We'll see about that, we'll see

about that. Don't be surprised if I have to ask for a
little more next month. (*To the* IBERIN SOLDIER:)
These simpletons have the haziest idea of politics.

FAT WOMAN: What? Higher rents?

IBERIN SOLDIER (*interrupting*): The question of the day
now is the Czichish purge. (*Reads from the paper*:)
"Iberin says expressly that our sole aim at present
is to exterminate the Peakheads, wherever they have
their nests!"

There is a sound of marching, singing is heard.

Listen, that's the Iberin Anthem.

HYMN OF YAHOO'S AWAKENING

Our great Iberin lowers rent
Yet keeps the landlords opulent.
Our great Iberin helps the farm
Yet keeps the millers from alarm.
The small shopkeeper's Iberin's care—
But the big store magnate keeps his share.
Praised be our Iberin, working for each man's salva-
        tion
Trusting we wait
For the glorious fate
Which he has decreed for our nation.

MADAME CORNAMONTIS (*to the* IBERIN SOLDIER): Let's
see them, those brave lads of ours off to finish those
clodhopping Sicklemen. (*Exit with* IBERIN SOLDIER.)

FAT WOMAN AND PALMOSA (*together*): I can't leave my
shop, here comes a customer. (*They go back into
their shops.*)

NANNA (*comes out of Madame Cornamontis' café with a
letter in her hand*): Mr. De Guzman has just passed
down the street. He is taking his walk before lunch
and will be back in a few minutes. I must speak to
him. My mother writes that my father is in bad com-

pany. Not being able to pay the rent for his farm,
he hás joined the Sickle League. I will try and get
Mr. De Guzman to let him off paying his rent. I think
he still cares for me enough to do that for me, although it's nearly three years now since we were at
all intimate. He was my first lover and it was through
him that I, a simple farmer's daughter, came into
service in such a respectable house as Madame Cornamontis'. He's done a lot for our family; I really don't
like asking him to do any more; but I must. Here he
is. But there are three men with him. Mr. Peruiner is
one of them. I won't have a chance to talk to him.
(*She beckons to* DE GUZMAN *who comes up to her.
His three friends stop and wait for him.*)

DE GUZMAN: Hello, Nanna.

NANNA: There's something I want to talk to you about.
Please step in here a moment. (*They go into the doorway.*) My father writes that he cannot pay his rent
again.

DE GUZMAN: I'm sorry, but he'll have to pay this time.
My sister is entering the San Barabas Convent and
has to have her novice money.

NANNA: But you wouldn't like my parents to starve on
account of it.

DE GUZMAN: My dear Nanna, my sister is about to devote
herself to a life of renunciation among the Needy
Sisters of San Barabas. You should respect her intentions because, even if it is not given to all girls
to live chastely, they should at all events think highly
of those who do.

NANNA: If you offered her a lover perhaps she might
change her mind—

DE GUZMAN: Nanna! You've changed for the worse, Nanna!
I hardly recognize you!

NANNA: I suppose it's no good my telling you that the
reason why my people can't pay their rent is that
they simply must have a horse.

DE GUZMAN: They can hire one.

NANNA: But that costs more money in the end.

DE GUZMAN: Well, that's the way things are in this world.
My horse also costs money.

NANNA: You don't love me any more, Emanuele!

DE GUZMAN: What have horses got to do with our love?
I'll pay you a visit this afternoon and you'll see that
my feelings toward you haven't changed. Now I must
go.

NANNA: Wait here a second. The Huas are coming. They
might attack you for being a Czich.

FIRST HUA: Wherever one goes, one finds Czichs, but now
this street seems to be clear of them.

SECOND HUA: Don't be downhearted.

NANNA: It seems to me, Emanuele, that you have always
used me as a handkerchief. I think you might at least
pay me for the liberties I have allowed you.

FIRST HUA: I hear voices.

NANNA (*loudly*): Excuse me, Sirs, but don't you think a
poor girl has a right to expect the man who has led
her astray to give her some consideration.

DE GUZMAN: I'm surprised at you, Nanna!

The three HUAS *approach.*

FIRST HUA: There's a fine looking gentleman, let's look and
see what kind of a knob he has.

SECOND HUA: I admire your hat, Sir, I should like to have
a hat like that myself. May I have a look inside and
see the name of the maker. (*He knocks the hat off
De Guzman's head. The latter's peakhead stands re-
vealed. The three* HUAS *set up a regular howl.*)

THREE HUAS: A Czich!

SAZ: We must interfere. Our friend De Guzman is in a tight
corner.

PERUINER (*holds the speaker back*): Don't attract attention. I am a Czich myself.

The three rich landowners hurry away.

THIRD HUA: I thought I caught a whiff of another Czich.

SECOND HUA: Well, we've got this one. He must come before the court.

Two HUAS *drag* DE GUZMAN *off and the third remains with* NANNA.

THIRD HUA: I think, Miss, you mentioned something about his having owed you money.

NANNA (*sulkily*): Yes, and he won't pay.

THIRD HUA: They're all like that, the dirty Czichs.

Exit the third HUA. NANNA *slowly enters Madame Cornamontis' café. Landlard* CALLAMASSI *has been brought to his window and the* FAT WOMAN *to the door of her shop by the commotion in the street. The tobacconist can also be seen in his doorway.*

CALLAMASSI: What's the noise about?

FAT WOMAN: They caught an apparently very well-to-do Czichish gentleman molesting one of Madame Cornamontis' waitresses.

PALMOSA: Is that not permitted now?

FAT WOMAN: They said it was a Czuchish girl. The gentleman, it seems, was one of the Big Five.

CALLAMASSI: You don't say so!

PALMOSA (*going back into his shop*): One of the Big Five has been attacked and carried off.

POLICE INSPECTOR (*taking his leave of the clerk*): That has nothing to do with the police.

FAT WOMAN: The rich are getting it in the neck now.

CALLAMASSI: Do you think so?

PALMOSA: It's going to be no joke for the landowners.

CALLAMASSI: But there's a campaign against the farmers who won't pay their rent.

PALMOSA: It said in the papers this morning that a new era has begun.

INTERLUDE

The street of old Yahoo is painted on a huge board. The Iberin soldiers run on the stage with tubs of whitewash and with long and short-handled brushes they start painting over the cracks and gaps in the walls of the houses.

THE WHITEWASHING SONG

Wherever walls are sagging, timbers rotting,
Something must be done to put things right.
Something to prevent the public spotting
How everything is crumbling in their sight.
Give us whitewash
Before the pigsty falls and it's too late.
Give us whitewash
To keep things covered till a later date.
Here's a new crack that mustn't show
It wasn't there a week ago.
Here's a new split's started
The bricks have parted,
That's why we need whitewash
Before the pigsty falls and it's too late,
To keep things covered till a later date.

3

AT A VILLAGE WELL

The Roundhead tenant CALLAS, *his wife and children, and the Peakhead tenant* LOPEZ, *his wife and children, have come to draw water.*

CALLAS AND LOPEZ: We have to fetch and draw till we're dead beat. The landlord won't give us horses so each of us has to be his own horse.

MISTRESS LOPEZ: The people from our village are joining the Sickle now.

The sound of many dogs is heard. A Roundhead tenant appears with a gun under each arm.

THIRD TENANT: In the terrible straits in which we all find ourselves, now that the price of corn has fallen so low, we farmers of Yahoo, every man who wears clogs, have joined together, and have resolved to take arms and fight under the banner of the Sickle against the landlords. Here Callas and Lopez, here are guns for you.

LOPEZ: You wanted to wait, Callas. You said you might get good news from your daughter.

CALLAS: Aah!—there is never any good news. I'm with you, boys.

LOPEZ: Give me your hand, Callas, give me your hand too! Today is the eleventh of September, a day that you must mark well, because it is the day the tenants shake the landlords off their backs.

They all join hands and sing the "Song of the Sickle."

SONG OF THE SICKLE

Men of the land
The hour is at hand.
Count not the hazard's cost
Life can but once be lost.
None will improve your lot
If you yourselves do not.
Men of the land
The hour is at hand.

ALL: The Sickle forever!

At this moment the bells begin to ring.

MISTRESS LOPEZ: Listen, what are those bells?

MISTRESS CALLAS (*calls back*): What's the matter, Paolo?

VOICES FROM BEHIND: Good news! good news! A new
government, friendly to the people, has come into
power!

MISTRESS CALLAS: I'll go and see if I can get more details. (*She leaves the others.*)

*A speech is heard over the wireless, "Proclamation
by the new Regent to the people on the land."*

IBERIN'S VOICE:

Oh, Czuchish folk! For many years your land Yahoo
Its rich, its poor have suffered,
Tormented by a base spirit,
The spirit of foul greed and discord:
O Czuchish folk! Why live you in such misery?
Oppressed and robbed? Who is it robs you?
Who grinds you down? Crawling in your midst
There is an inner foe, till now unknown,
The Czich! He is your curse,
Him you must extirpate.
But how can he be known? Oh, Czuchish folk,
His head betrays his soul, his head is peaked!

By that sign know the Peakhead Czichs.
I, Iberin, have resolved
To make a new division of the people
Putting the Roundheads and the Peakheads
In different camps, saying to all the Czuchs
Behold your mortal enemies the Czichs!
From this day on all greed, all discord ends
Between all brother Czuchs.
Rally, Czuchs, around the snow-white banner
Of Iberin, against the Czichish foe!

During this proclamation all present have more or less surreptitiously felt the top of their heads. The Roundhead children point jeeringly at the Peakhead children.

LOPEZ: That's only words after all. They're forever finding something new. What I want to know is what they're going to do against the landowners.

CALLAS: You're quite right.

MISTRESS CALLAS *has returned. She does not look at* MISTRESS LOPEZ *and gathers her children around her.*

LOPEZ: What's the news, Mistress Callas?

MISTRESS CALLAS: Our landlord, Mr. De Guzman, has been arrested!

LOPEZ: What for?

CALLAS: I don't think there's any need to ask, Lopez. It's pretty obvious he's been arrested for rack-renting.

LOPEZ: Then we're saved!

CALLAS: That's good news, Lopez. Our misery is at an end, children! (*He puts down his gun against the wall.*)

MISTRESS LOPEZ: This is a great day.

MISTRESS CALLAS: Not so fast, Mistress Lopez. Unfortunately the news isn't so good for you. Iberin has come into power and you are Czichs. In Yahoo a great anti-Czich campaign has already started. Mr.

De Guzman himself has been arrested only because he is a Czich.

LOPEZ: That's bad news, and a great misfortune.

CALLAS: I don't see that it's a misfortune, at all events not for everyone: it's not a misfortune for us for instance.

MISTRESS CALLAS: It is only a misfortune for you.

CALLAS: For us Czuchs, the news is very good.

MISTRESS CALLAS: At this moment we experience feelings which you, Mister Lopez, are unable to understand. You are probably a different kind of human being, I will not say an inferior kind.

LOPEZ: Until now my head was not too peaked for you, Callas.

CALLAS *does not answer. The two families have separated, on the one side stand the Peakheads, and on the other the Roundheads.*

Our burdens were the same. Five minutes ago, you were offering to fight with us under the Sickle to throw off the yoke of the landowners. That can only be done by force. Take the gun, woman.

MISTRESS LOPEZ *hesitatingly takes the gun into her hand.*

CALLAS: The odds are too great. If there were any chance of success, it would be the best way, but there is no chance.

LOPEZ: Why do you think now that the odds are too great?

CALLAS: Well, to tell you the truth, I am not so sure that it is the only course for me.

MISTRESS CALLAS: We naturally take it that we won't have to pay rent any more.

LOPEZ: I can understand what the slightest hope means to you. But you'll see: nothing will come of it. I have yet to hear of anyone being given anything by these people for having a head of certain shape.

CALLAS: Enough, Lopez, I have no cause for doubting the new government. It has been in office for only five hours and already my landlord has been arrested.

MISTRESS CALLAS: They say in the village that the Sickle League is now forbidden.

Five TENANTS, *including tenant* PARR, *come in in a state of great excitement. They are all Roundheads. One of them is carrying a flag with the Sickle device and all are armed with guns.*

PARR: What are you people doing? We were all to join together under the Sickle tonight, but since this new proclamation and the landlord's arrest perhaps we should wait and see?

CALLAS: I'll go into town and go straight to Iberin. If he gets horses for me and exempts me from rent, there's no reason why I should fight any more. De Guzman is a Czich and will have to keep his mouth shut.

FIRST TENANT: Yes, your landlord is a Czich but ours is a Czuch.

PARR: Still, our landlord may let us off our rent when the Czichs have been got rid of. He owes money to a Czichish bank which he probably won't have to pay now.

LOPEZ: They may let *him* off but he'll still want his rent.

THIRD TENANT: The people who support Iberin are the landlords.

PARR: They say it's not true. I've heard that Iberin lives very modestly. He doesn't drink or smoke. He's the son of a small farmer. He wants nothing for himself. He acts because parliament does nothing, and that's true.

FIRST TENANT: Yes, that's true.

Silence.

THIRD TENANT: So the tenants must keep quiet now?

PARR: The Czuchish tenants may rise up against the Czichish landlords.

LOPEZ: And what about the Czichish tenants? Should they rise up against the Czuchish landlords?

PARR: There are very few Czichish tenants. Czichs keep away from hard work.

FIFTH TENANT: Most of us are Czuchs.

PARR: The rain is coming through our roofs.

CALLAS: Our Czich landlord's been stuck in jail.

FIFTH TENANT: But the rain comes through my roof, too, and my landlord is a Czuch.

THIRD TENANT: What I want to know is whether Iberin will put all the landlords in jail, every one of them.

PARR: He'll put the Czich landlords in jail and force the Czuch landlords to ease off a little.

THIRD TENANT: That's no use. Czuch or Czich, a landlord is a landlord. Let Iberin send them all to the devil. I'm a Sickle man. I trust no one but myself. Do you want to free yourselves from the landlords—follow me under the banner of the Sickle. Iberin is a fraud. (*To the audience:*)

Landlord and tenant are to make their peace—
Those whose heads slope to the same degree.
I pay the rent, the landlord's funds increase,
But I'm to be content with unity.

CALLAS: You go if you want, I'll try my luck with Iberin.

OTHER TENANTS: Come with us, Lopez! Round head, pointed head means nothing to us. Rich man or poor man, that's the test for us. (*They reach out their hands to him, but he stays behind.*)

MISTRESS LOPEZ: I think we had better go home.

MISTRESS CALLAS: I don't think you'll be able to. As I passed the village pond, I heard people talking against you—then when I passed your house, I saw it afire.

MISTRESS LOPEZ: Oh! God!

LOPEZ: Callas, let my family hide in your house till this blows over.

Silence.

CALLAS: I'm sorry. I don't see how I can.

LOPEZ: Couldn't you just take my children for a few days?

CALLAS: I'd like to, but since you're in the Sickle League, it's dangerous for my own family for any of your family to be seen in my house.

LOPEZ: Well, we'll be going then, Callas.

CALLAS *is silent.*

TWO WOMEN:
Till now united by our common woes
Our different heads now make us foes.

The LOPEZ *family leaves.*

MISTRESS CALLAS: And now you, my man, must go as fast as you can to Yahoo. Refuse to pay your rent and get them to write out a deed that you don't have to pay it any more.

CALLAS: Right. I won't budge from there until I have it down in black and white.

4

IN THE REGENT'S PALACE

A trial is in progress in the courtyard. The parties in the case are the MOTHER SUPERIOR of San Barabas and the ABBOT of San Stefano. Illuminated bulletin: "The Sickle-men Are Marching On The Capital."

CHIEF JUSTICE: The Barefoot Beggar Monks of San Stefano versus the Needy Sisters of San Barabas. The Barefoot Beggar Monks claim damages to the sum of seven millions. Brother Abbot, state your case.

ABBOT: The San Barabas foundation has built a new church with the deliberate intention of drawing believers from our diocese, causing us damage which, by modest estimate, amounts to seven millions.

MOTHER SUPERIOR: We beg to inform the court that a glance into the books of the new welfare chapel of San Sebastian will show that the revenues in question do not amount to seven millions as the holy brothers declare, but scarcely four millions.

ABBOT: Yes, in the books! I beg to point out, however, that the Needy Sisters of San Barabas have already been before this high court for evading tax payments amounting to one and a half million. On that occasion the Needy Sisters also appealed to their "books."

The ABBOT and the MOTHER SUPERIOR shake their fists at each other. The CLERK of the court jumps up.

CHIEF JUSTICE: What's the matter? When such sums of money are before the court, everyone must act in a dignified manner.

CLERK: Your worships, there's a crowd at the gates. They have the landlord De Guzman. They want him arrested for raping a Czuchish girl.

CHIEF JUSTICE: Impossible: De Guzman is one of the Big Five. He was the victim of a false arrest and was released three days ago.

The crowd presses in. DE GUZMAN *is pushed in front of the judge.* MADAME CORNAMONTIS *and* NANNA *are swept in with the crowd. While the judge excitedly thumps the table, the crowd taunts and spits upon* DE GUZMAN.

VOICES: The price of his suit alone would support a family of six for a whole month. Look at his white hands. You can see he's never used a spade. Well, to suit his tastes, we'll hang him with a silken rope.

The HUAS *toss coins for the landowner's rings.*

A MAN: Your worship, the people of Yahoo demand that this man be punished.

CHIEF JUSTICE: Dear people, the case will be tried, but at the moment, we have a matter on hand of great urgency.

The MOTHER SUPERIOR *has approached the* ABBOT *in great agitation.*

ABBOT: We do not consider it convenient to settle our little difference before the general public. We agree to an adjournment.

CRIES FROM THE CROWD: No more putting off. The whole show should be burned to the ground. The judge himself deserves hanging.

A MAN: Let the court know that a new age has dawned in the land of Yahoo.

Illuminated bulletin: "The Deputy Regent In A Speech To Schoolteachers Describes The Struggle In The South As A Struggle Between Right And Wrong."

THE CROWD: Let's sit down and stay here until justice is
done and the landlord has been hanged. (*They sit
down on the floor, smoke, take out their newspapers,
spit and chat.*)

INSPECTOR (*comes up and speaks to the* CHIEF JUSTICE):
The Public Prosecutor asks me to say that you must
yield to the crowd and hold the trial. The court is
no longer bound to keep to the letter of the law,
but must be guided by the people's natural instinct
for justice. The fighting in the south is going very
badly for the government and the city population is
getting more and more restive.

CHIEF JUSTICE (*to the audience*): The strain is too much
for me. I have become physically weakened. For two
months now I have not been paid any salary. I must
think of my family. This morning I had nothing but a
cup of weak tea and a stale roll for breakfast. One cannot administer justice on an empty stomach. A man
who has not had a proper breakfast can't conduct a
case properly. He has no spirit. His justice has no
luster.

De Guzman's LAWYERS *come into the antechamber
with flying gowns followed by a few landowners.*

CZUCHISH LAWYER (*in the antechamber to the* SECOND
LAWYER): You stay in the antechamber. You as a
Czich had better not show yourself here.

CZICHISH LAWYER: Mind you have him put in prison for
eight days. I wish I was safe there myself.

The CZUCHISH LAWYER *and landowners enter the
courtyard.*

VOICES: Start the trial. It'll soon get too dark to hang him.

CHIEF JUSTICE: We must at least wait until you are all
properly seated. We can't preside in court like this.
(*To* MADAME CORNAMONTIS:) Who are you?

MADAME CORNAMONTIS: Madame Cornamontis, owner of the El Paradiso Café, Estrada 5.

CHIEF JUSTICE: What do you want here?

MADAME CORNAMONTIS: Nothing.

CHIEF JUSTICE: What are you here for then?

MADAME CORNAMONTIS: About half an hour ago a crowd appeared at the door of my establishment and demanded that one of my waitresses—here she is—should go with them to the court. As I refused to let her go alone, I was compelled to come here too. I've been brought into this affair the way Pontius Pilate was brought into the creed.

CHIEF JUSTICE (*to* NANNA): And you are the girl? Please take the stand.

Catcalls from the crowd.

CRIES: It's other people that should be here.

Illuminated bulletin: "The Government Troops Offer Stubborn Resistance To The Advance Of The Sicklemen."

CHIEF JUSTICE: I'm the one to decide who shall stand in the dock. (*To* NANNA:) You accosted the gentleman in the open street. You are aware that the penalty for that is three weeks' hard labor. (NANNA *says nothing but nods to* DE GUZMAN.) Please come forward, Mr. De Guzman. Was that so?

DE GUZMAN: Yes, your honor. I was accosted by her as I was taking my morning constitutional. She is the daughter of one of my tenants and asked me to exempt her father from paying his rent. (*Quietly.*) I ask you to put me under arrest, I am a Czich.

LAWYER: I am Mr. De Guzman's lawyer.

CHIEF JUSTICE: Have you brought witnesses?

LAWYER: Here are three gentlemen, Saz, Duarte and De Hoz.

CRIES: Landlords witnessing against poor people! (*Cat-calls.*)

CHIEF JUSTICE: Order! (*To the witnesses*:) What have you to say? I call attention to the fact that you can be prosecuted for perjury.

CRIES: That's more like it.

SAZ: Mr. De Guzman was accosted by this girl in the street.

LAWYER: I think my client's social position is enough to warrant the truth of his evidence considering that the opposing party is a mere café waitress.

VOICE FROM ABOVE: Oho, it may very well be the other way round. Just take off your cap, my young fellow, and let's see what kind of a head you've got.

SECOND VOICE FROM ABOVE: Take your cap off!

LAWYER (*taking off his cap*): My head is quite as round as yours, my good man.

VOICE FROM ABOVE: Ask your client why he makes her father pay such a high rent that she has to sell herself?

SECOND VOICE FROM ABOVE: One must always begin at the beginning.

CHIEF JUSTICE (*to* NANNA): Will you please go into the dock so that we can begin.

VOICES FROM ABOVE: Do nothing of the sort. You're here to get justice, not to be accused!

LAWYER: A transaction of this sort can't be done in the street. There are some very fine points here that need settling. Clever heads are wanted here.

VOICES FROM ABOVE: Yes, pointed heads, I suppose.

SECOND VOICE FROM ABOVE: We must have Iberin here.

VOICES: We demand that the following persons should be brought to the dock: the rack-renter, the pimp, and the law-twister!

VOICE FROM ABOVE: We want Iberin here.

VOICES: Iberin! Iberin! Iberin!

IBERIN *has a short while previously come in unob-*

*served and has sat down at the side, behind the
judge's bench.*

OTHER VOICES: There he is, Iberin!

SOME OF THE CROWD: Hail Iberin!

CHIEF JUSTICE (*to* IBERIN): Your Excellency, I allow
myself to be guided by the statement of some of the
most prominent landowners in the country.

IBERIN: Far better allow yourself to be guided by the war
news on the bulletin. (*Laughter.*)

*Illuminated bulletin: "The Inadequate Equipment Of
The Army Loyal To The Government And Lack Of
Munitions And Supplies Hamper The Troops In Spite
Of Their Magnificent Fighting Spirit."*

There is a commotion. Tenant CALLAS *enters the
courtyard amidst a crowd of people.*

VOICES: And here is the girl's father.

NANNA: My father! I must hide; I mustn't let him see me.
I've made a big mistake this time for which they'll
suffer at home.

CHIEF JUSTICE (*to* CALLAS): What do you want here?

VOICE FROM ABOVE: He wants justice!

CALLAS' COMPANIONS: We met this man in the street. He
asked us when and where the De Guzman case was
being tried. We told him that the case was now being
tried and that he had only to follow the crowd since
everyone is on his way here.

CALLAS: That's right. I'm here as a witness in the action
brought against my landlord for rack-renting.

CHIEF JUSTICE: The question of rack-renting is not before
this court.

CALLAS: I can prove that the rent was extortionate. The
land is marshy: the fields are too far apart. The tools
are almost useless. We've had to use the cow for

carting. We've had to work all summer from three
o'clock in the morning with the children helping. We
don't control the prices of corn; they've been different
each year, though the rent is always the same. The
rent should be written off for good, and the price of
corn should be fixed at a price that will enable us
to live by our labor.

VOICE FROM ABOVE: Quite right. (*Clapping.*)

THE MAN (*rises up and speaks to the crowd*): The father
of the molested girl, who is the tenant of the accused,
demands that farm rent should be abolished and that
there should be a fair price for corn. (*Applause from
the crowd is heard backstage.*)

CHIEF JUSTICE (*to* IBERIN): Your Excellency, how do
you want this case to be dealt with?

IBERIN: Do as you consider right.

*Illuminated bulletin: "All Sections Of The South
Report Forcible Seizure Of Land By The Tenants."*

CHIEF JUSTICE: According to the statutes, the girl is the
only person who has infringed the law. Outside the
bar where she works she has no right to address
any gentleman.

IBERIN: Have you nothing more to say? That's very little.

VOICE FROM ABOVE: Bravo. Do you hear how Iberin talks
to the Chief Justice? He says, "That's very little."

THE MAN (*facing the street at the back of the stage*):
Iberin has reprimanded the Chief Justice. He has
described the judge as lacking in knowledge.

IBERIN: Examine the girl's father. That the way to get
to the heart of the problem.

CHIEF JUSTICE: You say that your landlord has exceeded
his legal rights in assessing rent?

CALLAS: We could never earn the rent. We lived on crab-
apples and roots because we had to send all our corn
to the market. Our children run around nearly naked.
We have no money for repairs so that our house is

falling to pieces over our heads. The taxes are too high. I move that all taxes should also be written off the books for those unable to pay them. (*General applause.*)

THE MAN (*to the crowd as before*): The tenant moves that all taxes should be written off for those who are unable to pay them! (*Tremendous applause.*)

CHIEF JUSTICE: What is the rent? What do the taxes amount to?

IBERIN (*rises up so suddenly that his chair falls*): Can you think of nothing more important to ask? Doesn't an inner voice tell you what the people really want?

CALLAS: Horses! Horses, for example!

IBERIN (*sternly*): Silence! What are horses? Something more's at stake! (*To the* CHIEF JUSTICE:) You may go. Leave the post you are no longer fit to fill. I shall conclude the proceedings myself.

CHIEF JUSTICE *gathers his papers together and leaves the court.*

THE MAN (*as before*): The Deputy has relieved the Chief Justice of his office and is conducting the proceedings himself. Hail Iberin!

CALLAS: Did you hear what he said? What are horses? More is at stake!

THE MAN (*as before*): Now that the greatest rack-renter of all, the regent, has been got rid of, why shouldn't all the land be distributed to the tenants? (*Applause.*)

Illuminated bulletin: "In The Northern Districts Encounters With Rebel Tenants Are Reported."

IBERIN: As the court has been unable to pierce to the heart of the matter, I take the case into my own hands, in the name of the Czuchish people. This case shall serve us as an example of Czuchish justice.

A certain spirit must here be combated. Just as the troops will halt the rebellious tenants, the court will force the unbridled landlords to keep within the limits laid down by Czuchish law. Whether it be a rich man or a poor man, we judge by the crime alone. The same crime brings the same penalty. Landlord De Guzman and you (*pointing to* MADAME COR-NAMONTIS) enter the dock. This girl and her father will take their place on the plaintiff's bench.

THE MAN (*as before*): Iberin will give an example of Czuchish justice. He has already established order in the court. He shows the plaintiffs and defendants their places.

IBERIN (*to* CALLAS): Come forward. Look well at your daughter.

CALLAS: You are here, are you, Nanna?

IBERIN: Do you recognize her?

CALLAS: Of course I do.

IBERIN: I ask, because she must have changed a great deal.

CALLAS: No, she hasn't changed much.

IBERIN: Are those the clothes that you bought her?

CALLAS: No, of course not.

IBERIN: Am I not right in saying that those are not the clothes that a simple peasant, who has wielded the spade with blistered hands, buys for his daughter?

CALLAS: Of course I couldn't buy her clothes like that— what with the rent. . . .

IBERIN: And you would not, even if you could? Such finery would be alien to your simple, honest taste. Now how comes it that your daughter is able to buy such clothes?

CALLAS: She earns quite a lot.

IBERIN (*more sternly*): A terrible answer! I ask you once again, do you recognize in this fashionably dressed girl the happy little child who used to walk across the fields holding your hand? (CALLAS *gapes in aston-ishment, entirely at sea.*) Did you suspect that your

daughter had entered into illicit relations with your
landlord at a tender age?

CALLAS: Yes, I did, but all we got out of it was permission
to use the horses once or twice to cart wood. But
when (*he turns to the crowd*) you have to pay a rent
which is ten times too high, it's no help to have a
few privileges now and then—especially when you
can't count on them. What I want is horses of my own.

IBERIN: So the landlord, taking advantage of his economic
position, brought misfortune on your daughter.

CALLAS: Misfortune! The girl has decent clothes. She's
never had to work hard, but we. . . . I ask you, can
one plough properly without horses?

IBERIN: Are you aware that things have now gone so far
that your daughter lives in Madame Cornamontis'
establishment?

CALLAS: Yes. Good day to you, Madame Cornamontis.

IBERIN: Are you aware of the kind of establishment it is?

CALLAS: Yes, and I forgot to mention that later we were
charged for the use of the landlord's horses.

IBERIN (*to* NANNA): How did you come into that house?

NANNA: I was tired of working on the land. At twenty
a farm woman looks like a woman of forty.

IBERIN: The comfortable life which you came to know
through your seducer alienated you from the simple
life in your parents' home. Was the landlord your
first lover?

NANNA: Yes.

IBERIN: Describe the life in the café into which you came.

NANNA: I can't complain. Only the washing money is high,
and they take the tips from us. We're all in debt to
the landlady and have to work late into the night.

IBERIN: You say that you make no complaints about the
work. We must all work. But there was something
else about which you should complain.

NANNA: Yes, in bar rooms the staff are allowed to choose
their customers.

IBERIN: Aha! In this house you were forced to permit the embraces of one and all?

NANNA: Yes.

IBERIN: Enough. (*To* CALLAS:) What action do you bring against the accused as father of this girl?

CALLAS: Rack-renting.

IBERIN: You have cause to complain of more than that.

CALLAS: That seems to me to be enough.

IBERIN: You have suffered a far worse misfortune than extortion of rent. Don't you see that?

CALLAS: Yes.

IBERIN: What wrong has been done you?

CALLAS *is silent.* IBERIN *to* DE GUZMAN:

Do you admit that you abused your economic power when you seduced your tenant's daughter?

DE GUZMAN: She gave me the impression that she was not displeased at my taking notice of her.

IBERIN (*to* NANNA): What do you say to that? (NANNA *does not answer.* DE GUZMAN *is escorted from the courtroom.* IBERIN *to* NANNA:)

Will you state now whether you were pleased at De Guzman taking notice of you or not.

NANNA (*reluctantly*): I can't remember.

IBERIN: Hateful answer.

LAWYER (*to* NANNA, *then to* IBERIN):

Perhaps you were in love with him?
Sir, impenetrable are the ways of men.
We often do not know ourselves the grounds
On which we act, though plain to others.
Even the sharpest insight fails at times
To trace the tangled thread of human love.
Here stands a man accused, accused of what?
Of luring to his bed a gentle maid,
And paying her, thus purchasing
The unpurchasable. Milord, whoever
Speaks such words doth slander both,

For if he bought, the maiden sold.
Milord, I ask you is the language of the mart
Proper to describe the mystery,
The sweet and immemorial play
Of man and maid? 'Tis love that stands accused!

Sits down.

IBERIN (*to the* POLICE INSPECTOR): Fetch De Guzman in
  again. (DE GUZMAN *is brought in.*) Love? I see, and
  this man here aroused it! (*Laughter in the court.*)

LAWYER:
  Milord, what is love? What moves a man to love?
  One human being chances on another
  And falls in love, or again one, filled with love,
  Seeks out a partner.
  The first I call destiny; the second—
  Lust. Perhaps ours is the latter case—
  Crude, carnal lust?

MADAME CORNAMONTIS (*rises*): I should like to have a
  word. (IBERIN *nods to her.*) I must tell you that
  Nanna Callas is one of my best girls. She saves her
  money and sends it home.

IBERIN (*to the* LAWYER): You may go. Right is its own
  defense.

  The LAWYER *gathers his papers together and leaves
  the court.*

  (*To* DE GUZMAN:) Accused, admit that you abused
  your economic power?

  DE GUZMAN *is silent.*

  (*Suddenly.*) What are you?

DE GUZMAN: A landowner.
IBERIN: What are you?
DE GUZMAN: A member of the landed gentry.

IBERIN: I ask you, what are you?

DE GUZMAN: A Catholic.

IBERIN (*slowly*): What are you? (DE GUZMAN *is silent*.)
You are a Czich, and you have used your economic
position to seduce a Czuchish girl. (*To* MADAME
CORNAMONTIS:) And you, a Czuchish woman, did
nothing to prevent this Czuchish girl from selling
herself to Czichs. That is the pith of the matter. (*To*
DE GUZMAN:)

Behold the Peakhead who abused his power.
Power becomes an evil only when abused.
You who think to purchase the unpurchasable,
You who value what is alienated and know
Nothing that is inalienable,
Like the tree's growth which is inseparable
From the tree and the shape of the leaf that is
Inseparable from the leaf. You who are
A stranger to yourself, and more to us,
Your crime is judged.

To the others:

You see, my friends, how difficult it is
To separate the grains of what is right
From the chaff of what is wrong,
To recognize amid the debris
Of confusion, the simple truth.

HUA: Hail Iberin!

IBERIN: My judgment is: the maid shall be absolved from
blame. The café kept by Madame Cornamontis, in
view of the fact that a Czuchish girl has been seduced
by a Czich, shall be closed—to Czichs. The Czichish
seducer shall be sentenced to death.

CALLAS (*at the top of his voice*): And we shall be freed
from rent-paying. Ah Lopez, what do you say to
Iberin now?

IBERIN:

> What of your rent? That is the least
> That you have suffered. How insignificant
> Is all that you make most of, while you slight
> The central issue. Oh Czuchish father
> And Czuchish daughter oppressed by Czichs,
> You are henceforth free!

CALLAS: Free, hear that Lopez!

IBERIN:

> I give to you your child again, your child
> Whom once you led across your Czuchish fields.
> Explain to her the sentence of a Czuchish court,
> How we distinguish black from white,
> And Czuch from Czich:
> The Czichs destroy to let the Czuch live well.
> The Czuchs I raise as I
> Have raised this farmer from his ignorance,
> His daughter from her shame.

THE CROWD: Hail Iberin. (*The crowd claps as though possessed. As* NANNA *is carried out shoulder high,* THE MAN *announces to the crowd in the street.*)

THE MAN: The Deputy Regent has passed sentence of death against the Czich De Guzman for seducing a Czuchish girl. The girl, who was exonerated, is being carried triumphantly from the court. Hail Iberin!

The crowd takes up the cry and IBERIN *goes off hurriedly.*

ABBOT: That's a terrible sentence. The De Guzmans are one of the noblest families in Yahoo, and yet they throw him to the mob! And the sister of the accused is just about to take her vows.

DE GUZMAN *is led off. As he passes the group of rich landowners, they look away.*

DE GUZMAN:

> Oh help me, Don Duarte! You my friends
> Should stand by me today. How many times

Have we not dined together at a common board.
Alfonso, can you not put in a word for me?
You have a round head: that's what counts today.
Say that what I've done, you did yourself.
Why do you turn away? You will not own me?
You wrong me greatly. Look at this coat!
I am your cloth brother. Save me.

The landowners look away.

IBERIN SOLDIERS (*beating him*): Rack-renter. Dishonor
a Czuchish girl, would you! Hit him on his peakhead
and keep a good eye on his friends.

The landowners hurry away.

CALLAS (*pointing to* DE GUZMAN): To think that that was
once my landlord! Madame Cornamontis, my daughter gives you notice. She is not going to have anything to do with a house like yours any more.

PALMOSA: We have never seen anything like this before.
The new age has begun. The landowner is to be
hanged. The tenant is coming into his own, Madame
Cornamontis.

MADAME CORNAMONTIS: Mr. Palmosa, it is delightful
listening to the way you talk. You seem to have pre-
served intact the innocence of childhood.

CALLAMASSI: You seem to think, Madame Cornamontis,
that a poor man can never win against a rich man?

MADAME CORNAMONTIS: I'll give you my opinion on that
point. (*She sings the "Ballad of Tossing the Button."*)

BALLAD OF TOSSING THE BUTTON

A crooked man comes up to me
And he asks most timidly
"Does your fairest maiden love me well?"
And I say, "Such things are hard to tell."
Then I snatch and pluck a button from his habit,

Saying, "Friend, we'll let the fates decide it.
Let us toss it.
If the holes come up above
Then you cannot trust her love."
And I toss and looking say: "She doesn't."
Then he says,
"But these holes go right through."
And I say, it is so.
"Yes, luck's not yours, 'tis vain to try it."*

CALLAS: I don't think you can have washed your ears, this morning, madame. The Regent said quite clearly that rent was of minor importance. If I can get horses now, everything will be all right.

MADAME CORNAMONTIS *breaks out into loud laughter and points with her finger at* CALLAS *who behaves exactly as a man who has been struck blind. Illuminated bulletin: "The Battle In The South Continues."*

---

* The rest of the song is given on page 282.—E.B.

5

THE CONVENT OF SAN BARABAS

MOTHER SUPERIOR *and, facing her, nuns of the Needy Sisterhood of San Barabas;* ISABELLA DE GUZMAN *and her Czuchish* LAWYER.

LAWYER: Miss De Guzman wishes, before her application for admittance to the convent is taken up, to ask you one or two questions.

ISABELLA (*reads from a slip of paper*): Is the convent a strict one?

MOTHER SUPERIOR: The strictest convent there is, child, (*to the* LAWYER) and the most expensive . . .

LAWYER: We know that.

MOTHER SUPERIOR: And therefore the most select.

ISABELLA: Are there many fast days? How many fast days are there?

MOTHER SUPERIOR: Twice a week, before the High Feast days, then a fast week, and Ember day fasts.

ISABELLA: Are men really never allowed to enter? And is it never possible to leave the convent?

MOTHER SUPERIOR: Never.

ISABELLA: Is the food plain, and are the beds hard? And are the religious duties exacting?

MOTHER SUPERIOR: The food is plain, the beds are hard and the religious duties are exacting, my child.

ISABELLA:
The fleshly lusts and sensual delights
Which weak men often seek repel my soul.
Even my brother's eyes allowed themselves
To stray and steep in sin as oft I heard
Through his closed door . . . oh hateful memory!

I wish my bed unsoiled, my virtue sealed.
Oh chastity, perpetual joy; oh, royal poverty!
If unadorned the cell, and plain the fare,
And eyeless the walls, I ask no more.
Chaste I seek to be, and meek and poor.

MOTHER SUPERIOR:
That is how we live here, my child, and how
You'll live. And as are we
So you will learn to be.

(*To the* LAWYER:) But we must agree about the terms, Sir, what does the girl bring with her?

LAWYER: Well, I hope you won't be too exacting. Here is the list.

MOTHER SUPERIOR (*reading*): Three thousand chemises. Hardly enough. We require five thousand.

LAWYER: Now, now, now, let's say four thousand, that should be ample.

MOTHER SUPERIOR: And what about the linen?

LAWYER: Do you mean to say you want linen as well?

MOTHER SUPERIOR: You must remember that the young lady will be with us until she is eighty. I take it that the knives and forks are silver?

LAWYER: Solid silver, I assure you.

MOTHER SUPERIOR: My dear sir, one must always make sure. Also we prefer the cupboards to be of cherry rather than birch.

LAWYER: We won't quarrel about that. We now come to the most important question, madame.

MOTHER SUPERIOR: Yes.

LAWYER: You know what I refer to. You don't think there will be any difficulties?

MOTHER SUPERIOR: I am afraid there may be.

LAWYER: It is true we cannot vouch for the young lady's descent.

MOTHER SUPERIOR (*relieved*): Oh that, that is all right. I thought you had something else in mind. (*She goes up to* ISABELLA *and feels the top of her skull. Laughing:*) Peaked, there's no denying it. That won't matter here. A mere question of externals. If everything else is all right, that will not make any difference. But now about the important question, the weekly contribution. . . .

LAWYER: You have information of the income of the De Guzman estates?

MOTHER SUPERIOR: The rents are not high. A percentage of course will have to be made over to our convent. Twenty-five per cent.

LAWYER: That is quite impossible. The young lady's brother has the family name to keep up and he depends entirely upon the rents.

MOTHER SUPERIOR: As far as I am aware, Mr. De Guzman is not exactly in a position at the moment to keep up the family name.

LAWYER: All the same, the young lady will live very simply here, won't she?

MOTHER SUPERIOR: Simply does not mean cheaply.

LAWYER: Moreover, the fact that the new government has come into power makes it possible not only that the regular collection of rents will be assured, but also that they may be raised.

MOTHER SUPERIOR: I am very glad to hear it, but one cannot wholly rely on that.

LAWYER: It is quite true, I don't see myself how the already overburdened tenants are to be made to pay more. It may turn out to be impossible for us to keep Miss De Guzman here. Miss De Guzman, hadn't you better think it over?

MOTHER SUPERIOR: Yes, think it over, my child. You know what it costs.

ISABELLA (*to the* LAWYER): Is it really too expensive?

The LAWYER *takes* ISABELLA *into the corner. He interrupts to ask the sisters again.*

LAWYER: Six thousand? (*The sisters shake their heads and look straight ahead. To* ISABELLA:) The life that you have chosen costs a lot of money.

ISABELLA (*weeps because the beautiful life is so difficult to attain*): I want it, I want it.

LAWYER (*to the* MOTHER SUPERIOR): You must remember that on account of the good harvest the corn is bringing in practically nothing this year. Even the landowners are denying themselves luxuries these days.

MOTHER SUPERIOR: We have fields of our own, so we suffer from that ourselves. You must remember, however, that the family will be greatly benefited by the young lady's entering our convent. We have already mentioned her descent.

LAWYER: Very good. I had one other question. (*He reads from his slip of paper.*) Would the estate pass formally into the hands of the convent? Would the Needy Sisters, if necessity arose, start legal proceedings?

MOTHER SUPERIOR (*nodding to each question*): That will be taken care of.

LAWYER: Then I think we're agreed. We have only to see now that we get our money. That is not so simple in the midst of civil war. Here are the books and title deeds of the De Guzman estate. (*He hands them to the* MOTHER SUPERIOR *who locks them up.*)

MOTHER SUPERIOR: Well, dear child, we are pleased to welcome you within our silent precincts. You will live in peace here. The storms of life do not penetrate to this sanctuary. (*A stone breaks the window.*) What's that? (*She runs to the window.*) What are those people with the arm bands doing on our grounds? (*She rings and a* NUN *enters.*)

NUN: Good Mother, outside. . . .

MOTHER SUPERIOR: I've seen it all. Tell the De Guzman's coachman to drive up.

NUN: It's dreadful. The hooligan at the head of the mob, the one with the painted woman beside him, unhar-

nessed Mr. De Guzman's horses. He said they were
his. He said he was Mr. De Guzman's tenant and
needed them for his farm. He hit the coachman on
the head and drove the horses away, saying that Mr.
De Guzman could go to the gallows on foot.

MOTHER SUPERIOR: Scandalous.

LAWYER: Madame, under the circumstances I should like
to ask you to take the young lady immediately under
your protection.

The MOTHER SUPERIOR *looks at the other nuns.*

MOTHER SUPERIOR: It seems to me that the property of the
De Guzman family is in more danger than the family
itself.

LAWYER: You mean to say that you refuse asylum to the
young lady?

MOTHER SUPERIOR: I am responsible for the peace of these
walls, good sir. I hope you can understand the situation without my having to say what is not pleasant
to say.

ISABELLA: Let us be going, then.

LAWYER: And what about our agreement over the estates?

MOTHER SUPERIOR: We shall keep to our word wherever
we can.

The parties bow to one another. The LAWYER *and*
ISABELLA *leave the room.*

6

MADAME CORNAMONTIS' CAFE

Afternoon. The three rich landowners SAZ, DE HOZ *and* PERUINER *are sitting at a small table between large chests.* CALLAMASSI *is in the background, behind a newspaper.* MADAME CORNAMONTIS *is behind the bar smoking and knitting.*

SAZ:
It was a good plan to wait here till our train pulls in.

PERUINER:
If any train will pull in.

DE HOZ:
Here one is unobserved, which in these days is much
to be desired, to such a pass we've come!

SAZ:
What's the war news? That's the main thing now.

PERUINER:
Bad. This journey does not lure me. . . .

DE HOZ:
The regent is to blame. And wise Duarte
Who brought this Iberin to his notice.
All this blah of round and pointed heads
Was meant to bring the tenants from the Sickle flag
Only to clap their clogs to Iberin.

Noise without.

PERUINER:
What's that noise?

SAZ (*ironically*):
The national hero!
The story of Callas and the horses
Has gone round Yahoo.

PERUINER:

A nasty business.

SAZ:

The sort of thing that spreads.

PERUINER:

I quite agree.

Tenant CALLAS *and his daughter come down the street. He is leading two horses. Tenant* PARR *and three* HUAS *are with him, within a crowd.* CALLAS *ties up the horses and enters the café. The crowd calls: "Long live Iberin! Long live Callas!"*

ONE HUA: Go on Callas! In with you, you old sinner!

ANOTHER HUA: Dear people. You see here, "Callas and his horses." The victor according to the sentence of a Czuchish court.

MADAME CORNAMONTIS: Good day, Nanna. You are welcome as a guest in the house where you served so long.

CALLAS (*introducing* PARR): This is my friend Parr, also a tenant. Yes, about the horses! A couple of days ago I was walking along the road with my daughter. The case had been won and the landlord was to be hanged. But I myself had not got anywhere in this business. I was just as poor as before, except for the honor, so to speak. I had been given my daughter back, so to speak, but that only meant another mouth to feed. I caught sight of the horses in front of the convent of the good-for-nothing nuns of San Barabas. "Oh," I said to my daughter, "aren't these the horses he promised you when he seduced you?" "They are," said my daughter, only she was not sure whether people would believe us or not. "Why not," I said, and I led off the horses. I've had enough of being sat upon.

PARR (*in admiration*): He didn't wait to ask. He just took them.

CALLAS: I thought—But what one has, one has. (*Sings the "But What One Has, One Has" song.*)

BUT WHAT ONE HAS, ONE HAS

Once a certain man
To mourn his lot began
They said to him: just wait.
So he waited, the good man,
Though the waiting had no date.
Hail Iberin! Ave!
But what one has, one has.

The man began to waste,
With bankruptcy was faced.
He was a ruffian bold.
Men acquiesced in haste.
A promise he did hold.
Hail Iberin! Ave!
But what one has, one has.

As no kind friends began
To fetch things for our man
He thought he'd help himself
And now takes what he can
And scorns all men with pelf.
Hail Iberin! Ave!
But what one has, one has.

SAZ: Blatant rebellion, I call it.

HUA: From the Czuchish standpoint it is one of the greatest deeds of heroism, and its emulation is recommended.

MADAME CORNAMONTIS *brings* NANNA *a cup of coffee.*

MADAME CORNAMONTIS: Would you like a cup of coffee, Nanna?

NANNA: No thanks.

MADAME CORNAMONTIS: Do have a cup.

NANNA: I didn't order any.

MADAME CORNAMONTIS: There's no charge for it. (*To* SAZ *in a whisper as she passes by his chair:*) Look out.

SAZ (*turning away from her, to the* HUAS): Do you really think that that is in the spirit of Mr. Iberin?

HUA: Yes, my good sir, it *is* in the spirit of Mr. Iberin. You think, I suppose, that a person who goes about in clogs is inferior to you? To put you right on this point we'll take the liberty of singing the "New Iberin Song."

NEW IBERIN SONG

The landlord ponders day and night
On how to satisfy each whim.
And when he thinks of it, presto,
The tenant runs and fetches it for him.
He brings him a dish
Of meat or fish
And at a sign
Pours him wine:
The rarest are for him; his smoke, Havana;
His drink, champagne; his fruit, banana.
Everything he wants
Is simply there.
The rich man said: that's the way for me,
The way, thank God! it should always be.

Then, my dear friends, the tenants went to their friend Mr. Iberin and Mr. Iberin went to the landlord and showed him. The landlord became so humble that henceforth he has treated his tenant like a brother and:

The tenant ponders day and night
On how to satisfy each whim.
And when he thinks of it, presto,
The landlord runs and fetches it for him.
He brings him a dish

Of meat or fish
And at a sign
Pours him wine:
The rarest are for him; his smoke, Havana;
His drink, champagne; his fruit, banana.
Everything he wants
Is simply there.
The tenant said: that's the way for me.
The way, thank God! it should always be.

The HUAS *act the song with* PARR. *In the first verse they make* PARR *bow down before the landowners; in the second verse they lift him up on the table, put Mr. Saz's hat on his head and give him Mr. De Hoz's cigars and Mr. Peruiner's glasses.* PARR *accompanies with a clog dance.*

HUA: Horses and modern farm implements will soon be distributed among the tenants. After that the land will be distributed. Callas has merely put himself first on the list.

PARR (*to* CALLAS): It's just what the Sicklemen are after.

CALLAS: It's more. According to the Sicklemen, the village is to get the horses. But listen to me: Take time by the forelock. With all due respects to Mr. Iberin, and needless to say my confidence in him is unbounded, if during the next few days you should come into the possession of any horses, let's say by chance as in my case, that certainly wouldn't be a bad thing. Safer that way, see what I mean?

PARR: I see what you mean. Hail Iberin, but what one has, one has. Callas, you have opened my eyes. I know now what I must do. (*He goes off in haste.*)

HUA: And now I ask all present to drink the health of Callas and his horses.

The HUAS *stand up. The rich landowners, excepting* PERUINER, *remain seated.*

DE HOZ (*under his breath*): I'm not going to drink to the health of a horse thief.

SAZ: Then we had better go home.

The landowners pay, get up and leave.

HUA: I can hardly believe my eyes. They wouldn't drink your health, Callas. That looks bad. I bet they're Czichs.

CALLAS: Why, they're the ones who were at De Guzman's trial. They testified that my daughter had molested him. They're De Guzman's pals, the same sort as he is.

HUAS: You stay here, Callas; we'll bring them back and have a confidential talk with these gentlemen in your presence. (*They follow after the landowners.*)

MADAME CORNAMONTIS (*hurrying after the* HUAS): For God's sake, don't do anything against the biggest landowners in the country.

CALLAS (*to his daughter*): Nanna darling, can't you find me a little loose cash? I'm pretty hungry.

NANNA: There's nothing I can do now. For three days the whole of Yahoo has feted me like a queen. People drink my health and compliment me on my rise in the world. For three days not a man has done more than tip his hat to me. I can no longer earn anything. Men look at me now with respect instead of with desire. I am ruined.

CALLAS: But there's no reason for you to go back to that sort of thing. Look, I have horses now, and I got them without lifting a finger.

NANNA: I'm not sure they're yours yet.

The two De Guzman family LAWYERS *come in and rush toward* CALLAS *with outstretched arms.*

LAWYERS: Ah, here you are, my dear Mr. Callas, we have a most attractive proposition for you. Things are pan-ning out very satisfactorily. (*They sit down beside him.*)

CALLAS: Well.

LAWYERS: There's a certain family you know of. You can guess the name. Well, they are ready to meet you half way in the matter of the horses.

NANNA: What do you mean?

CALLAS: You refer to a certain Czichish family, I suppose.

LAWYERS: You must realize that you will eventually face a lawsuit over the horses.

CALLAS: I don't know.

LAWYERS: You will, my dear man. Not a stone will be left unturned by the family involved, a family of high standing, to have their present sentence remitted, after which certain other actions will follow. . . .

CALLAS: From the Czichish side.

LAWYERS (*laughing*): From the Czichish side. We are in possession of an affidavit testifying that your daughter had had relations with another gentleman before she made the acquaintance of the Czichish gentleman in question, so that the charge of seduction falls through.

NANNA: That's a lie.

LAWYERS: If you were to admit it we could immediately discuss the question of compensation.

CALLAS: To that I have only one answer.

NANNA: Wait. (*To the* LAWYERS:) Let me have a few words alone with my father.

LAWYERS: Well, not to beat about the bush, we want you to know you can have legal possession of the two horses if you act prudently. (*They stroll toward where the horses are tied.*)

CALLAS: Iberin is on our side. That's why they're making us propositions. They want us to sell our good name for a ham sandwich. What do you think?

NANNA: I think we should take the horses. The question

is not what side Iberin is on but how the fighting is going.

CALLAS: And how is the fighting going?

NANNA (*excitedly looking through the paper*): This is all lies but it is quite clear that the Sicklemen are winning. Even here it says that they got outside the town of Mirasonnore, that's where the power station is that supplies Yahoo. If they take it, Yahoo will go dark and everything will stop running.

CALLAS: Dear daughter, I drain my glass to our good friend Lopez. He's fighting like a tiger. The land-owners begin to give their horses away. But I must stay here, because what one has, one has.

NANNA: But, the tide may turn. There are too few with the Sickle League. Too many ran away as you did.

CALLAS: I am of a different opinion. (*He beckons to the* LAWYERS.) Sirs, my answer to the De Guzman family is: no, I do not need to make any compromises. Read today's papers. Tell them I see no reason to lick their boots.

LAWYERS: And the two horses?

CALLAS: I have the horses. They are standing outside. And I have no intention of selling the honor of a Czuchish girl.

LAWYERS: As you wish. (*Exeunt.*)

CALLAMASSI (*who has been sitting at the next table*): Are you angry, Mr. Callas?

CALLAS: On the contrary. These Czichs are a soft lot. They're out to bribe me; but I caught them. They wanted to make me a present of the horses I already have, in payment for a dishonorable act toward my own daughter. That's Czichs all over. They think one can't do anything except for money. The Deputy was absolutely right. Good Sir, the days when I had to sell my honor are past. Today I no longer look at things materialistically. How stupid these Czichs are. They think they'll make out that I got the horses

because the Czich had my daughter. Not everyone
would get a bargain like that. My daughter looks as
well as any other girl of her age. But just look at
the horses. I have them tied up outside. And between
ourselves, there was never any question of my getting
the horses for the girl.

NANNA (*sees that he is drunk*): We'd better go, father!

CALLAS: It's absurd: Who would offer two horses like
that for a girl? You must really see those horses.

CALLAMASSI: Mr. Callas, I should esteem it a great honor
to be allowed to look at your horses.

NANNA *pulls her father out by the coattails.* CALLA-
MASSI *follows them. A radio announcement is heard:*
"*The Mirasonnore power station is threatened by the
Sickle troops. The current may be cut off in the
capital at any moment.*" *The rich landowners* SAZ, DE
HOZ *and* PERUINER *come in through the back door.
They are wounded.* MADAME CORNAMONTIS *goes up
to them.*

MADAME CORNAMONTIS: You would have done much
better to swallow your pride and stand up with the
others to drink the health of Callas. He is now a
national hero.

SAZ: Pull down the blinds, the Huas are after us.

PERUINER: Water and bandages!

MADAME CORNAMONTIS *brings water and bandages.
The gentlemen begin to bind their wounds.*

SAZ: When the Sicklemen have been crushed, we'll have
these fellows hanged.

PERUINER (*to* MADAME CORNAMONTIS): I can't use my
arm. Bandage my head, will you?

MADAME CORNAMONTIS: I don't see any wound there, sir!

PERUINER: There's no wound, but don't you see it's
peaked!

There is a knock at the door and a man enters.

DOCTOR: I have been called here. I am a doctor.

PERUINER (*shouts*): Take your hat off.

The DOCTOR *takes off his hat. He has a peak head.*

PERUINER: You're a Czich!

DOCTOR (*shouts*): I am a doctor!

SAZ: If you're found here, we'll get it in the neck. Get out!

Exit the DOCTOR.

DE HOZ (*to* PERUINER): You *would* be a Czich. If you weren't, nothing would have happened to us.

PERUINER: I'm not of that opinion. Not now. It's our clothes. That's why the mob is after us. We should never have allowed De Guzman, a fellow landlord, to get into their clutches. We gave him up as Czich, but the mob attacked him as a landlord; and now they're after all of us.

DE HOZ: Well, let's go. But where? The station would be a trap for us.

There is a knock at the door. MADAME CORNAMONTIS *opens cautiously.* MISSENA *enters.*

MISSENA (*warmly*): Delighted to find you here.

SAZ: And we, Sir, are most obliged to you. Your good men, your Hua crowd, have nearly made hash of us.

DE HOZ: What's the war news?

MISSENA: Bad.

SAZ: The truth now.

MISSENA: The battle's lost. Our troops are routed. We can't get them to make a stand.

PERUINER: Where's the battlefield?

MISSENA: The fighting is around the Mirasonnore power station.

SAZ: So near?

MISSENA: Yes, we need money. We must have money, money do you hear?

PERUINER: Money, money, money, money, easily said!
But what will you use it for?

SAZ: Iberin's boys have attacked us!

MISSENA: That's why we need money, my friends. He has
to feed his men. Don't you get the idea? He hires
one half of the poor against the other half. Czuch or
Czich, it makes no difference. What we need now is
money to feed the half that helps us keep the other
half down. Otherwise all is lost.

The light flickers out.

SAZ: What's the matter?

MISSENA: Mirasonnore has fallen, my friends!

MADAME CORNAMONTIS (*brings in a candle which she
lights*): God save us, sirs, what's going to happen
now? Soon the Sicklemen will be in Yahoo.

DE HOZ: What can save us?

MISSENA: Cash!

SAZ: Cash comes with confidence! In whom can we have
confidence now? I'll lodge no complaint of assault
and battery; if only my goods are safe, a knock or
two won't bother me. The question that concerns me
is our rents. What about our rents?

MISSENA: Rents are property and property is sacred.

PERUINER: What about Callas and his horses?

MISSENA: What do you want?

SAZ: That this "hero" be brought before the law! At once,
and publicly.

MISSENA: Agreed! You bring the cash and we will sue. I
know that Iberin is outraged by this low-down, grasp-
ing spirit the tenants show. But what's the good of
grumbling? Wait till we've overcome the Sicklemen.
In the meanwhile give him and others like him a free
hand. Help Iberin crush the Sicklemen and De Guzman will get his horses back. At the trial we'll only
take up the question of the horses. Let's go to Iberin!
But I want to warn you. Careful how you discuss

money with him. His unworldly soul shrinks from all material things. He thinks the Czuchish soul itself is enough to win. Therefore in offering him the financial help he needs, be tactful. Then he'll take it in a spirit of renunciation and self-sacrifice.

PERUINER (*indicating his head*): A head like this he'll hardly welcome.

MISSENA: In time of need, he'll learn to prize your worth.

PERUINER: He doesn't take money from Czichs.

MISSENA (*smiling*): He does, I'll bet you he does. Come, we have no time to waste.

7

THE REGENT'S PALACE

The court is again in session. The courtroom, however, is greatly changed. A large chandelier, a carpet and the new clothes worn by the officials all speak of wealth. The CHIEF JUSTICE *is wearing a new gown and smoking a fat cigar. The* POLICE INSPECTOR *is no longer barefoot. As the clerks arrange the courtroom furniture, under Missena's direction, the* CHIEF JUSTICE *sings to soft music the song of the "Life-giving Power of Gold."*

LIFE-GIVING POWER OF GOLD

Gold is much despised on this our planet.
Though where 'tis absent things fall flat,
While our state with money-bags to man it
Prospers and we all grow fat.
Our poor land's ruin by gold was stayed.
The frozen ponds are running water.
Sunrise lights the Eastern quarter.
In the house the fire is made.
Yes, the world now looks as different as it can.
Hearts faster beat, and loads are lighter.
Boards are better spread and garments brighter.
And man is quite a different sort of man.

Oh, how terribly are those mistaken
Who believe that gold's of no account.
Fruitfulness with plague is overtaken
When the stream stops in lucre's fount.
Each man shouts and takes what can be taken.
Everything is plunged in darkest night;
Those who starve not are not sated;

Hearts are dead and love has lost its light;
Kin by nearest kin are hated,
See the hearths—they are no longer bright.
The atmosphere is one we can't extol.
Malice rules with envy close beside her.
None will be ridden, each the rider
And the world's a world without a soul.
Quickly wanes all virtue on this earth,
For hungry men care naught for worth.

But if the good man has a little gold
Then with the saints he'll be enrolled.
Once more one sees what human nature can attain.
"Edel sei der Mensch," as said the famous writer.
Men's minds are growing now. They had begun to
    wane.
The heart is firmer and the outlook brighter.
All know who's the ridden, who the rider,
Who's the in—and who outsider.*

The INSPECTOR *writes in large letters on a blackboard: "Convent of San Barabas versus Tenant
Farmer Callas, in re: Two horses."*

Illuminated bulletin: "Government Troops Advance."

IBERIN *comes out of the palace.*

IBERIN: How goes the fighting?
MISSENA: Better. The Sicklemen are repulsed; we are at-
    tacking. We have fresh troops and new equipment.
    Mirasonnore will be the turning point. Around the
    power station, the battle rages. You'll take the case
    yourself?
IBERIN: I'm not thinking of the case. Nothing's decided.
    When there is victory, I'll pass judgment, not before.
MISSENA: We'll begin then, shall we?

* Another version of this song is to be found in Brecht's
Selected Poems (Evergreen Books), pp. 82-85.—E.B.

IBERIN: Do as you please. (*Returns to the palace.*)

MISSENA: Always vacillating. We'll begin. Your Worship, a word with you. (*Takes the* CHIEF JUSTICE *aside and speaks to him. When the parties in the case appear, he leaves.*)

POLICE INSPECTOR: The Convent of San Barabas versus Tenant Farmer Callas. Matter in dispute, two horses.

CALLAS, *his daughter,* ISABELLA DE GUZMAN, *the* MOTHER SUPERIOR *of San Barabas and the* LAWYERS *are admitted into the court.*

CALLAS: I'll hold a candle up to him now and we'll see how he carries out his ideas in practice. He'll tell us whether a Czich has the right to deprive a Czuch of horses that he needs for his farm.

NANNA: According to that you might take any horse you happened to find standing in the street.

CALLAS: Any horse belonging to a Czich.

CZUCHISH LAWYER: How goes the fighting?

MOTHER SUPERIOR: Well, since this morning.

LAWYER: Good, everything depends on how it goes.

ISABELLA: Ah, Mother, if only this base wrangle
       For earthly goods were done!

NANNA: Good-for-nothing Peakhead, but pious I suppose. She makes up for her peakhead with a round bottom. It's plump like a queen's. She's well fed; she ought to have plenty of staying power; but she'll never have to use it. No work for her. (*To* CALLAS:) It's you who pays for her.

CALLAS: I? I shall pay nothing. (*To* ISABELLA:) You'll get nothing out of me.

MOTHER SUPERIOR: My dear child, take refuge in our quiet precincts. It will be good for you.

NANNA: Yes, it will do her good. She needs a long rest from doing nothing.

CALLAS: Czichish scum.

NANNA: The old judge is back again. That's bad.

CALLAS: The public's not admitted. That's a bad sign too.

NANNA: Her brother will be strung up anyway. (ISABELLA *shows signs of fainting.* NANNA *at the top of her voice*:) I suppose you need the two horses to bring your chamber pot into the convent.

MOTHER SUPERIOR: Never mind them, poor child. You're safe now. (*Goes up to* CALLAS.) You're probably counting on the fact that your head is round. You think that that excuses you from paying? Do you know to whom you are in debt?

CALLAS: I won't pay anything to Czichs.

The MOTHER SUPERIOR *strokes her own head.*

NANNA: What's the idea?

MOTHER SUPERIOR: You'll see. Let me inform you that our heads are also round.

NANNA (*to her father*): At the front things go badly for the Sicklemen, and here they go differently for us from what they did eight days ago. They've smartened up the place, but I'm afraid not for us.

CALLAS: I trust Iberin.

Bulletin board: "The recently announced death sentence on a large landowner has made a good impression. Members of the Sickle League are returning to their farms."

CHIEF JUSTICE: Iberin is very busy. However he will give judgment in this case since it has been so much discussed and brings up basic questions of property rights.

CALLAS: I should like particularly to mention that I rely on the Deputy Regent's statement that rent in the future will be of secondary importance; and also on his remark, "What are two horses?" and finally on the fact that I have been wronged.

CHIEF JUSTICE: Everything in proper order, please. First of all we shall hear the De Guzmans' family lawyer.

CZUCHISH LAWYER: Your honor, I insist that this man has not the slightest legal claim to the horses, which he took by violence from the rightful owners.

NANNA: The young lady could claim that she has to pray on horseback.

CHIEF JUSTICE: Defendant Callas, explain why you took the horses.

CALLAS: When my daughter was seduced by the landlord, it was agreed that I should have the horses.

CZUCHISH LAWYER: Then it was a commercial transaction?

CALLAS *does not answer.*

A commercial transaction by your own account.
Your daughter for two horses—a thing impossible!
Or was it possible for you?

CALLAS: It wasn't anything like that.

CZUCHISH LAWYER: What was it then?

CALLAS (*to* NANNA): What does he say?

NANNA: Say the horses were a present.

CZUCHISH LAWYER: When?

CALLAS: What does he mean, when?

CZICHISH LAWYER: Before or after?

CALLAS: I don't answer Czichs. (*He looks round for applause but encounters only stony stares.*) You're trying to get me into a trap, with your trick questions. Questions like that are hatched only under peaked skulls.

CHIEF JUSTICE:
If you had first contracted out your daughter—
And I can scarcely credit that you did—
You would have been your daughter's own procurer.
The court assumes the deal was later made
And that the landlord, to buy your silence,
Gave you the horses,—a salve for your paternal pain.

CALLAS: Yes, it was afterward he gave me the horses. Yes, I'd say he gave them as a sort of salve for my wounded feelings, just as you say.

Illuminated bulletin: "Offensive In The South Success-ful, Sicklemen Retreating."

CZICHISH LAWYER (*quietly to the other*): No word about Czich and Czuch today.

CZUCHISH LAWYER: I've noticed that. (*Addressing the court.*)
Your honor! Gentlemen of the Court!
It is my firm conviction
The question we must here consider
Is one of first importance to our land.
It might be said two horses, more or less,
Could hardly be of much account
To my defendants; but 'tis clear
If these two horses will not be restored
Then tenants will feel free
To take anything they see.

NANNA: And this smooth dame will not be able to retire for her beauty rest into the convent.

MOTHER SUPERIOR (*in a very loud voice*):
From our stable in the South a tenant
Drives our horse and confiscates our plough;
Then shouting that he is wronged he further
Takes our fields and calls it an injustice
That horse and farm were yesterday another's.

CZICHISH LAWYER: Your Worship, there is a prisoner who can give testimony in this case. He is also a tenant: may he be called?

The CHIEF JUSTICE *nods.*

POLICE INSPECTOR (*calling*): Tenant Parr.
NANNA: What do you want Parr for?

CALLAS: Nothing at all, it's a trick.

PARR *is brought in in heavy chains.*

CZUCHISH LAWYER: You came into Madame Cornamontis'
café with Mr. Callas when he brought the horses
there, is that so?

PARR: Yes, sir.

CZUCHISH LAWYER: You are also one of Mr. De Guzman's
tenants?

PARR: Yes, sir.

CZICHISH LAWYER: After leaving the café, you walked five
hours to your village and drove two horses from De
Guzman's farm?

PARR: Yes, sir.

CZICHISH LAWYER: On what grounds?

PARR *is silent.*

CZUCHISH LAWYER: You have no daughter, have you, Mr.
Parr?

PARR: No, sir.

CZICHISH LAWYER: Then they were not a present from
Mr. De Guzman?

PARR *is silent.*

Why did you appropriate the horses?

PARR: Because I need them.

The LAWYERS *smile.*

CHIEF JUSTICE: But that is no reason for taking them, my
man.

PARR: It would not be for you, sir, but for me it is different.
As my farm is all bogland, I need horses to plough
it. That should be clear to anyone.

CZICHISH LAWYER: Mr. Callas, is your farm also bogland?

CALLAS: It is indeed.

CZUCHISH LAWYER: And did you also need the horses?

CALLAS: Yes, that is to say, no. I did not take them because I needed them, but because they were given to me as a present.

CZUCHISH LAWYER: You therefore do not approve of your friend's action?

CALLAS: No, I certainly do not. (*To* PARR:) You just went and took the horses! What right did you have to them, eh?

PARR: As good as yours! If I had no right to the horses I took, you had no right to the horses you took.

CZUCHISH LAWYER: What's that? What do you mean? Callas had no right?

PARR: Because the horses were not given to him.

CALLAS: How do you know?

PARR: De Guzman must have a lot of horses if he's going to give a pair away every time he has a woman.

CZUCHISH LAWYER: Your Honor, tenant Parr is expressing in the plainest terms the opinion current among tenants with regard to situations such as that between De Guzman and Nanna Callas. Your Honor, may I call a witness whose testimony I think will enlighten the court. This witness will transmit Mr. Callas' own opinion as to whether landlords give away horses for a tenant girl's favors.

NANNA: Who have you blabbed to now? You let off a lot of wind in the café.

CALLAS: The whole show is spoiled. Damn that idiot Parr.

CALLAMASSI *comes in.*

CZUCHISH LAWYER: Please repeat what you heard Mr. Callas say in the café.

CALLAMASSI (*all in one breath*): Mr. Callas said: Between ourselves there was never any question of my getting the horses for the girl. It's absurd, who would offer two horses like that for a girl? Take a look at the horses.

CHIEF JUSTICE (*to* CALLAS): Did you say that?

NANNA: No, he didn't.

CALLAS: Yes, that is to say no, I was drunk, Your Worship, everyone drank my health that day. I had plenty to drink but nothing to eat, and you know what drink does to a man on an empty stomach.

CHIEF JUSTICE: That doesn't sound so well, Mr. Callas. Perhaps you will consider returning the horses of your own free will.

NANNA: You'll do nothing of the sort.

CALLAS: Never, Your Worship, as I am not in a position to do this. (*Loudly.*) I move that the Deputy himself give judgment in this case as it is not ordinary horses but Czichish horses that are in dispute.

Illuminated bulletin: "The Deputy Will Soon Announce Good News From The Front." IBERIN *enters from the palace.*

CHIEF JUSTICE: Your Excellency, tenant Callas asks for your judgment in the case concerning the horses belonging to the Convent of San Barabas.

IBERIN (*to* CALLAS):
What do you want of me? Have I not done all
That you could require of me? Have I not
Restored to you your honor and condemned
Him who had wronged you, despite
His wealth and your poverty. Did I not
Raise you up? But did you stay erect?
I know your plot, and warn you!

CALLAS: I should like to call your attention to the fact that the horses which I need for ploughing were in Czichish hands.

MOTHER SUPERIOR: And I would like to call attention to the fact that you are now in Czuchish hands.
Sir! We are the horses' owners,
And we are Czuchs. But even if they were
Czichish, still, property is property
Which none may alienate. Sir, imagine two horses

In a field. Walk round them, pinch them,
Look them in the mouth. Can anywhere
A Czichish sign be seen? No, Sir, it can't
By any means, for what's a horse, sir?
Is it a Czichish or a Czuchish thing?
It's neither, it is something that is worth
A hundred pesos odd. It might be
A piece of cheese, a pair of boots and still
But be so many pesos worth. In short
A hundred pesos graze upon the meadow
And they are convent pesos which by chance
Are covered with a horse's skin. And as
The skin lies on the horse, thus on it
Our claim lies. It is convent property.

CZUCHISH LAWYER:

Because by transference of right one half
Of all the goods and chattels of the farm
From which these horses come are convent property.

CALLAS: When I took the horses they did not belong to
the convent.

ISABELLA (*suddenly excited*): But neither did they belong
to you, you beast. Take your hat off!

NANNA: You weren't asked for your opinion.

CALLAS: The whole gang doesn't even know how to harness
a horse to a cart.

ISABELLA: Take your hat off! They are our horses. Take
your hat off!

CALLAS: I refer to the Deputy's statement that here there
are neither rich nor poor.

ISABELLA: Take your hat off!

IBERIN: Yes, take it off. (CALLAS *does so*.) Enough of this
dispute. (*To the landowners*:)
I hear that there is now a rumor current
That because I judged a Czichish landlord,
I am the landlords' enemy. Nothing
Could be more false. The sentence that I passed
Was passed against abuse of power, and you,

Peasant, scorning the things that move a Czuch
Thought only of gain.
Do horses pay you for your honor?
A Czuch should blush for shame!

CZUCHISH LAWYER: Your Excellency, my clients, the Convent of San Barabas, wish to bear witness to the fact that the defendant is a disaffected element.

CZICHISH LAWYER: The defendant himself condemned horse theft when it was committed by another, by the tenant Parr. (*To the witness,* CALLAMASSI:) You say that the defendant sang a certain seditious song in the café?

CALLAMASSI: Yes, it was the prohibited song, "But what one has, one has."

NANNA (*to her father*): You're done for now.

CZUCHISH LAWYER: I move that the defendant be asked to sing the song.

IBERIN (*to* CALLAS): Did you sing that song?

CALLAS: No, that is to say, yes. I was drunk, Your Excellency. Everyone drank my health but nobody gave me anything to eat, and you know what drink does to a man on an empty stomach.

IBERIN: Sing it, please.

CALLAS: I'm very hoarse today.

CZUCHISH LAWYER: We are not expecting to get any aesthetic pleasure from it.

IBERIN: Sing!

CALLAS: I only once heard it, so I can't remember it word for word, but it goes something like this. (*He sings the song without emphasis on any word except the word Iberin.*)

MOTHER SUPERIOR: Blatant rebellion, I call it.

CHIEF JUSTICE: The song is outright defamation of the government.

IBERIN: The defendant is to be deprived of the horses.

CHIEF JUSTICE: You are deprived of the horses. (*Leaves.*)

CALLAS: Then I am not to have the horses?

IBERIN: No, right is right, for you, as for everyone else.
CALLAS: Then I should like to say that I spit on your
     right if I am not to have the horses that I need for
     my farm. There is nothing right about that. It's not
     right for me if I am not to have the horses which I
     need. That is landlord justice. I realize now that I
     would have done much better had I joined the Sickle
     League.

At this moment the bells start ringing.

VOICE FROM BEHIND: The Sickle League is defeated.
CZUCHISH LAWYER: Victory!

     MISSENA *appears with a microphone.*

MISSENA: Your Excellency, the tenants' rising
          Is, with the help of God, wiped out in blood.
MOTHER SUPERIOR (*applauding genteelly*): Bravo.
IBERIN (*at the microphone*):
     The Sickle flag lies in the dust.
     Arms outstretched for others' goods
     Are hewn to the ground. It is a Czuchish trait
     To reverence the rights of property.
     A good Czuch will sooner starve to death
     Than eat what lies upon another's dish.
     But there are in Yahoo a baser sort
     That sucks with parasitic mouth the state's welfare
     And mumbles, "We are not to blame."
     "Give us to eat, there is no work." And we
     Throw them a crust, but spurn their claim to
          Czuchship.
     Let them be fed, at the abasing beggar's dish
     But those who claim that since they till the land,
     The land is theirs, and seize the landlord's property,
     Because they say they need it—such thieves, I say,
     We'll scatter and destroy, for such as they
     Divide our land, against all natural laws,
     Into two camps, with greedy aims in view

Which only greed engender. We must crush
The last of these foul rebels, nothing trust
Till every Sickle flag is trodden in the dust.

At this moment the lights go on in the chandelier.

VOICE FROM BEHIND: The town of Mirasonnore has been
 retaken. The power station is in the hands of the
 government! Long live Iberin!
IBERIN: Ah, light at last! (*To* CALLAS, *holding the micro-
 phone to his mouth.*)
And you, peasants, go home and plough the land.
Leave state affairs to men
Who see things as a whole. If you are poor
It is because your work is insufficient.
Industry we need and not complaints.
The fields need laborers.
Go, give your best and do not vainly yearn
And thus the honored name of peasant earn.

He turns away into the palace followed by MISSENA.
All leave except CALLAS *and* NANNA.

*Illuminated bulletin: "Sicklemen Routed. Tenants Are
Abandoning The Farms They Illegally Appropriated."*

CALLAS: Did you hear? The swine sentenced me to death!
NANNA: I didn't hear anything of the kind. He said you
 were to be deprived of the horses.
CALLAS: It's the same thing.

The bells continue ringing.

8

A STREET IN YAHOO

The bells are still ringing. The tobacconist is standing in the doorway of his shop. The door of the provision shop to the right opens and the FAT WOMAN comes out with boxes and portmanteaus.

FAT WOMAN: What are all the bells for, Mr. Palmosa?

PALMOSA: Bells of victory, Madame Tomaso. The Sickle League has, with God's help, been crushed. It's a great victory!

FAT WOMAN: I shall have to move, I can't pay rent.

PALMOSA: Couldn't you manage to hold out till the government projects begin?

FAT WOMAN: No. (*She sits down for a moment on her trunk.*) And I've lived here thirty-five years!

PALMOSA: I shall also probably have to move. Luckily my son, who is in the Czuchish Legion, will soon get a good salary.

FAT WOMAN: Mr. Iberin has greatly disappointed me. He looks so energetic.

PALMOSA: Give him time. Rome wasn't built in a day. You have to make your little sacrifice, Madame Tomaso, along with the others, in order that Yahoo may attain prosperity.

FAT WOMAN: The only good thing Iberin did was to get rid of the Czich who had the provision shop over there!

A man with a diffident manner and a large hat has come down the street. He opens the door of the provision shop to the left; it is the Czichish shopman.

244

(*Leaving with her boxes:*) It's beyond me!

Bells ring. The Czichish shopman comes out of the provision shop to the left again. He also has shut up his shop and had only come back to fetch his portmanteau. CALLAMASSI *comes down the street.*

CALLAMASSI: I've just come from the trial. Great news. Callas has been deprived of the horses.

PALMOSA: You don't say. And what about the landowner?

CALLAMASSI: There was nothing said about him.

PALMOSA: Do you think he will go free?

CALLAMASSI: Am I to understand that as a criticism of the government, Mr. Palmosa?

PALMOSA: Mr. Callamassi, my business is to sell cigars and not to criticize the government.

CALLAMASSI (*entering his office*): You had better be careful, Mr. Palmosa. The Deputy spoke very sharply against disaffected elements. Moreover, you haven't paid your rent yet.

PALMOSA *runs over to the café and rings until* MADAME CORNAMONTIS *comes out.*

PALMOSA (*regarding* MADAME CORNAMONTIS *with a strange look*): Madame Cornamontis, Callas has been deprived of his horses.

MADAME CORNAMONTIS: Then I can expect a visitor soon. (*Goes in again.*)

PALMOSA (*goes back into his shop*): Well, well, times change.

CALLAS *comes down the street with his daughter who is carrying a portmanteau.*

NANNA: Now we're back here where we were before. Here is the house. This is where people asked, how is it a Czuchish girl ever came into such a house? "It is unworthy of a Czuch!" they cried, but as one cannot eat fine words, I must be thankful if they'll take me back again.

CALLAS: They will be very pleased to see you.

NANNA: I don't know.

CALLAS: Luckily none of these Iberin people can see us. If they did they would lock me up for not behaving like a national hero. (*They ring.*) Why does nobody open?

NANNA: Perhaps it has been closed for good by the police.

CALLAS: This is a nice how-d'-ye-do. I'll have to feed you all through the winter.

MADAME CORNAMONTIS (*appearing at the door*): Ah! Nanna, it's you.

NANNA: Good day, Madame Cornamontis.

CALLAS: Good day, Madame Cornamontis.

NANNA: Madame Cornamontis, the hopes which my father had with regard to his future have not materialized. I could have told him they wouldn't from the beginning, but a sensational trial in which we both figured—I'm sure you remember it—gave him exaggerated hopes. My father wishes to ask you whether you will take me back.

MADAME CORNAMONTIS: I don't know whether I ought to.

NANNA: Strange are the ways of the world, Madame Cornamontis. Two days ago people were carrying me out of the courthouse on their shoulders, and incidentally tore a pair of new silk stockings. But I can count myself lucky as that kind of thing generally turns out worse. All the small folk who were outdoors shouting yesterday and today will soon wake up out of their happy dream. Earning eight pesos and kicking up an eighty peso row can't go on forever.

MADAME CORNAMONTIS: All that is in God's hands. (*Inspects* NANNA *critically.*) To think that you only left my establishment a couple of days ago, and have already become so run down. I shall have to start your education all over again from the very begin-

ning! What was the good of spending so much money
on you when in two days all your make-up is ruined.
Your stocking is hanging down. And what have you
been eating all this time? Your complexion is ruined!
And that new smile of yours. You'll have to do more
than wash that off! This girl had a smile like a Venus
and now she just grins! And those disgusting hip
movements, like a common woman of the streets. I
shall have to think it over before taking you back.
The only thing in your favor is that gentlemen prefer
girls who only yesterday seemed to be unattainable.
Well, perhaps I'll try you again. (*She goes inside.*)

CALLAS: Now, dearest Nanna, the hour of parting has
again arrived. I'm glad to have met you again and to
have satisfied myself that you are not in such a bad
way, at all events not in such a bad way as your poor
parents! If you could send us anything small in the
way of a present from time to time, we should be
very glad of it. I and your dear mother have always
done all we could to help toward your advancement.
Don't forget that.

NANNA: Good-by, father. We've had a good time, anyway,
for a few days. Now, you go straight home and try
to keep out of trouble. (*She goes inside.*)

PALMOSA (*comes out of his shop, where he has been
listening*): You're not Horseman Callas, are you?

CALLAS: Yes, that's what they called me, Horseman Callas.
But the horses were a dream. The Sickle League was
winning then . . . but now. . . .

PALMOSA: Were you successful at least in having your rent
written off?

CALLAS (*suddenly remembering*): The rent? Of course!
We forgot all about it in the horse business. I must
find out about the rent.

PALMOSA: Where will you go?

CALLAS: Yes, where?

PALMOSA: Why don't you go straight to Mr. Iberin?

CALLAS: To Iberin? Never again. But I'll clear the matter up all the same. (*He leaves on the run.*)

PALMOSA: Where are you off to? (*He goes back into his shop, shaking his head.*)

ISABELLA DE GUZMAN, *the* MOTHER SUPERIOR *of San Barabas and the* LAWYERS *pass on their way from the trial.*

MOTHER SUPERIOR: I think the worst is over. Mr. Peruiner has sent a secret greeting to your brother, and Mr. Saz told me when our troops come to the capital they'll have a surprise in store for Mr. Iberin. You should have heard Saz laugh.

CZUCHISH LAWYER: Yes, all is well.

The POLICE INSPECTOR *and a* HUA *come down the street with* EMANUELE DE GUZMAN *in chains. De Guzman has a huge placard hung from his shoulders, reading, "I am a Czich, I have dishonored a Czuchish girl for which I rightly go to the gallows."*

ISABELLA: What's that?

CZUCHISH LAWYER: Mr. De Guzman, I congratulate you. All is now well.

MOTHER SUPERIOR: We got back our horses.

CZUCHISH LAWYER: The property is saved.

DE GUZMAN: And I?

CZUCHISH LAWYER: That question we shall now consider. It wasn't mentioned at the trial.

ISABELLA: Emanuele, why do you not speak? So pale and so bowed down with chains? This placard, what means it?

MOTHER SUPERIOR: A mere form. Don't let it disturb you.

ISABELLA: Speak, brother, where are you being led?

DE GUZMAN: Dearest sister, I am lost. I'm headed for the prison of the Holy Cross.

ISABELLA: No!

CZUCHISH LAWYER: Is it true?

POLICE INSPECTOR: That's bad. No prisoner has ever left the Holy Cross alive.

DE GUZMAN: Oh God! I'll go no further, not a step further. (*He sits down on the ground.*)

ISABELLA: It's true then, Good Mother. All the time a fear lurked in my mind. And now I know it. In all this business of the horses, we forgot my brother. We saved the horses for him but he is lost to us.

DE GUZMAN: Yes, they'll hang me.

CZUCHISH LAWYER: Nonsense. After our victory!

MOTHER SUPERIOR: Listen to the bells. Victory!

ISABELLA: I'm frightened. I remember now. A man came up to me and told me quietly my brother should be kept in mind. The law, he said, was apt to run its course mechanically. He offered help. He frightened me.

CZUCHISH LAWYER: What sort of man?

ISABELLA: Big and brutal. He made me shudder.

CZUCHISH LAWYER: That must be Zazarante, Iberin's right hand man.

POLICE INSPECTOR: Prison Governor of the Holy Cross!

CZUCHISH LAWYER: Did he want to make an appointment —any specific time and place?

ISABELLA: Yes, five in the morning. (*Pause.*)

DE GUZMAN: Sister, save me!

ISABELLA: Oh, Emanuele . . .

DE GUZMAN: You take his fancy. It's' a rendezvous. Five A.M. Men don't discuss public affairs at five A.M. I know that kind of appointment. Sister, you must go.

ISABELLA: Brother!

DE GUZMAN: Do not refuse me.

MOTHER SUPERIOR: This is too absurd, landlords are not hung. You are a landlord, friend.

DE GUZMAN: No, I'm a Czich.

CZICHISH LAWYER: Of course it was a bargain, an attempt

to force the maid to yield to him. But that was when
The Sickle was on top. Then it might have been
forced on us, but now, with the Sickle down, we can
find other ways out.

ISABELLA: What does this mean?

MOTHER SUPERIOR: Yesterday, my child, you would have
had to go. Today you need not.

DE GUZMAN: Oh, yes, you must. Sister, do it for me. I'm
a Czich, there's no remedy for that.

ISABELLA: Yes, we're Czichs, look at his head, it's peaked.
Can we shake off our peaked heads?

DE GUZMAN: She doesn't understand.

ISABELLA: I understand.

DE GUZMAN: That I must hang?

ISABELLA: Oh! They want to hang him.

DE GUZMAN: And now, as quickly as possible. Now that
we know the abyss we're in, and must stand loss,
we must decide how to yield least to save the most.
Life must be saved—and anything is less than life.
Sister, save me.

ISABELLA (*looks at her brother, horrified*): Brother,
what's come over you? The man who spoke to me
was a beast.

DE GUZMAN: What was I to the tenant's daughter? A beast
maybe, too. Of course it's not easy. Do you think
it was easy for the tenant's daughter? Look at my
paunch! And she was young like you.

ISABELLA: You asked her?

DU GUZMAN: Of course I asked her.

ISABELLA: I should have refused.

DE GUZMAN: That may be. I asked; and this man has
asked. It's up to you to make your choice. If I am
hanged, you'll get no rents. Then you can take your
chastity to market.

ISABELLA: Ask me anything else, my brother!

DE GUZMAN: This is no time to play the saint. They want

to hang me. Neither for the whore nor for a virgin
do I care to die.

ISABELLA: Oh brother, it's your dreadful plight that makes
you wicked. (*She runs away.*)

DE GUZMAN (*shouts after her*): No one would blame you,
sister.

CZUCHISH LAWYER: She'll never do it.

MOTHER SUPERIOR: I'll follow her. (*Exit.*)

CZUCHISH LAWYER: I must have a word with Peruiner.
Tomorrow morning, early, every landlord must be
called to the execution grounds. De Guzman, you're
a landlord. (*Exit.*)

HUA (*who has been sitting on the iron ball to which De
Guzman's foot is chained, stands up*): Stand up. Who
won this victory, anyway? As soon as it was announced, they cut our pay.

POLICE INSPECTOR: We must be moving, Mr. De Guzman.

DE GUZMAN (*gets up*): I'm lost.

CZUCHISH LAWYER (*to the POLICE INSPECTOR*): He's a bit
nervous. (*Exeunt.*)

PALMOSA (*who has again been listening, runs to the café
and rings until MADAME CORNAMONTIS and NANNA
come out*): Miss Callas, you've missed something.
De Guzman has just passed on his way to the Holy
Cross. You will at least have the satisfaction of knowing that he'll hang.

NANNA: Will he?

PALMOSA: You don't seem to be particularly pleased over
it.

NANNA: The fact is, Mr. Palmosa, I have seen Mr. Iberin
at work. Yesterday, the regent was sentencing us;
and today the deputy sentences us. Today it is the
Mother Superior of San Barabas who gets the horses.
Who knows, tomorrow it may be De Guzman? (*She
sings the "Ballad of the Mill Wheel."*)

BALLAD OF THE MILL WHEEL

Many great ones through the ages
Have attained to earthly power.
Yet they all but had their hour,
Sad it is when fate has failed to speed them.
But for us whose job it is to feed them,
Whether this one's high and that one low,
The loads, on our shoulders, always go.
    Still the mill wheel turns, it turns forever,
    Though what is uppermost remains not so.
    The water underneath in vain endeavor
    Does the work but always stays below.

Many are the different masters
Who've ruled us in their day.
Eagles, Tigers and Hyenas,
Even Swine have had their say.
Which of them was better than the other?
Every boot's the copy of its brother.
And each boot trod us well, d'you catch what's here
    intended?
We do not seek new masters, we want all mastery
    ended.
    Still the mill wheel turns and turns forever.
    What is uppermost remains not so.
    While the water underneath in vain endeavor
    Does the work but always stays below.

And they beat their heads till they are bloody,
Scrambling after booty.
Each calls the other rascal,
And himself the slave of duty.
The time has come, away to speed them.
Each in lasting conflict with his brother.
Only our resolve that we'll not feed them,
Brings them to peace with one another.

Still the mill wheel turns and turns forever.
What is uppermost remains not so.
While the water underneath in vain endeavor
Does the work but always stays below.*

* Another version of this song is to be found in Brecht's
Selected Poems (Evergreen Books), pp. 88-91.—E.B.

9

MADAME CORNAMONTIS' CAFE

ISABELLA *at the door*.

ISABELLA: Now that I know they'll hang my brother, I
realize what I must sacrifice for him. But first I want
the advice of those who know something about these
things. I must know if I should be proud during
the ordeal, or pleading. I must know what clothes to
wear, and whether I should come a little late. Should
I pretend that I've come willingly, make him believe
he's caught my fancy too, or be sad, and act like
one submitting to a hard fate. If I acted willing—
as if he were the man of my dreams—that would be
a way of keeping it from being a mere base transaction. Or, perhaps, it might be more in keeping
with my dignity never to let him forget that innocence is being violated, and be cold and passive, re-
maining, even in his arms, remote and unattainable.
Also I must know what such men think of the girl
yielding, whether they blame her or not. Maybe a
girl need do so little that even resistance might be
mistaken for something else. Also, practiced girls
don't become pregnant. I must know what they do.
There's certainly a lot to learn about these things.
(*She knocks.*)
NANNA (*opens*): You! What do *you* want here?
ISABELLA: Good day, Nanna, you must know me. We used
to play together at my father's farm.
NANNA: Yes, and what can I do for you?
ISABELLA: I hope I'm not intruding. Are you busy?
NANNA: No. It's all right.

ISABELLA: I must have your advice. My brother's execution has been fixed for five o'clock tomorrow morning. There's a possibility of saving him, but at a certain sacrifice. I'm put in a terrible situation, and I don't know what to do. In what is before me, I have no experience. Oh, I feel faint—

NANNA: Sit down. Take it easy.

ISABELLA (*sits down*): May I have a glass of water.

NANNA *fetches a glass of water.*

A proposal has been made to me by the Governor of the Holy Cross. He wants me—well, you can guess what he wants. I don't know what to do.

NANNA: I see.

ISABELLA: I know nothing about lovemaking.

NANNA: I can well believe it.

ISABELLA: Please don't think me cynical. What I'm going to ask you, I ask because I am compelled to do so, and I turn to you because you can advise me from your professional experience.

NANNA: Certainly. Fire away. Only you'll have to pay my manager for the time you use up.

ISABELLA: Very good, I shall be glad to pay for your time.

NANNA: I can imagine what you want to know. I'd advise you to consult Madame Cornamontis; she's a woman who's had lots of experience.

ISABELLA: Can she be trusted to keep a secret?

NANNA: Absolutely, that's her business.

ISABELLA: Please call her then.

NANNA *fetches* MADAME CORNAMONTIS.

NANNA (*whispers to* MADAME CORNAMONTIS, *then in a loud aside*): Fleece her well, she has money. (*They both come up to* ISABELLA.)

MADAME CORNAMONTIS: Do not tell me your name but question me as frankly as though I were your father confessor, my child.

ISABELLA: This is the situation. My brother's life depends on my giving myself to a certain highly placed gentleman who appears to have taken a fancy to me. I do not know how to conduct myself, since, I suppose, nothing like this has happened before.

MADAME CORNAMONTIS: Oh, no. It happens quite often.

ISABELLA: Really?

MADAME CORNAMONTIS: Yes. And what are your questions, child?

ISABELLA: If he was disappointed with me, might he not refuse to keep his part of the bargain?

NANNA: He might.

ISABELLA: How can one guard against it?

MADAME CORNAMONTIS: Men break their promises, and there is no remedy against it. They deceive us, they beat us. If they did not need us for the same uses later, they'd kill us after they'd had their pleasure.

ISABELLA: Since so much depends on it, I must ask you whether you don't consider the dress I have on unsuitable.

MADAME CORNAMONTIS: Most suitable, my child.

ISABELLA: It is the dress of a novitiate.

MADAME CORNAMONTIS: All the better.

ISABELLA: Do you really mean it? It's cold linen.

MADAME CORNAMONTIS: Linen above all. Nothing could be better.

ISABELLA: And I have a nature as cold as the linen I wear.

MADAME CORNAMONTIS: Perfect. The colder the better.

ISABELLA: And do you think I'll be awkward during . . . You know what I mean.

MADAME CORNAMONTIS: Not at all.

ISABELLA: But I know less about these things than, I think, you realize.

MADAME CORNAMONTIS: There's less to know than you imagine, my child. That's the sad thing about it. It's our tragedy, as professionals, that the more practice the less zest we can take—and give. Don't you worry.

You will be enjoyed, all right. For these furtive enjoyments, practically anyone will do.

ISABELLA: So there's no reason why, so to speak, I should not drink this cup to the dregs?

MADAME CORNAMONTIS: None. (*Pause.*) Oh yes, there is, though.

ISABELLA: What is it? Please tell me.

MADAME CORNAMONTIS: Your money, my dear. That is a very good reason. Why should you, in your position, make such a sacrifice? Why do anything for which you have no inclination? It would be unseemly for you, for whom other much less sensitive people earn money in the sweat of their brows, to do anything to lower yourself in these people's eyes! I think it would be most unseemly. What would you say if one day the rain started falling from the ground to the sky? Wouldn't you consider it unnatural? You would certainly think it unseemly. No, you should certainly not do what you have in mind.

ISABELLA: But a certain highly placed person requires it of me.

MADAME CORNAMONTIS: And quite rightly, my child, one can't say anything against that. Why shouldn't he require it of you if he is highly placed? And why should he not be given what he requires? But what has that got to do with you who are also highly placed and have means to arrange the whole business entirely *comme il faut*.

ISABELLA: What have you in mind?

MADAME CORNAMONTIS: I have ourselves in mind, of course. In how much better position are we, debased as we are, to endure debasement? Look at this lazy creature here, starting to blink because work for her is in question. Nanna, leave us for a moment and wait outside.

NANNA *leaves the room.*

The best of my girls will go for you.

ISABELLA: Impossible. You don't know who he is.

MADAME CORNAMONTIS: Whoever he is, he won't notice.

ISABELLA: It is the Governor of the Holy Cross.

MADAME CORNAMONTIS: That's of no account. She will
go in your clothes and will imitate your manner. But
she will be more successful than you could be. Your
brother will be set free and the rain will not fall from
the earth to the sky. But it will cost you a thousand
pesos.

ISABELLA: But will she consent to go for money?

MADAME CORNAMONTIS: Delighted, my dear. (*Calls.*)
Nanna. (*To* ISABELLA:) You need not mention the
cost to the girl.

Enter NANNA.

Nanna, change clothes with the young lady, will you?
You'll take her place with the governor.

NANNA: And what will I get for it?

MADAME CORNAMONTIS: You shameless hussy. You'll be
paid regular rates. Now change clothes.

The girls start changing their clothes.

ISABELLA: Please let me have a screen.

NANNA: It's all right, I'm not looking.

ISABELLA: Just the same, I would like a screen.

NANNA *brings her a screen.*

MADAME CORNAMONTIS: Now, Nanna, you are in her
clothes, but look to your deportment. Let's rehearse
it. I'll take the part of the big shot. Good morning.
What can I do for you, mademoiselle? . . . Answer!

NANNA: I have come again, sir, to ask you to do something
for my brother.

MADAME CORNAMONTIS: To beseech you!

NANNA: To beseech you!

MADAME CORNAMONTIS (*to* ISABELLA): Is that what you would say?

ISABELLA: I wouldn't say anything.

MADAME CORNAMONTIS: You'd keep mum and let him guess? That's a good plan.

NANNA: I wouldn't know how to carry off anything like that. I don't like this business at all.

MADAME CORNAMONTIS: Hold your tongue. He'll probably ask you your reasons for joining the Needy Sisters of San Barabas. How would you answer?

NANNA: I have money. If I do not deposit it in the safe-keeping of the convent, it will be taken from me. I have a peakhead, you see. A marriage wouldn't help me. It would do me no good marrying a Peakhead; he couldn't offer me security these days; and a Round-head wouldn't have me legally. I shall be quite well off at the convent. No work—good food, freedom from worry. . . .

MADAME CORNAMONTIS (*to* ISABELLA): Is that right?

ISABELLA: Those are not my reasons. But why should she necessarily say what I would? I would rather not give my reasons.

MADAME CORNAMONTIS: But *she* will have to give them. If we don't prompt her she will speak like a scullery-maid without any refinement. Tell her what to say.

The landlord's sister instructs the tenant's daughter in the three principal virtues: temperance, obedience, and poverty.

ISABELLA (*softly*):
Ah, but I wished my childhood ne'er would leave me,
Wished that my days were free, my nights unmolested.
To live in a chamber alone, safe from men's glances,
Safe from the vice of the world was all I requested
So that for me there should be one alone
Whom I could trust and as my lover own.

MADAME CORNAMONTIS (*Weeps*): There's refinement for
you, you farm hussy!

NANNA (*saucily*): Sure, her childhood's never left her—

MADAME CORNAMONTIS: We don't need your remarks.
Remember the sort of person you're supposed to be.

NANNA: I'll remember.

MADAME CORNAMONTIS (*to* ISABELLA): Please go on, it's a
real lesson to me.

ISABELLA:

Of all the virtues, brightest and best is obedience.
How can I know what is good for me? One
     consolation
Stays with me always, the Lord will provide for his
     children
And so I bow down to his will in self-abnegation
Knowing He will love his little maid
And will forgive her if her feet have strayed.

MADAME CORNAMONTIS (*to* NANNA): Now repeat it and do
try to say it like a lady.

NANNA *repeats Isabella's words.*

ISABELLA:

But chief of the things that are needful is poverty holy
And I shall find it neither affliction nor burden.
Therefore demand of Thy handmaid the hardest
     ordeal—
The rapture of doing Thy will shall be my guerdon—
That and the riches that the Lord will give
To those who choose in poverty to live.

NANNA *repeats Isabella's words.*

MADAME CORNAMONTIS: Goodness me, we have forgotten
the most important thing of all! She is a Czuch, she
has a round head, and, as it happens, the higherups
somehow have a weakness for Czich girls. The figure,
the carriage, is the same, but the head is different. He'll

pat her on the head and then everything will be done for.

NANNA: Give me a hair pad and my head will get by. Anyway, I don't think that's what interests him.

NANNA *is given a coiffure that gives her head the same shape as Isabella's.*

MADAME CORNAMONTIS: Well, Nanna, you're like her in appearance, try to behave like her. Forget everything you know. Act as though nothing was required of you beyond your mere presence. Imagine, if you can, how a wooden board would offer to be embraced. Don't respond at all, but pretend you are responding too much. The man won't have any fun, but he'll feel under an obligation to you. Now go upstairs and wash your hands again and you'll find my lavender water on the dressing table. No, that's not necessary. It's more genteel not to smell of anything.

NANNA *goes upstairs.*

(*To* ISABELLA:) Meanwhile you wait here until Nanna comes back, then you can return in your own clothes.

MADAME CORNAMONTIS *goes out and sits down behind the bar.* MISTRESS CALLAS *comes in with her four small children.*

MISTRESS CALLAS: Ah, Madame Cornamontis, when we heard you had new times here, my husband came into town in order to get his bit. We've heard our landlord has been sentenced to death for rack-renting. Yesterday our cow was taken away, as we hadn't paid our taxes, and my husband is still away. We've searched for him everywhere, and my children can go no further and are starving, but I have no money to buy food for them. Formerly Nanna used to help us when we were in a bad way, but we hear now that she has bettered her position, and is not with you any longer. Of course our daughter could not have stayed with you forever, Madame Cornamontis, but all the same you might know where she is.

MADAME CORNAMONTIS: Oh, Nanna is back with us again, though she can't be seen right now. I can let you have some soup.

MADAME CORNAMONTIS *brings the soup and the family takes it sitting on the doorstep.* NANNA *comes in in her nun's clothes and makes her way through the family.*

MISTRESS CALLAS: You are the landlord's daughter, aren't you? Children, say your little rhyme.

CHILDREN:
Mr. De Guzman, we've been sent
To ask you to let us off our rent.

NANNA (*aside, under her veil*):
My latest job is to be guardian of propriety
And keep sustained a pillar of society.
A Czuch must save a Czich's repute,
A nun's kept pure by a prostitute.

10

PRISON

In one condemned cell, TENANTS *are sitting, among them* LOPEZ. *They are having their hair cropped by* HUAS. *In the other condemned cell, landlord* DE GUZMAN *is sitting. Outside gallows are being erected.*

HUA (*to the* TENANT *whom he is cropping*): Was it worthwhile joining this Sickle League?

TENANT: Yes.

HUA: Who'll help your wives through the winter now?

TENANT: We don't know.

HUA: And who will plough your fields in the spring?

TENANT: We don't know.

HUA: Will your farms be there at all in the spring?

TENANT: We don't know that either.

HUA: But you think the Sickle will win in the end, do you?

TENANT: Yes, we know it.

POLICE INSPECTOR (*approaches* DE GUZMAN *with a measuring tape, and measures his neck*): This case really deserves our sympathy. They say that there are large numbers of tenants in town who are only waiting for the landlord to be hung. Then on the first of the month they will all refuse to pay their rent together. What do they want to hang him for! Neck—16—that means the height of the fall must be eight feet. If I'm not mistaken, there'll be an uproar again this time. I remember the row they kicked up when Cobzoni was hung last year and the trap door was out of order. They didn't make as much fuss when it was discovered that he was perfectly innocent.

The two LAWYERS *enter.*

CZUCHISH LAWYER: The condemned man's sister could save his life. Where did she go?

POLICE INSPECTOR: Probably she's the veiled lady who just went into the governor's office.

The LAWYERS *breathe more freely.*

CZICHISH LAWYER (*to* DE GUZMAN *who has heard nothing owing to his perturbed state of mind*): Good news, De Guzman. Your sister is with the governor.

CZUCHISH LAWYER: One can count on not being disturbed, for an hour or so, by Zazarante.

POLICE INSPECTOR: All the same, we had better go on with the barbering.

The HUA *crops the landlord.*

CZUCHISH LAWYER (*to the other*): We are not out of the soup yet, by any means. And to think that this should happen to one of the biggest landowners in the country. Now what will the poor tenants do if their landlord is hanged?

DE GUZMAN: Yes, what's to be done about this hanging?

LAWYERS:
It is something far too urgent to neglect.
And though we have good reason to expect
That some brave member of the lower orders
Will be found to bear the burden even here
This time circumstance has overawed us
And we really wish the proxy would appear.

Through an iron-barred opening in the wall at the back, tenant CALLAS *appears.*

CALLAS (*beckoning*): Mr. De Guzman, Mr. De Guzman, I'm your tenant Callas. I want to know about the rent.

CZUCHISH LAWYER: The rent's to be paid to the Convent of San Barabas.

CALLAS: I didn't ask you. Mr. De Guzman, you *must* let me off paying rent.

CZICHISH LAWYER: Come in here, we'll see what we can do for you, we're human beings after all.

CALLAS disappears from the window.

I believe we've found the proxy.

Enter CALLAS.

CALLAS (*to the audience*):
When I left my piece of land
My expectations were not grand.
I thought of rent I'd now be free
And I'd plough for my family.
But after entering the town
I soon achieved renown.
All the bells began to ring
As though I were a kind of king.
And those who harmed such men as I
They said would be condemned to die,
And so the frog leapt from his pool
And sat upon a golden stool.
Although 'twas pleasant,
I remained a peasant.
There is no joy sitting in a famous seat
For those who have no bread to eat.
Since they've evaded my suggestion,
It is the landlord I must question.
Good news or bad news, I'll know what's his intent,
Am I exempted or must I pay the rent?

In passing by he sees his former friend LOPEZ in a condemned cell.

CALLAS (*shouting at LOPEZ who looks at him without saying anything*): Hold your tongue. (*In front of DE GUZMAN's cage.*) Mr. De Guzman, if you don't let me off my rent, I'll hang myself, things have got to that pitch.

LOPEZ: And yet there was a time, Callas, when you held everything in your hands.

CALLAS (*shouts at him*): Hold your tongue.

CZUCHISH LAWYER: Mr. Callas, we have a proposal to make to you! (*Brings a chair for* CALLAS.)

CZICHISH LAWYER: You are very fortunate. Mr. De Guzman has his reprieve as good as in his pocket, though the prison authorities do not know about it yet. He is to be reprieved under the very gallows owing to the return of an important personage who is expected any moment. The only thing we are afraid of is his going to the gallows in the state he is in at the moment. He is too nervous for our liking. Would you take his place in return for being exempted from your rent for one year? There is no danger at all, practically no danger.

CALLAS: You mean I'm to hang for him?

CZICHISH LAWYER: Nonsense, no one would ask you to do that.

CZUCHISH LAWYER: Decide yourself. You are completely free. There is no slavery in Yahoo. You're not under any compulsion. But you must realize what the offer means and whether you can afford to turn up your nose at a year's rent.

CZICHISH LAWYER: Just now you said you'd hang yourself.

CZUCHISH LAWYER: You understand the situation. A rich man is not fitted, constitutionally, to go through such an experience. He has become softened by comfortable living and it tells on such occasions as this. Between you and me, he is a regular old woman. Now you farmer folk are different stuff. You would take it like a man. (*He beckons to the Iberin soldier who has just finished cropping the heads of the condemned tenants.*) Hello there, come and crop this man too. Zazarante has ordered it.

CALLAS: But they'll hang me.

CZICHISH LAWYER: You can think it over, but in the meanwhile you had better have your hair cut, as otherwise it will be too late.

CALLAS: But I haven't said "yes."

Sitting on a chair beside the cage in which his landlord was cropped, tenant CALLAS is also cropped.

HUA (*who is cutting the Sicklemen's hair*): What are you going to do with your shoes?

TENANT: Why?

HUA: You see these boots? They were given to us but we have to pay to have them soled, that's why they're no good to me any more.

TENANT: You can have mine.

CALLAS (*after turning the matter over in his mind, tremulously*): At least two years' rent. After all I risk my head.

CZICHISH LAWYER: Mr. De Guzman, your tenant Callas is willing to take your place, but you must meet him half-way about the rent.

HUA (*who is cutting Callas' hair*): Oh, Callas, Callas, don't bargain like a Czich.

CZICHISH LAWYER: He says the rent is too high.

DE GUZMAN (*overhears*): What about the rent?

CALLAS: It's too high. We have no chance of making a living.

DE GUZMAN: And how do you think I am to live? Don't be so lazy, there's no reason why you should beg.

CALLAS: If I am lazy, how about you?

DE GUZMAN: If you're going to be insolent, the whole matter is closed.

CALLAS: I am not insolent. I am in trouble. I can't pay the rent.

DE GUZMAN: The farm is a very good one. I wonder you aren't ashamed of yourself—always complaining, always asking for gifts.

CALLAS: I am not asking for any gifts, but I don't want to give anything away either.

DE GUZMAN: You can go if you wish. You are entirely at liberty.

CALLAS: Yes, I can go away, but where to?

DE GUZMAN: Enough. I shall keep what belongs to me.

CALLAS: Is that your last word? (*To the* HUA): Stop cutting my hair, please.

CZUCHISH LAWYER: Mr. De Guzman is quite sure that there is no risk, or practically no risk.

CZICHISH LAWYER (*to* DE GUZMAN): You must really make a small concession. After all, you're not absolutely certain and a year's rent is not too much under the circumstances.

CALLAS: Two years', since my head is at stake.

DE GUZMAN: Your head? (*As though waking up.*) What is it you want?

CZUCHISH LAWYER: Mr. Callas is taking your place since, as we have tried to impress upon you, there is no danger. Isn't that so?

DE GUZMAN: So you tell me.

CALLAS: And I want to be freed from rent for *two* years. I may have to swing for it.

CZUCHISH LAWYER: One year.

CALLAS (*to the* HUA): Stop cutting my hair.

POLICE INSPECTOR (*calls from behind*): Ready, please! The governor wishes to see the prisoners before they are brought out.

CZUCHISH LAWYER: Very good, a year and a half, Callas! (CALLAS *is silent.*)

DE GUZMAN: Two years.

CALLAS: But I haven't said I would—yet.

Meanwhile the two tenants of the Sickle League have been brought out.

CZUCHISH LAWYER (*to* CALLAS): Say yes, my good man, there is no other course open to you.

CALLAS:
> Czuch or Czich! Unjust or just
> The poor man must die because his master says
>   he must.

CZICHISH LAWYER (*whispering to the other*): It's to be hoped the regent will arrive in time—otherwise he will hang.

CZUCHISH LAWYER (*answering in a whisper*): Yes, he has every cause now to pray God to save his landlord.

11

THE REGENT'S PALACE

It is early morning. Gallows have been erected. In the court there is a board on which is written, EXECUTION OF ONE LANDLORD AND 200 TENANTS. Between the POLICE INSPECTOR *and a* HUA, *a man is standing with a cap over his face. They are waiting. The sound of the pattering of many clogs can be heard.*

POLICE INSPECTOR (*to the* HUA): I can't think why the execution order has not arrived yet. The Sicklemen will soon be here.

HUA: How do you know they are Sicklemen? If you are judging from the sound of the clogs, plenty of us Iberin soldiers are wearing clogs now.

POLICE INSPECTOR: Hold your tongue. You'll be getting us into trouble. You'd much better fix up the gallows.

The HUA *goes sulkily behind to do what he is told.*

It all comes from hanging the person they want to see hanged! It makes them uppish. (*To the* HUA:) What are you taking so long about?

HUA (*returning*): Everything is ready, you can hang away now.

The Deputy enters the court followed by MISSENA *and Messrs.* SAZ, PERUINER, DE HOZ *and* DUARTE. *They can be heard shouting at some distance.*

SAZ: Where are your senses, man? This is a landlord and not a Czich. If you make him swing, people will say it's for rack-renting.

270

PERUINER: On every farm belonging to Czich landlords,
peasants will refuse to pay their rent. That will sound
good to the peasants of the Czuch landlords and they
too will stop paying rent.

IBERIN: Well?

DUARTE: And he answers, "Well?"

MISSENA: You must remember that the man condemned,
though certainly a Czich and one whose crime we
can't condone, is after all a landlord, a man like ourselves.

IBERIN: A man like ourselves?

MISSENA: Who lives on rent.

IBERIN: I do not live on rent.

SAZ: What do you live on then?

DUARTE:

    Who pays the court?
    Who gave the money for this gallows here?
    Who paid this man? (*indicating the* HUA)
    Who fitted out the army
    That crushed the Sicklemen?

PERUINER:

    The landlords, man, who gather in their rent. . . .
    But don't let's shout at him. It's not unnatural
    That he should be a little obstinate.
    He's spoken so much of Czich and Czuch,
    Too much, perhaps. Well, we don't complain.
    It served its purpose. We're not against you.
    You've done your job quite well and carried out
    Your promise to crush the rebel tenants.
    With profit, even, we might imitate
    The methods you have shown, and now I see
    Ahead all kinds of prospects, cunning plans,
    Oh, very cunning plans that might be launched
    Immediately.

IBERIN: What plans?

MISSENA (*warningly*): Hm.

PERUINER: All kinds of plans. But that must wait. Meanwhile we ask that you be reasonable and change your attitude.

MISSENA: If there are difficulties, tell us who could give the Czich reprieve.

IBERIN (*stubbornly*): Not I, anyway.

MISSENA: Who could? (*Pause.*) The regent could.

PERUINER: We'll put off the execution till he comes.

IBERIN: Till he comes. What do you mean?

MISSENA:
The Regent,
Our most beloved and exalted liege,
Has now resolved to take his place again
As ruler of our land.
No doubt to you this news will be most welcome.

IBERIN: He's coming back?

MISSENA:
This very night the army
Greeted him in camp and made him promise
To lead them into Yahoo
Today, in triumph.

IBERIN (*after a painful pause*):
Really?—
And I was not consulted.
I think I earned that much.

MISSENA: I ask you now.

IBERIN (*after a bitter inner conflict*):
And what if I myself
Were to agree to set the Czichman free?

MISSENA: You?

IBERIN: I do agree.

MISSENA:
That's rather sudden.
And what about your Czuch and Czichish theory?

IBERIN: That's my business and need not worry you. But as regards this entry into town, I'd like to have a word with you, especially as to who's to lead it.

Trumpets and marching soldiers are heard.

MISSENA (*smiling*): The army's here, already, and at its head . . .

The REGENT *enters, smiling, and very debonair, with a steel helmet and soldier's cloak over his dinner jacket. All bow down to him.*

MISSENA (*quietly to* IBERIN *who also bows*): Your sovereign!

REGENT: Hello, Iberin.

MISSENA: Milord, you're welcome. You could not have arrived more opportunely. We two were in a great predicament. Our Iberin, in following up a case which was to have shown clearly to the people the firm distinction between just and unjust, has got us in a fix.

REGENT: I know the case. Allow me, Iberin, to show you now the fishes that your net has caught. A wealthy man, who, having diddled a poor man's daughter, is doomed to die. The culprit is a Czich, I understand. This is the wealthy Czich.

POLICE INSPECTOR: Yes, Milord, this is the Czichish landlord.

REGENT: Are you sure he is? Why is he wearing clogs? (*He tries to lift the cap from the man's face but the man holds it tight.*)

MAN: Let me be.

The POLICE INSPECTOR *pulls the cap from his face.*

MISSENA: It is the Czuchish tenant.

REGENT: What are you doing here?

CALLAS: I was promised exemption from two years' rent if I would do this. I was told that the landlord would never be hung.

REGENT: They deceived you, my friend. Fetch the other.

Exit POLICE INSPECTOR.

IBERIN (*to* CALLAS:) What, for a few pesos you risked hanging? You menial!

CALLAS: No, for two years' rent.

REGENT: Mr. Iberin, once in the past the daughter of this man yielded to this Czichish landlord whom you condemned to death. You did not know, but I shall tell you, to please your sense of righteousness. A Czichish maid, just like the Czuchish maid, has come to her brother's rescue, making the same sacrifice, yielding her virginity to aid her kin. A second fish caught in your net—the Czichish girl, sister to the landlord. She now approaches.

NANNA *is brought in wearing Isabella's clothes. The clothes are torn and she walks unsteadily, but she is still wearing her veil.*

What has happened to her?

POLICE INSPECTOR: Milord, we found her lying in the passage, gagged, and when we questioned her she said the soldiers had molested her as she left the governor.

REGENT: Is that true? (NANNA *nods.*)

RICH LANDOWNERS: How horrible! How shameful! Iberin, you'll pay for this. A woman whose blood is of the noblest in the land, so insolently used. A maid so famed for chastity abandoned to the mob!

REGENT: Things would be bad if they were as they seemed. But, I suspect, a happy chance again has averted misfortune. Of course it can't have been a nice experience even for this maid who is standing here, but if my suspicions do not trick me, it is not rare in her profession. And now we'll test my surmise. (*He lifts up her veil.*)

MISSENA: The tenant's daughter!

RICH LANDLORDS: Ho, a Czuchish maid. (*They burst out laughing.*) That's a good joke you've put upon us,

Iberin! This is the crowd you boosted all this time.
Honor indeed! She's dragged it in the mud. There's
Czuchish virtue if you like! Now own up, she's just a
tenant's daughter, nothing more, and Czuch or Czich
is quite beside the point. Hey, tenant, here's your
daughter.

REGENT: Enough now! It's his daughter and everything's
in order.

DE GUZMAN *is brought with his sister beside him.*

And here come the true-blue Czichs. De Guzman,
you are free because your tenant didn't want you to
be hanged. He himself was ready to pay your penalty.
Also the tenant's daughter was so unwilling to have
you die, she endured defilement to save your head. I
liberate you as one beloved of the people. Likewise
I set the tenant free so that he may pay his rent. Yes,
Callas, rent you must pay to set a good example! Also
the costs of the lawsuit over the horses. Release them.
The selfsame justice must be meted out, liberty for
both, and life! (*To* IBERIN:) Do you agree? (IBERIN
nods. *The fetters are removed from landlord and
tenant.*)

ISABELLA: Emanuele, are you really free!

DE GUZMAN: Of course I am, dear.

CALLAS: And I must pay the rent?

REGENT: You must, my friend. The contract you made
with De Guzman is contrary to public order. Therefore it is null and void.

NANNA:
Although both live, one shall sit down to eat,
The other slave to furnish him with meat.
And if one's free to choose his own abode,
The other's free to put him on the road.
You'd see the difference in their liberation,
If you but knew their different destination.

REGENT:

Yes, peasant, one small thing I had forgotten.
I know you are not wealthy. Listen here.
I've now come home but not with empty hands.
I see, friend, that your hat's a little ancient
And so I recommend the latest style,

Places his steel helmet on his head.

I also offer you this soldier's cloak.
What do you think of it? For the present,
Go plough your fields, but soon,
We shall be calling you to higher tasks.
You've taken the first step, Mr. Iberin,
But now some longer strides are needed.
This new state you have built these last few weeks,
Unless it can expand, will shrink to nothing.
As you are well aware, across the sea,
There dwells the nation we were born to hate,
The heads of whose inhabitants are peaked,
A fact which hitherto has been ignored.
Now you must teach your Callases new tasks
For such a bloody war we'll have to launch
That every single able-bodied man
Will be required. And now to dinner, friends.
I think we'll take this judge's bench, on which
Justice has so often been administered,
And let it serve us as a dinner table.
Tenant, wait awhile, we'll give you soup.

CALLAS: Nanna, did you hear, they're going to make war?

The dinner is served, and the REGENT, MISSENA, *and
the rich landlords sit down to it.*

REGENT (*serving the soup with a huge ladle*): First comes
the tenant, is that right, Iberin? He is a soldier, we
must feed him now. More plates, please, we're getting hungry.

POLICE INSPECTOR: Milord, you will excuse me, but the

condemned Sicklemen are waiting to be hanged. Or
are they also to be set free?

REGENT: Of course not.

POLICE INSPECTOR: I thought perhaps the general amnesty
in honor of your return was to be extended to them.

REGENT: Has not Iberin passed judgment on them? They
must die, but our Callas here shall be given soup.
Bring him his soup.

The HUA *brings* CALLAS *and his daughter their soup,
which they drink sitting on the floor. The* HUA *goes
up to the blackboard on which is written: "Execution
of One Landlord and 200 Tenants" and rubs out the
word "One Landlord and" with his sleeve. He then
takes up his position behind* CALLAS.

HUA:

Eat your soup, Callas, it doesn't need stirring.
You were always far cuter than these lads, preferring
To follow the wiser course and that's the reason why
You're having your supper while they go to die.

*The Sicklemen are brought under the gallows. Drums
beat.*

LOPEZ (*to* CALLAS *from the scaffold*):

Those who won't bow are made to swing.
You get the soup and we the string.
But we would rather meet this fate
Than beg for soup from the master's plate.
You left your good gun to rust
And put your foot in legal dust.
You stole two horses on your own,
Made off with them, like a thief, alone.
Your fishing was a one-man affair,
You thought that way you'd secure your share.
But you had your horses only as long
As the Sickle army was whole and strong.

You thought as a Roundhead you'd get some prize
But you know now it was delusion.
See round and peaked heads hung before your eyes
By round and peaked heads in collusion.

While LOPEZ *has been speaking,* CALLAS *and* NANNA
*have stopped drinking their soup. They stand up. The
tenants at the gallows sing the "Song of the Sickle."*

SONG OF THE SICKLE

Men of the land
The hour is at hand.
Fear not grim circumstance.
Death can be met but once.
None will improve your lot
If you yourselves do not.
Men of the land
The hour is at hand.

THE TENANTS: Long live the Sickle!

*The drums beat louder and louder till they drown
every other sound.* CALLAS *has emptied out his and*
NANNA's *plate and lays his steel helmet and soldier's
cloak on the ground.*

CALLAS (*loudly*): Lopez, Lopez, I wish it was the eleventh
of September again.

Exeunt CALLAS *and* NANNA. *As the sunrise begins to
color the palace court, the Roundhead and Peakhead
landlords continue their meal, while the Roundhead
and Peakhead tenants are prepared for the gallows.*

REGENT:
It now remains for me, Mr. Iberin,
To express my greatest satisfaction
With the outcome of your regency.
It is no exaggeration if I say

That your theory of the heads
Has saved the realm.

IBERIN:

Milord, I think without great arrogance
I may say that the symbol of the Sickle
And the disaffection which it represents
Has, in Yahoo, been rooted out forever.

REGENT (*smiling and wagging his finger at him*):

Therefore, good friend, no more Czuch and Czich.

IBERIN: Good, Milord.

MISSENA:

Although there is an element
Of this theory which we might well retain,
That is, that we have learned to feel like Czuchs
And now as Czuchs we must campaign for peace,
For peace shall now be Yahoo's only slogan.
Peace, peace, and peace again shall be the cry,
At the elections. No anemic peace,
However, but a manly Czuchish peace.
And anyone who works against such peace
Will be dealt with like the Sickle League.

During his speech the barrel of a large cannon is lowered over the table.

REGENT (*raising his glass*):

Drink, friends, to things as they are.

The landlords sitting back and smoking, sing the following song.

THE LANDLORDS' SONG

Perhaps the shades will pass that have disturbed us
And the rumors which have much perturbed us.
Perhaps they long will leave us unmolested
As we would leave them unmolested too.
And many friendly meals will be digested

Before we die of measles or of flu.
Perhaps all men will praise and not defy.
Perhaps the nights will trespass on the days.
Perhaps the moon will cease to change its phase.
Perhaps the rain will fall from earth to sky.

When the song is ended, the HUA *takes away a board which is leaning up against the wall, as he needs it for the execution. This reveals on the newly whitewashed wall a large red sickle. All look at it transfixed. The tenants sing quietly, under their caps, the "Song of the Sickle."*

TWO NOTES

1

Bertolt Brecht began work on *Roundheads and Peakheads* in 1931 or 1932. A version of it was completed in the following year, and can today be found as Experiment 17 in Book Eight of the Experiments (*Versuche*). In 1933 it had only got as far as galley proof when Hitler came to power and all Brecht's writings were banned. The version that was published in 1938 by the Malik Verlag (official address: London; printing house: Prague) reflected changes made in 1933 and 1934. Before, however, this first German printing had come out, the play had been twice published—if in abridged forms—in English. The first English-language presentation appeared in *The International Theatre*, Moscow, August 1935, under the title *The Round Heads and the Sharp*. The second—reprinted in the present volume—appeared in *International Literature*, No. 5, Moscow, 1937. No further rendering in English has followed (1937-1965), though Brecht's Notes appear in *Brecht on Theatre*, edited by John Willett, New York: Hill and Wang, 1964, pp. 100-103. English-language books on Brecht (Willett, Esslin, etc.) contain short accounts of the play, but an extended treatment, based in part on study of unpublished versions, is to be found only in German, namely, in *Bertolt Brecht: von der Massnahme zu Leben des Galilei*, by Werner Mittenzwei, Berlin: Aufbau Verlag, 1962, pp. 154-192.

As necessary to the student of this play as any critical commentary is a copy of Shakespeare's *Measure for Measure*. Brecht had been asked by the stage director Ludwig Berger to adapt Shakespeare's play for production by the Berlin Volksbuehne, and *Roundheads and Peak-*

heads was the end result. Mittenzwei tells that Brecht's first script was called *Mass für Mass oder Die Salzsteuer*— "Measure for Measure or The Salt Tax."

2

The music of most of the songs has been published with the German words in Hanns Eisler's *Lieder und Kantaten*, volumes I and II.* Two songs that are totally omitted from this adaptation are to be found in my record album *"Songs of Hanns Eisler"* (Folkways, FH 5433), under the titles "The Love Market" and "There's Nothing Quite Like Money." (In the play, the former is sung by Nanna in Scene 2, the latter by Madame Cornamontis in Scene 9.) One song in the Goold-Verschoyle text is given in so truncated a form that one suspects a printer's error. This is the "Ballad of Tossing the Button" in Scene 4.

Our text ends with the first line of a four-line refrain. The whole refrain, literally translated, reads: "And I say, luck has decided against you./If you perceive this, you are sparing yourself nothing but torments./Love isn't given you as a present here below./If you need love, you must pay." Second and third stanzas follow: "A stupid man comes up to me/And doubtingly asks of me/Whether his brother might honorably share with him./I say: it can happen. No question./But then I tear a button from his collar/And say: Friend, let us question fate!/We want to see:/If the holes face upwards/Perhaps he will cheat you/And act for his own advantage./Let me see if you are out of luck!/And I throw the button and say: You are./Then you say: But these holes/ Go right through! Then I say:

---

* The songs are numbers 19, 25, 40, and 46 in Volume I; numbers 1 and 54 in Volume II. The two volumes are part of what is, to date, an eight-volume series which came out at irregular intervals between 1955 and 1965, as published in Leipzig by VEB Breitkopf & Haertel.

That's how it is./ (Refrain): And I say, luck has decided against you./If you doubt it, you'll have nothing but torments./If you want peace and a halfway quiet time/You must pay your brother for them."/Third stanza: "A poor man comes up to me,/Angrily announces to me:/A rich man is destroying my heart and home,/Shall I get anything in return?/I begin by tearing a button from his collar/And say: Friend, let us question fate!/ We want to see:/If the holes face upwards/Perhaps you will get nothing at all/And needn't wait around./ Let me see if you are out of luck!/And I throw the button and say: You are./Then you say: But these holes/Go right through! Then I say: That's how it is./(Refrain): And I say, luck has decided against you/And you'll see this happen too many times./ Whatever you may start, friend, here below/Of just or unjust, you will pay!"

—Eric Bentley